Caroline Franks Davis graduated in philosophy from Queen's University, Canada, in 1980. After a period of postgraduate study in philosophy and theology at the University of Tübingen, West Germany, she won a scholarship to the University of Oxford, where she completed a doctorate in philosophy. She is the author of several articles in the philosophy of religion.

THE EVIDENTIAL FORCE OF
RELIGIOUS EXPERIENCE

THE
EVIDENTIAL FORCE
OF
RELIGIOUS EXPERIENCE

Caroline Franks Davis

CLARENDON PRESS: OXFORD
1989

Oxford University Press, Walton Street, Oxford OX2 6DP
Oxford New York Toronto
Delhi Bombay Calcutta Madras Karachi
Petaling Jaya Singapore Hong Kong Tokyo
Nairobi Dar es Salaam Cape Town
Melbourne Auckland
and associated companies in
Berlin Ibadan

Oxford is a trade mark of Oxford University Press

Published in the United States
by Oxford University Press, New York

British Library Cataloguing in Publication Data
Davis, Caroline Franks
The evidential force of religious experience
1. Religious experiences
I. Title
291.4′2
ISBN 0-19-824436-3

Library of Congress Cataloging in Publication Data
Davis, Caroline Franks.
The evidential force of religious experience
Caroline Franks Davis.
Bibliography: p.
Includes index.
1. Experience (Religion) I. Title
BL53.D37 1989   291.4′2--dc19   88-37442
ISBN 0-19-824436-3

Set by Pentacor Limited, High Wycombe, Bucks.
Printed in Great Britain by
Biddles Ltd., Guildford and King's Lynn

ACKNOWLEDGEMENTS

This book grew out of research undertaken over several years at Brasenose College, Oxford. Space does not permit me to name all those at the college and elsewhere who provided academic, moral, and financial support; but a few deserve special mention.

Professor Basil Mitchell saw the project through from beginning to end, despite retirement, and gave unfailing encouragement and advice. His successor, Professor Richard Swinburne, examined the first draft with considerable skill and care, and provided crucial assistance throughout the final stages. I am deeply indebted to them both. Any errors and inadequacies which have persisted despite their able and constructive criticism are entirely my own responsibility.

I owe many thanks to Margaret Yee, without whose theological insight, inspiring discussions, and timely encouragement, this book would probably never have been written.

For additional helpful discussions and correspondence, I am grateful to Michael Argyle, John Berry, David Brown, Richard Gombrich, Crawford Knox, Mettānando Bhikkhu, Olivera Petrovich, and Rob Prevost.

To my husband, Gary, I owe a special debt of gratitude. Despite his own busy schedule, he gave invaluable technical assistance and constant moral support.

This research was funded by the Commonwealth Scholarship Commission and the Social Sciences and Humanities Research Council of Canada.

Thanks are due to Oxford University Press for permission to quote from *The Spiritual Nature of Man* by Alister Hardy (Oxford: Clarendon Press, 1979).

C.E.S.F.D.

CONTENTS

ABBREVIATIONS

Hardy
: Alister Hardy, *The Spiritual Nature of Man: A Study of Contemporary Religious Experience* (Oxford: Clarendon Press, 1979).

James
: William James, *The Varieties of Religious Experience: A Study in Human Nature* (The 1901–2 Gifford Lectures; Glasgow: Collins Fount Paperbacks, 1977).

Swinburne
: Richard Swinburne, *The Existence of God* (Oxford: Clarendon Press, 1979).

INTRODUCTION

It is only comparatively recently in the history of civilization that there has been widespread scepticism regarding religious experiences. People were concerned to distinguish 'genuine' religious experiences from 'illusory' ones, but the religious framework within which this distinction was made was rarely questioned. Experiences judged 'illusory' would be more likely to be explained in terms of other supernatural factors such as 'the devil' than in the naturalistic terms which so often rival religious explanations today. Just as we distinguish veridical sense experiences from misperceptions and illusions without (except in philosophy lectures) doubting that the experiences judged 'veridical' really do give us some kind of access to a stable external world, and just as the early Israelites had only to convince others that Yahweh was the supreme God, alone worthy of worship, without having to convince them that there were such things as gods, so most cultures have taken it for granted that genuine religious experiences are what they appear to be: apprehensions of the divine. An argument to show that religious experiences in general can be considered evidence for religious claims would have been unnecessary.

With arguments against the plausibility of religious doctrines and reductionist accounts of religious experiences now widely accepted, and with many people leading atheistic lives which are to all appearances perfectly adequate, religious individuals can no longer assume that experiences judged to be 'genuine' by fellow believers are immune from further attack. They are challenged on all sides, by philosophers, psychologists, sociologists, anthropologists, members of other religious traditions, and even by members of their own tradition with widely differing views. But 'arguments from religious experience' have been largely unconvincing, and religious experience continues to be regarded as something rare and obscure, inaccessible to ordinary routes of inquiry. A critical reassessment of the value of religious experiences as support for religious claims appears to be called for.

Such a reassessment will necessarily be interdisciplinary. Challenges come from so many fields that a thorough, well-grounded account of religious experience must draw upon the sciences as well as philosophy and religious studies. It will also be multi-cultural. The fact that religious experiences are found in all the religious traditions of the world makes it essential to consider non-Christian as well as Christian experience. But this inquiry is not merely a philosophical and psychological account of 'the varieties of religious experience'; its goal is to discover the role which religious experience can legitimately play in the defence of religious doctrines. Neither is it a traditional 'argument from religious experience'.[1] Such arguments typically proceed from some narrow conception of religious experience to "the existence of God"; and, since their proponents are Westerners (Eastern religious traditions have nurtured highly developed systems of philosophy, but the issue of the justification of religious belief has not commanded very much attention there), this has usually been the traditional Judaeo-Christian God. Although religious experiences do, as we will see in the end, provide good evidence for a broadly traditional theism, there seems to be no *a priori* reason why they should not prove to support a very different conception of divinity. Rather than taking the traditional approach, therefore, I have preferred to start with more basic principles: I look at the way experiences in general are used as evidence for claims about the world; investigate the extent to which all perceptual experiences involve 'interpretation' in accordance with prior beliefs and other factors; ask what counts as a religious experience and provide a brief survey of the representative types; and—the most demanding part—attempt to give sound, empirically grounded responses to the sceptic's challenges.

Some may think it strange to talk of using an experience of alleged direct perception of a state of affairs as 'evidence' for the claim that that state of affairs obtains. J. L. Austin maintains, for instance, that one only needs 'evidence' if one has not directly witnessed a thing oneself.[2] Smoke may be taken as evidence of a fire, but when one is perceiving the fire directly, one does not need evidence. (It should be remarked that many people—I am not accusing Austin of being one—seem to feel this way about

---

[1] Though it does to some extent follow the same format and build upon the same principles as Richard Swinburne's argument in *The Existence of God*, ch. 13.

[2] *Sense and Sensibilia* (Oxford: Clarendon Press, 1962), pp. 115 ff.

ordinary perceptual experiences only, and have no qualms about regarding an experience of a numinous presence as possible 'evidence' for the subject's claim to have encountered a divine reality.) However, the reason these people feel it is odd to talk of direct perceptual experiences as 'evidence' is, I suspect, an underlying idea that if x is 'evidence' for y, then y must have been consciously *inferred* from x—as when we infer fire from smoke, the identity of the murderer from fingerprints, and so on. We do not usually *infer* the existence of percepts from our perceptual experiences in this way. But 'evidence' can be used in a wider sense to mean anything we use to back up a claim, whether the claim was inferred from it or not. After all, we do use the phrase 'the evidence of our senses'. We may cite religious experiences as evidence for the existence of God (or some divine power) without God thereby being treated as an inferred entity.

Another potential objection to any study of religious experiences as 'evidence' could come from those who believe religious experiences are non-cognitive, like emotions or pains. Chapter I, which lays some of the philosophical foundations for this inquiry, will defend the view that reports of religious experiences often involve religiously significant claims about the world, even when they are couched in metaphorical language.

The most powerful challenges to religious experience will prove to be the 'conflicting claims challenge', that subjects of religious experiences cannot agree on a single, consistent account of the alleged percepts, and the 'reductionist challenge', that religious experiences can be explained more plausibly by reference to natural (and often pathological) factors alone than by explanations which allow certain religious experiences to be veridical. Together, these challenges restrict the evidential force of religious experience somewhat, so that it cannot play the straightforward evidential role it had in those early homogeneously religious cultures. Despite such challenges, it will be seen that religious experience provides substantial evidence for certain crucial and fundamental religious doctrines; but its most important place will be within a 'cumulative argument', where it works in conjunction with evidence from a wide range of sources to support the belief systems of specific traditions. Religious experience is therefore far from "self-authenticating", but this does not imply that it is "nothing but interpretation"; like all experiences, it is woven into the fabric of our lives with a complex pattern of cognitive, perceptual, and personal factors, and any argument which does it justice must take that complexity into account.

I

SOME PRESUPPOSITIONS

Many philosophers and theologians who are themselves religious
see religious experiences as completely non-cognitive and hence
useless as evidence for anything beyond the subject's own
psychological states. This view is usually bound up with a radically
demythologized or non-realist picture of religious language. In
order for an investigation of religious experience as evidence for
something beyond purely autobiographical claims to get off the
ground, we must defend the presupposition that religious experiences and religious utterances can and ought to be treated as capable
of having cognitive content.

I will not deal here with the account which logical positivists
hostile to religion have given of religious utterances, according to
which they are meaningless or at least not factual assertions. The
various forms of the verificationist principle have been argued
against so effectively by so many philosophers that yet another
refutation would be superfluous. Of interest here are the views of
those who are *sympathetic* to religion and who yet maintain that
religious utterances are not intended to be factual assertions. These
views may take three forms. (i) Religious experiences occur within
the framework of an autonomous language-game. (ii) Religious
utterances have an emotive or conative function, but not a
cognitive function. Experiences which are described as direct
perceptions of some 'supernatural' state of affairs should be given
demythologized descriptions. (iii) Religious experiences, particularly of the numinous and mystical varieties, are radically ineffable,
and so there are no verbally expressible claims for which they could
be evidence.

(i) The language-game view of religious utterances (which
include reports of religious experiences) originated with Wittgenstein, and is now held by such philosophers as D. Z. Phillips. On
this view, religious experiences could be used as 'evidence' for

doctrines within one language-game if they conformed to the rules of the game, but they could not be considered veridical or even be assessed at all from the viewpoint of another language-game such as science, or humanism. This view of language does contain some important insights: as we shall see later, some aspects of religious experiences can only be appreciated if one understands something of the specific traditions out of which they emerged, just as one can only understand what counts as a 'goal' in soccer if one understands the rules of the game; and the specific criteria by which one assesses experiences of ordinary sense perception are not all applicable to religious experience (see Chapter III.3). But a thoroughgoing language-game interpretation of religious utterances does not do justice to the facts. There is not space here to argue against such an interpretation—that has been done elsewhere[1]—but these few remarks should show why I do not consider it the best approach to religious experience. (a) On the language-game view, there ought to be not just one language-game called 'religion', but one for each different religious tradition. The radical cultural relativism thus envisaged ought to preclude any dialogue between the traditions. Such dialogue has, however, proved possible. (b) Certain religious insights *are* considered superior to others on the basis of criteria which we apply to non-religious insights as well (e.g. coherence). (c) The language-game view is ultimately prescriptive rather than descriptive. Subjects of religious experiences usually consider them to be truly reality-depicting and their religious claims to be valid universally, not valid just for the players of one language-game.

(ii) It was very common in the wake of the logical positivist attack on religious language for philosophers sympathetic to religion to point out that meaning is not determined by verifying observations or procedures alone, but also by the *use* to which language is put.[2] Religious language may have an *emotive* function which gives its utterances meaning; like laughter or a song, it can express and elicit feelings. An apparently assertive statement such as "the universe is the handiwork of God" can arouse in the hearer a

---

[1] See e.g. Kai Nielsen, *Contemporary Critiques of Religion* (London: Macmillan, 1971), ch. 5, where it is argued that this view of religious language leads inevitably to religious scepticism.

[2] See N. Schedler, "Talk About God-Talk: A Historical Introduction" in N. Schedler (ed.), *Philosophy of Religion* (New York: Macmillan, 1974), pp. 221–50; and Frederick Ferré, *Basic Modern Philosophy of Religion* (London: Allen & Unwin, 1968), ch. 12.

sense of wonder at the world and a feeling for the intrinsic worth of all 'creation'. Religious language may also have a *conative* function; like a promise, it can express a commitment to a certain course of action. A statement apparently entailing the existence of a transcendent being, such as "I love God", might express the intention to follow a religious way of life involving love of one's neighbour and so on.

These are important non-cognitive functions of religious language, but some philosophers of religion consider them the *only* functions of religious language. They thus deny the two statements above any factual significance. R. B. Braithwaite writes, for instance, in a well-known lecture, that

a religious belief is an intention to behave in a certain way (moral belief) together with the entertainment of certain stories associated with the intention in the mind of the believer.[3]

The 'stories' or 'parables' need not be believed to be effective; novels may be just as effective as biographies at inspiring good behaviour. Ostensibly factual assertions such as "Jesus rose from the dead", it is claimed, do not impart information; they only encourage morality. Believing that something is the will of God, for instance, may make it much easier for a person to do it.

The most explicit application of such non-cognitive views of religious language to religious *experience* is that found in T. R. Miles's book, *Religious Experience*.[4] For Miles, religion is "silence qualified by parables", and religious experiences are those experiences which occur when the subject 'tries to come to terms with cosmic issues'. They may be described using the vivid and compelling imagery of religious myths, but to be seen in their true light the descriptions should be radically demythologized, leaving out reference even to "God". They do nothing so absurd as to 'put people in touch with a non-material world'. Rather, their real value lies in the way they illuminate one's understanding of oneself, one's relation to others, and one's place in the world. An "experience of God" means an experience of love or a sense of 'holiness' in the world, expressible in terms of the world and human beings; an "experience of the Virgin Mary" should be understood as a parable

---

[3] "An Empiricist's View of the Nature of Religious Belief", in John Hick (ed.), *The Existence of God* (New York: Macmillan, 1964), pp. 229–52.

[4] London: Macmillan, 1972.

rather than as a vision of a person who was alive many centuries ago; and an "experience of the risen Christ" should be seen as the subject's 'recognition of the compelling nature of the demand to carry Jesus in his heart' rather than as anything to do with a 'spiritual body' of Christ. To ask whether a religious experience was veridical would, on Miles's view, show as much insensitivity to the true nature of such experiences as asking whether some poetic utterance was literally true would show to the nature and function of poetry.

Again, there is much that is useful in these 'non-cognitive' accounts, particularly in their condemnation of a crude realism. But as general accounts of religious language and experience, they are unsatisfactory, for the following reasons.

(a) The emotive and conative import of a religious utterance are often parasitic upon its descriptive content. Religious utterances are not all strings of nonsense syllables like "Wow!"; it is the descriptive content which elicits the response. We are moved to recognize the intrinsic worth of all things by "the universe is the handiwork of God" because of what it tells us about the world and God's relationship to it; Isaiah's terrible imagery leads to reform because it is taken to be the description of an angry God; the assertion, "God so loved the world, that he gave his only-begotten Son . . ." inspires a sense of security because of the belief that there really is a divine power of infinite love somehow at work in the world, in our lives. The meaning of such religious utterances cannot consist entirely in their conative or emotive function.

(b) It follows from the previous point that a person who holds that religious utterances and experiences are non-cognitive must also claim, firstly, that the utterances often are not merely exclamations or declarations of intent but 'useful fictions' which only guide us because we act *as if* they were true in some way, and, secondly, that religious experiences are widely misinterpreted by their subjects as if those useful fictions were true. But why should we use such ontologically and spiritually misleading 'parables' to describe our moral convictions and our 'coming to terms with cosmic issues'? Why think in terms of *religious* categories at all? As Ian Barbour says, "It would be unreasonable to adopt or recommend a way of life unless one believes that the universe is of such a character that this way of life is appropriate."[5] A mature

---

[5] *Myths, Models and Paradigms* (London: SCM, 1974), p. 58.

person ought to find other aids to his or her moral behaviour than 'parables' which give unacceptable reasons for that behaviour and which even enjoin behaviour (such as worship) which would be pointless unless the 'parable' were reality-depicting to some extent. By the same token, the good 'fruits' of religious experience, such as peace and renewed hope, may be outweighed by the disadvantages of the false beliefs which such experiences tend to induce in their subjects. Religious experiences and beliefs may even be dangerous, instilling in the subject a false sense of security. There seems to be little reason for proponents of this account of religious language and experience to remain 'religious'.

(c) Any survey of religious experiences will show that an account such as Miles's is *prescriptive* rather than *descriptive*; people do take their experiences to give them access to something beyond the material world. Reports of experiences can usually be 'demythologized' to some extent, but often a 'sense of presence' remains which Miles would not be able to get rid of without classifying the experience as illusory in some fundamental way. We are attempting to evaluate people's religious experiences as evidence for their religious claims with as few controversial presuppositions as possible; religious experiences must thus be taken in the first instance just 'as they appeared to the subject'. To impose what Ninian Smart calls a 'hetero-interpretation'[6] on them from the outset would be to bias the inquiry and beg many questions.

It is true that subjects of religious experience often claim that the 'fruits' of an experience, such as the new ability it gives them to cope with life, are far more *important* than any cognitive content. They may feel that the cognitive content is insignificant because it is taken for granted, or they may feel that to concentrate on it in an 'academic exercise' does not do justice to the practical importance of the experiences in their lives. However, as long as there is some alleged content, such experiences are valid data for this study—and the 'fruits' will not be ignored (see especially Chapter IX).

(d) Miles's view implies that the religious person must choose between radical demythologization and a rather crude belief in a supernatural being who performs miracles and makes his will known in visions and voices. This is too strong a dichotomy; there are many shades of religious understanding between the non-cognitive and the naïvely literal. The next section expounds a

[6] In "Interpretation and Mystical Experience", *Rel. Stud.*, 1 (1965), 75–87.

'critical realist' view of religious language which does away with that crude dichotomy and provides a more sensitive understanding of religious language and experience.

2. CRITICAL REALISM

It is widely accepted that religious language should not be understood at a naïvely literal level, and much has been written on the role which models, metaphors, myths, and other non-literal elements play in religious thought. What is not so widely accepted is the possibility that irreducibly metaphorical utterances can themselves state truths about the world. If one can *never* speak of God in literal terms, it is argued, then the word "God" does not really refer, and alleged statements about God must merely have non-cognitive functions. Against this, the "critical realist" account maintains that models and metaphors can have important cognitive functions, and that it is not necessary to "break out of the circle of metaphor" if one's statements (religious or otherwise) are to be reality-depicting. A person may thus find it impossible to describe a religious experience without recourse to religious models and metaphors, and yet be describing a veridical perceptual experience.

I can do no more here than give a very brief sketch of "critical realism". For a more detailed exposition, the reader should turn to such works as Ian Barbour's *Myths, Models and Paradigms* and Janet Martin Soskice's *Metaphor and Religious Language*.[7] The latter is an especially good account, and I will follow it closely here.

It is important to recognize that the problem of irreducible models and metaphors is not unique to religion. Both Soskice and Barbour show, for instance, that models are as indispensable to science as they are to religion; even in science, they are much more than useful fictions or heuristic devices which can be discarded once a theory has been formalized. Scientific models such as the 'billiard ball' model of gas molecules aid the interpretation of data, suggest avenues for further research, and are viewed by scientists as (inadequate and symbolic) representations of an aspect of reality.[8]

---

[7] Oxford: Clarendon Press, 1985. Many of my examples are drawn from this book.

[8] See Barbour, ch. 3 and Soskice, ch. VI.2; see also Mary Hesse, *Revolutions and Reconstructions in the Philosophy of Science* (Brighton: Harvester Press, 1980), ch. 4.

Moreover, both science and religion rely on a multiplicity of models in tension; individual models are rarely "descriptively privileged".[9] Models interact, supplementing, complementing, and limiting each other, generating fruitful questions for research and preventing the development of inappropriate analogies (in religion, for instance, the model of God as 'spirit' shows that the physical aspects of the 'fatherhood' model are inapplicable). Barbour even suggests that the models of God as immanent and personal on the one hand and transcendent and impersonal on the other (traits typically revealed by numinous and mystical experiences respectively; see Chapter VII) may have the same sort of complementary relation as the wave and particle models of light have in physics.[10]

Irreducibly metaphorical statements are not unique to religion, either.[11] It should be pointed out first of all that such statements need not resist all attempts at clarification. One may not be able to point to the intended referent or to paraphrase them in literal language (which uses terms in their standard, familiar senses), but it is usually possible to rephrase or explain them in terms of other, less obscure metaphors. The distinction between 'literal language' and 'metaphor' is in any case somewhat vague: some metaphors have become so familiar that they are now regarded as literal terms (e.g. the 'stem' of a glass) and have lost most of their original associations (such terms are 'dead metaphors'—itself a good metaphor!). Even 'reducible' metaphors (e.g. 'ship of the desert') cannot normally be translated into literal language without some loss of content, since one is stripping off a subtle and potentially vast network of associations. But often we cannot put our apprehensions of the world (be they secular or religious) into language at all without using metaphors, employing existing linguistic terms in a new context. As Soskice points out, it is a mistake to view metaphors as nothing more than colourful or emotive linguistic ornaments, or to see metaphorical sentences as utterances which cannot "really" be true until they are expressed in literal terms. Metaphors often function as vehicles of cognitive information which cannot be conveyed in any other way. They may, for instance, fill the lexical gap when something is invented or

---

[9] See Soskice, especially p. 103; and Barbour, chs. 5 and 8.
[10] Barbour, ch. 5.3.
[11] See Soskice's discussion, ch. v.3.

discovered ('white noise'), suggest a new way of looking at things ("rosy-fingered dawn"), guide investigation into the nature of something (the 'flow' of electricity), describe 'private' experiences (a 'sharp' pain), or describe experiences which few have had and for which therefore few standard terms are available (a seeing person in a blind community trying to describe colour). Though the terms are used in non-standard ways, they are understood as metaphors within the context of the speaker's intentions, the particular situation, and the shared set of associations which both speaker and hearer bring to the discourse;[12] they require all participants to "go beyond the words given". (We will see in a later chapter how all perception involves 'going beyond the information given'; it is hardly surprising that understanding speech involves this too.)

It is often maintained that successful reference to an object requires literal and accurate descriptions of that object, and that this is impossible in the case of 'God'. It has been shown, however, that descriptions do not need to be literal, exhaustive, or unrevisable before a speaker can use them to refer. Events, experiences, and other phenomena may be 'dubbed' before their nature is properly understood, but the term used continues to refer as the theories about it are changed and corrected[13] (unless it must be completely abandoned, as "phlogiston" was). Donnellan's example, in which one successfully refers to a certain man by "the man drinking a martini" despite the fact that he is actually drinking water,[14] and Kripke's 'Columbus' example both show that in an appropriate context, incorrect descriptions can refer:

in Kripke's example, a speaker who knows of Columbus only that he was the man who discovered that the world was round or that he discovered America really refers when he mentions Columbus, even though Columbus did neither of these things. The reason the speaker refers here, even though all his particular beliefs about Columbus are incorrect, is because the relevant linguistic competence does not involve an unequivocal knowledge, but rather depends on the fact that the speaker is a member of a linguistic community which has passed the name from link to link.[15]

[12] The crucial contribution of context to the meaning of *any* discourse, metaphorical or literal, is stressed in current psycholinguistic studies such as P. N. Johnson-Laird's *Mental Models* (Cambridge: CUP, 1983), especially ch. 15.

[13] As happened with the term "gene", for instance; see Soskice, p. 126.

[14] Keith S. Donnellan, "Reference and Definite Descriptions", *Phil. Rev.*, 75 (1966), 281–304.

[15] Soskice, p. 127.

Linguistic continuity, shared associations, and causal links with experiences and events can all enable the grounding of a reference. Metaphorical and inadequate references to God can thus be considered to be reality-depicting if they are grounded in community history and experiences.

Models and metaphors are often very closely related. Some metaphors suggest explanatory models (e.g. the 'flow' of electricity, mentioned above); others are generated by models (the model of the brain as a computer has spawned many such metaphors). Many metaphorical descriptions of religious experiences can be understood in terms of models, and many ground-breaking religious insights have consisted in the suggestion of a new model of divinity, which then generates new metaphors.

Over time, in both religious and secular spheres, a network of interlocking models and metaphors, rich in associations, becomes embedded in community tradition. These models have been selected by the community as particularly appropriate to their experience; they are continually revised and embellished, often acquiring new and illuminating associations.[16] They may also be completely overthrown, if they come to be seen as irrelevant or incorrect. Models and metaphors considered appropriate by one generation may be rejected by the next; those appropriate within one cultural community may be rejected by another; new experiences, new knowledge, changing social conditions, and the ideas of influential individuals may lead to revisions. A model originally grounded in experience may become so embedded in a community and so reworked that most people have no knowledge of its sources; in both religion and science, "we rely on authoritative members of our community to ground referring expressions".[17]

Religious descriptions are usually recognized as being 'inadequate' as well as irreducibly metaphorical—for how could our limited language adequately describe 'ultimate reality'? No one model or metaphor captures all its aspects. Yet, as this section has pointed out (and Soskice has shown), single models are rarely descriptively privileged; metaphorical, inadequate, and even inaccurate descriptions may successfully refer; and where reference is

---

[16] Ian Ramsey describes such a process in his *Models for Divine Activity* (London: SCM Press, 1973).
[17] Soskice, p. 149.

grounded in experience, linguistic continuity, and shared associations, religious metaphors can be understood as 'reality-depicting'.
'Critical realism' thus avoids both the naïve realist's unsupportable
claims about the primacy and incorrigibility of a particular model
of God (together with possible dangers of anthropomorphism) and
the non-cognitivist's radical programme of demythologization,
which reduces reports of religious experiences to poetically
embellished statements about the human condition.

This is not to say that all religious language is metaphorical, nor
that all descriptions of religious experiences are. Terms are often
used in very straightforward ways—e.g. "I had a vision of a cross",
"I felt a comforting presence". Nor is it to say that when metaphors
are used, they are always of the irreducible kind—"My heart
burned with love" and "I . . . have my 'spiritual' batteries
recharged",[18] for example, use reducible metaphors. And it
certainly does not imply that quasi-physical visions are only naïve
realists' misinterpretations of experiences. For instance, a person
may have a vision of God as a mighty king, use 'mighty king' non-
metaphorically in the description of his experience, and yet realize
that his vision only took that form because his community uses
'kingship' as one model for God.

3. THE INEFFABILITY OF RELIGIOUS EXPERIENCES

We must now deal with claim (iii), the claim that religious
experiences, particularly the numinous and mystical ones usually
appealed to most in arguments from religious experience, are so
radically ineffable that no cognitive claims can be based on them.
The non-cognitive views of religious language just examined imply
both that religious experiences are not suitable as justification for
religious beliefs and that religious beliefs do not *require* justification;
this view merely implies the former. But are religious experiences
actually *radically* ineffable? In this section I will look at the reasons
why experiences may have seemed so, with particular regard to
mystical experiences. The investigation will lead to the conclusion
that, though mystical experiences are often claimed to be ineffable,
they are generally not ineffable in the radical sense which would
prevent them from being cognitive experiences.

---

[18] The latter is quoted by Alister Hardy in *The Spiritual Nature of Man*, p. 116.

William James goes so far as to call ineffability "the handiest of the marks by which I classify a state of mind as mystical",[19] and Tennyson certainly echoes a common complaint when he writes: "I am ashamed of my feeble description. Have I not said the state is utterly beyond words?"[20] Yet vivid and detailed descriptions of mystical experiences abound, descriptions which include cognitive claims and which are sufficiently precise for others to be able to recognize that they have had 'the same sort of experience'. Why then do mystics so often claim ineffability?

(a) Poetic hyperbole: in many cases, expressions such as "unspeakable bliss" and "the experience is beyond the power of mere words to describe" should be treated in the same way as "unbearable pain" which is nevertheless borne and "impossible feats" which are nevertheless performed; the exaggeration conveys the intensity or immensity of some feature far better than a literal description could on its own. The claim that a mystical experience is ineffable emphasizes the fact that it was tremendously significant, involved overwhelming emotions—difficult enough to articulate normally—and was highly unusual. For instance, the addition of "The description is quite inadequate" to one of Hardy's correspondents' reports that "the main sensation was of being loved, a flood of sweetness of great strength, without any element of sentimentality or anything but itself,"[21] alerts us to the fact that the actually very useful description is to be taken seriously, and not just as a colourful description of an ordinary experience of 'being loved'.

(b) A second possible source of 'ineffability' is the fact that, to some extent, emotions and sensations must be experienced to be understood; a verbal description cannot convey the experience adequately to one who has not had it. The Persian mystic al-Ghazali expresses this view when he writes,

. . . [I] progressed, as far as is possible by study and oral instruction, in the knowledge of mysticism. It became clear to me, however, that what is most distinctive of mysticism is something which cannot be apprehended by study, but only by immediate experience, by ecstasy and by a moral change. What a difference there is between *knowing* the definition of health and satiety . . . and *being* healthy and satisfied! What a difference between being acquainted with the definition of drunkenness . . . and being drunk!

---

[19] *The Varieties of Religious Experience*, p. 367.
[20] Quoted by James, p. 370 n.
[21] In Hardy, p. 58.

. . . What remained for me was not to be attained by oral instruction and study but only by immediate experience and by walking in the mystic way.[22]

This type of ineffability is not peculiar to mysticism, nor is it usually radical, as metaphors and analogies can often be used to give the hearer some sense of what the experience is like. Experiences such as being in love, reaching safety, 'going wild with joy', floating on water with one's eyes closed, and 'losing oneself' in some intensely absorbing activity, are close enough to certain mystical states that, with suitable care, a mystic can enable sensitive readers both to understand what he or she went through to some degree and to recognize their own experience as being of the same kind, should the readers ever be fortunate enough to have such an experience. Even if they are particularly gifted at expressing themselves, the mystics' ability to make themselves understood will be greatly enhanced if they belong to a community with a rich variety of standard metaphors employed by previous mystics, in the same way that we are often helped to articulate such common human experiences as pain, joy, and love by means of a common metaphorical vocabulary.

(c) Sometimes mystical revelations are so fundamental and all-encompassing that subjects are unable to articulate them, though they are left with an impression of having "understood everything": "So that is what it is all about!"[23] St Teresa of Avila explains this predicament with a real-life analogy: she was taken into a room with a magnificent display of *objets d'art*, "set out in such a way that you can see almost all of them as you enter". "Although I was there for some time," she writes, "there was so much to be seen that I could not remember it all, so that I could no more recall what was in those rooms than if I had never seen them, nor could I say what the things were made of; I can only remember having seen them as a whole."[24] Perhaps if subjects were able to describe mystical experiences while they were occurring, they would be able to make more explicit knowledge claims, instead of merely retaining the frustrating but exhilarating impression of *having* understood the secret of the universe.

[22] al-Ghazali, *Deliverance from Error*, in *The Faith and Practice of al-Ghazālī*, tr. W. Montgomery Watt (London: Allen & Unwin, 1953), pp. 54–5.

[23] Quoted in Hardy, p. 110.

[24] *Interior Castle*, tr., and ed. E. Allison Peers (Garden City, NY: Doubleday, 1961), p. 152.

Experiences which are ineffable in this way are of little use as evidence for claims about the external world—except for the claim that people sometimes *have* such experiences. However, we must remember that some people are more gifted than others at articulating their thoughts, more adept at analysing experiences and 'intuitions'. A great many mystics are able to put their alleged revelation into words, albeit usually only partially and inadequately. Some, such as R. M. Bucke (quoted in Chapter II.4, below), give a veritable encyclopaedia of insights attained, ranging from eternal life to love as the fundamental guiding principle of the universe—despite saying that it was "an intellectual illumination impossible to describe"![25]

(d) There is a view, championed by William Stace in particular, that mystical experiences are described as ineffable because they are inherently paradoxical.[26] The mystic seems to experience the dissolution of the subject–object distinction, see God as both personal and impersonal, and so on—apparent contradictions.

[The mystic] is embarrassed because he is, like other people, a logically minded man in his nonmystical moments . . . When he returns from the world of the One, he wishes to communicate in words to other men what he remembers of his experience. The words come from his mouth, but he is astonished and perplexed to find himself talking in contradictions. He explains this to himself by supposing that there is something wrong with the language. He says that his experience is ineffable.[27]

Stace is probably right that this is one reason why experiences which can actually be accurately described are alleged to be ineffable. We need not go as far as he does, however, in saying that the paradoxicality of mystical experiences is such that they really *do* contravene the laws of logic. Mystics may 'find themselves' saying that the experience was "both *a* and not-*a*", but subsequent reflection on the experience usually leads them to interpret that phenomenon in a coherent way. As Chapter VII will show, there is a rich tradition within the world religions of analysis of the apparently contradictory aspects of the divine, and enough plausible solutions have been proposed for us not to feel trapped by apparent self-contradictions. Paradoxes do not have to lead to a

[25] Quoted in James, p. 385.
[26] William Stace, *Mysticism and Philosophy* (London: Macmillan, 1960), pp. 304–5.
[27] Ibid. p. 305.

sense of unfathomable, non-logical mystery in religion any more than they do in the sciences; in both realms they have encouraged reflection, questioning, and the development of concepts to make sense of puzzling experiences.

(e) Proponents of the view that mystical experiences are radically ineffable often draw heavily upon texts from apophatic or *via negativa* mystics. There are plenty of suggestive passages to choose from. Dionysius the pseudo-Areopagite writes that the Divine

is not soul, or mind . . . It is not immovable nor in motion, or at rest . . . nor is It Godhead or goodness . . . nor does It belong to the category of non-existence or to that of existence . . . nor can any affirmation or negation apply to it. . .[28]

And Gregory of Nyssa says that

The true vision and the true knowledge of what we seek consists precisely in not seeing, in an awareness that our goal transcends all knowledge and is everywhere cut off from us by the darkness of incomprehensibility.[29]

The writer of the *Book of Tao* concurs: "The Tao that can be expressed is not the eternal Tao;" for "how can [words] represent the all-embracing, true Tao and the nameless name?"[30] Every great religious tradition would be able to supply examples.

However radically apophatic these mystical utterances seem, though, they must be rejected as indications that mystical experiences are so radically ineffable that they are non-cognitive. A truly radically ineffable experience could not be represented in the memory beyond being 'relived', and could not be expressed at all in words. Even metaphors would be useless; only silence would be appropriate—and indeed, there are mystics who have felt pushed to this extreme. But it is difficult to see how, if *no* description is possible, subjects could even confidently describe their experiences as 'mystical'. And an object that was truly radically ineffable would be beyond human experience. Stace writes:

Absolute ineffability . . . would mean that the something called ineffable would be outside our consciousness altogether in the sense in which God is

---

[28] *The Mystical Theology*, ch. V, from *Dionysius the Areopagite: On the Divine Names and the Mystical Theology*, tr., C.E. Rolt (London: SPCK, 1920), pp. 200–1.
[29] *Life of Moses*, ii. 162–4, in J. Daniélou, *From Glory to Glory*, tr. H. Musurillo (London: John Murray, 1962), p. 118.
[30] *Tao Tê Ching*, ch. 1, line 1, tr. by Ch'u Ta-Kao (London: Unwin Books, 1970; 1st edn. 1937); and commentary by Ch'u Ta-Kao, p. 11.

presumably outside the consciousness of a dog. It may plausibly be
supposed that God is *absolutely* unknowable to a dog. A dog could not
think "God is unknowable to me." Only a being conscious of God, or at
least conscious of some meaning which he attributes to the word "God,"
could say "God is unknowable to me."[31]

This does not mean that apophatic mystics have been deluding
themselves. A closer look at their writings reveals that their
negative language often conceals a 'positive' purpose (see Chapter
VII) and that they do use positive imagery as well. Negative
language emphasizes the fact that no descriptions can possibly be
adequate to the infinite, holy ground of all existence, and that we
can never know God 'as he is in himself': he cannot be "gotten and
holden" by the understanding. But we must remember here the
'critical realist' discussion of religious models and metaphors
(section 2, above). The divine may be far greater than anything the
human constitution can directly experience or the human mind
fully encompass, but we *can* speak of it.

In his early work on logical positivism, A. J. Ayer made this
stark pronouncement: "If a mystic admits that the object of his
vision is something which cannot be described, then he must also
admit that he is bound to talk nonsense when he describes it."[32] We
have shown above that "cannot be described" should normally not
be taken in such a strict sense. The mystic's descriptions may not be
adequate; they may be inextricably bound up with models and
metaphors, and the divine may remain ultimately beyond the grasp
of human concepts, but that does not mean that the often eloquent
attempts of the mystic to communicate his 'vision' are not intended
to give us some indication of an ultimate reality beyond his own
personal life.

4. SOME REMARKS ABOUT 'EXPERIENCE'

An 'experience', for the purposes of this study, is a roughly datable
mental event which is undergone by a subject and of which the
subject is to some extent aware.

(i) By the qualification "roughly datable" I exclude the senses of
'experience' in expressions such as "the accumulated experience of a

---

[31] Stace, p. 291.
[32] *Language, Truth and Logic* (London: Victor Gollancz, 1936), p. 180.

lifetime" and—the bane of job-hunters—"experience required". Since a continuous or lifelong "awareness of the divine presence" is normally manifested in numerous episodic experiences, this restriction should not blind us to any important aspects of religious experience.

This should not be taken to imply that experiences can occur in isolation or that they are "episodic" in the sense of having sharply defined boundaries. (Nor does it imply, when we get to the specifically religious experiences, that I will be dealing only with the more extraordinary or intense experiences.) As Chapter VI will show, experiences do not take place in a vacuum, but are always the product of interaction with other experiences, beliefs, the environment, and the subject's 'set'.[33]

(ii) Experiences are *undergone*. This does not mean they are involuntary; I can cause myself to have an experience of pain by sticking my hand into the fire. It also does not mean that the subject of an experience is simply a passive recipient or recorder, for, as we shall see in Chapter VI, a great deal of unconscious interpretation must be performed in perceiving. It does, however, exclude mental activities directed by oneself, such as thinking, calculating, and daydreaming. While reaching the conclusion of an argument may be considered an 'experience' on some accounts, I do not wish to do so here. Thus, a sudden 'flash of insight' on looking into a glorious sunset that "a benevolent power created all this" would be a religious experience, but the arrival at that same conclusion after a chain of reasoning would not. Thoughts which are very sudden, unexpected, or overwhelming may seem to the subject to be 'given' or placed in the mind by some external power rather than to be produced under his or her own power or direction; they are thus 'experiences' on this account, and many of them come into the category of religious 'revelatory' experiences discussed below.

(iii) Subjects must be *aware* of experiences to some extent. This is part of what it is to be a mental event. Events which are undergone by totally oblivious subjects do not constitute experiences (e.g.

---

[33] It is interesting to note that, just as English-speaking philosophers have had to struggle to clarify the distinction between 'knowing' a fact and 'knowing' a person while other European languages provide separate words for the two kinds of knowledge (e.g. the German *wissen* and *kennen*), I have had to make a distinction here between 'episodic' and 'accumulated' senses of 'experience' which would have been obvious to a German speaker: 'experience' here means *Erlebnis* rather than *Erfahrung*.

surgery while the subject is under general anaesthetic); neither do events of which the subjects are aware only in the sense of knowing that the events are happening to them (e.g. being attracted to the earth by the force of gravity, and, for many believers, being continually sustained by God.) Subjects need not be aware at the time of the experience that they are having an experience of a certain sort, though they may characterize it as an experience of that sort when they remember it (e.g. the memory of an event witnessed while one was half-asleep); and they need never have any knowledge of the cause or true nature of their experience, for an experience to have occurred (e.g. when the subject is taken in by a hallucination).

(iv) Being mental events, experiences are 'private' in the sense that the subjects are in a better position to say how things *seem* to them to be (in Chisholm's 'epistemic' sense of 'seem'; see below) than anyone else is. Others must infer what the subject is experiencing from his behaviour, verbal reports, and so on.[34] Some experiences are also 'private' in the sense that the subject is in a better position to say how things really *were* than anyone else; these are experiences of the subject's own sensations, emotions, and states of mind, to which the subject has 'privileged access'. Such experiences I call 'nonperceptual experiences'. In the case of *perceptual* experiences (I am using 'perceptual' here not as an 'achievement' term, implying that the experience was veridical, but rather simply as a label for experiences which are putative perceptions) the subject is not necessarily in the best position to say how things really were, since the object of the experience (the alleged percept) is an external object, event, or state of affairs, beyond the subject's mental life (sensations, etc.), and something to which other people should be able to gain just as direct access.

Not all external percepts are 'public' in the sense that anyone fulfilling certain physical and conceptual conditions will have an experience of its seeming to them that the percept is there. If there is a God (and this goes for other 'supernatural' beings as well), one would expect him to be able to choose to whom he reveals himself. Thus, although many religious experiences are perceptual experiences, one person may have such an experience while "his neighbour equally attentive and equally well equipped with sense-

---

[34] When we speak of people having 'the same experience', it is the *type* to which we are referring, not the token.

organs and concepts" may not.[35] In this study I will be interested primarily in perceptual religious experiences, since only they can offer direct evidence for a religious reality beyond believers' own minds. Nonperceptual religious experiences will not be ignored, however, since it will be seen at the end that even they have a certain evidential function.

Both perceptual and nonperceptual experiences may have sensory and cognitive components. My experience of anger, for instance, may consist of certain sensations plus the belief that I have just been insulted, and my perceptual experience of an apple may involve visual, tactile, and gustatory sensations plus various beliefs about apples and the belief that there really is an apple there. Some nonperceptual experiences have no cognitive component (e.g. a sudden tingle), while some perceptual experiences have no sensory component, though this is more unusual. Examples of the latter are the phenomenon of 'blind-sight', where people who have no visual sensations from some portion of the visual field can nevertheless say where objects are in the 'blind' region,[36] and nonsensory experiences of the apparent presence or action of a divine being. Most of the cognitive elements of both perceptual and nonperceptual experiences are the result of 'incorporated interpretation', an important concept which will be introduced below and discussed further in Chapter VI.

Because of the sense in which all experiences are private, we rely heavily on subjects' own descriptions of their perceptual experiences. These descriptions may be—using Swinburne's terminology[37]—'internal' or 'external'. An 'external' description such as "I was aware of the presence of Christ near me, comforting me," entails that the alleged percept existed or occurred as described; to use *that* experience as the basis of an argument from religious experience would beg the question. An 'internal' description is less ambitious; "I had an experience of its seeming to me that Christ was near me, comforting me," does not entail anything about an external object, event, or state of affairs, but only about the way things seemed to the subject to be. Both believers and nonbelievers would accept that the subject had that experience, and so we have an uncontroversial starting-point from which to build the argu-

[35] Swinburne, p. 249.
[36] L. Weiskrantz, "Varieties of Residual Experience", *Quarterly Journal of Experimental Psychology*, 32 (1980), 365–86.   [37] pp. 244–5.

ment. It is true that people rarely report their experiences in 'internal' terms, but this is due to what Grice calls 'conversational implicature':[38] in ordinary conversation, it is assumed that a weaker statement will not be asserted where a stronger statement could have been. In common usage, for instance, "I believe" implies "I doubt; I am not sure; I do not know"—whereas philosophers maintain that believing is a necessary condition of knowing! In this study, the word 'seems' (and similar terms such as 'looks' and 'appears', all of which in normal conversation would imply "but it isn't" or "but it may not be") will be used in Chisholm's 'epistemic' sense,[39] in which the subjects are inclined to believe what 'seems' to them to be so, and in which its seeming to the subjects that x is present is a necessary condition of their perceiving that x is present.[40] (The inclination to believe can be overridden—one may strongly suspect one is hallucinating, for instance—but it may also be followed without question.) Although internal descriptions would be misleading in ordinary conversation, then, we will use them here when appropriate.

We must also distinguish between 'auto-descriptions', the descriptions subjects themselves would give of their experiences (which will sometimes be called 'experiential reports'), and 'hetero-descriptions', descriptions others would give. The terms are based on Ninian Smart's 'auto-interpretation' and 'hetero-interpretation',[41] but since 'interpretation' can be used in so many ways when applied to experience (as we shall see), I have preferred to make this distinction in terms of descriptions. Hetero-descriptions are referentially transparent; that is, co-referring expressions may be substituted without altering the truth-value of the description. For instance, if we know that the bird Jones saw was a thrush, then we can give the hetero-description, "Jones saw a thrush," even though Jones did not know at the time that the bird he was looking at was a thrush. The (external) auto-description in this case might be, "I saw a bird." Any alternative expression which the subject would have recognized at the time as co-referring can be substituted in an auto-description, but auto-descriptions are otherwise opaque. External

---

[38] H. Paul Grice, "Logic and Conversation", in Peter Cole and J. L. Morgan (eds.), *Syntax and Semantics*, vol. 3 (New York: Academic Press, 1975), pp. 41–58.

[39] R. M. Chisholm, *Perceiving* (Ithaca, NY: Cornell Univ. Press, 1957), ch. 4.

[40] As long as one takes "perceiving" in the 'opaque' sense.

[41] In "Interpretation and Mystical Experience".

descriptions of the form "S perceived *that p*" (as opposed to "S perceived *x*) and all internal descriptions are opaque and must be auto-descriptions. (An auto-description in this sense need not be stated in the first person singular; it must, however, use what would be 'the subject's own words'.)

The transparency of hetero-descriptions is not limited to expressions referring to the alleged percept; they can also describe the experience's true nature and causes. Thus Jones's experience of its seeming to him that there is a bird in his visual field might be described as the hallucination of a bird brought on by a high fever and Jones's childhood fear of birds. Hetero-descriptions of religious experiences given by sceptics are often of this form.

Both auto and hetero-descriptions can vary in degree of ramification and completeness. The latter term should be clear enough; it is the difference between, say, the experiential reports, "I saw a dog" and "I saw a large black dog with floppy ears". The former term is more difficult. (It is also borrowed from Ninian Smart,[42] though I do not agree with everything he says about it.) Very roughly, the more highly ramified a description is, the more it entails beyond what was actually observed. Highly ramified descriptions may involve highly theory-laden terms (e.g. "a glaciated landscape") or very specific terms (e.g. "beagle" as opposed to "dog" or "animal"), or employ specialized knowledge (e.g. "This is the pen which the prime minister used to sign the treaty"). A 'maximal' auto-description (my term) describes the way things seemed to the subject to be at the time, with whatever degree of ramification that was. A 'moderated' auto-description retreats from that degree of ramification to statements which commit the subject to less beyond what was actually observed (e.g. "a landscape of such-and-such a description"), and a 'minimal' auto-description attempts to describe the sensory component alone. Moderated and minimal auto-descriptions often do not do justice to the experience, as when the witnessing of a goal is described in terms of the players' movements; and they can be difficult to give—artists are trained to see things in the minimally ramified terms of shapes and colours, but most people would be unable to describe in less ramified terms the experiences which make them claim, "I see that you are unhappy" or "I hear my husband's voice on the telephone".

[42] In "Interpretation and Mystical Experience".

It is not always obvious what degree of ramification is intended by the speaker. For instance, although the term 'God' is generally quite highly ramified, a person may use it without having any more precise meaning in mind than 'an overwhelming holy power', and certainly not intending to imply the whole corpus of traditional Christian thought. Expressions may acquire a network of associations within a certain tradition, but even a person from within that tradition may not always use the expression with those associations in mind. This fact will prove important when we come to compare accounts of experiences from different traditions.

The veridicality of a perceptual experience is closely bound up with its auto-description, among other things. Perceptual experiences are veridical if the object was present, the event occurred, or the state of affairs obtained as it seemed to the subject (as described in his auto-description) and there was an "appropriate" causal relation between the percept and the percipient. The causal condition is crucial, and will be elaborated below. The other condition shows the importance of description. There is no 'one right way' to describe a particular experience. Which features are relevant and what degree of ramification and completeness appropriate depends largely on the context of utterance. In one context it may prove important to describe an experience as an experience of its seeming to me that John was unhappy or that there was an animal on the road; in another, I may have to remember how John was dressed or that the animal was a fox. Such experiences might well be veridical under one description and unveridical under another; veridicality is only an all-or-nothing affair if one restricts it to experiences under their most complete maximal auto-description.

Experiences which are unveridical under a certain auto-description are often veridical under a moderated or less complete auto-description. For instance, if I claim to have seen a rabbit, and the percept turns out to be a rock, the experience was still veridical under the description, "I saw a small dark object". Such experiences are 'misperceptions'. If there is no auto-description under which a perceptual experience is veridical (e.g. if it is a hallucination), then it is a 'nonperception' (not to be confused with 'nonperceptual experiences'). Many religious experiences may be misperceptions, and still be of use as evidence for some less ramified religious claims, as later chapters will show.

Just as it is possible for experiences to be unveridical under one description and yet be evidence for a moderated experiential claim, it is possible for experiences to be veridical and yet have little or no evidential force. It is for this reason that this work is an examination of the 'evidential force' of religious experiences and not primarily of their 'veridicality'. This point will be explained further in Chapter IV, where a general account is given of the way perceptual experiences can be used as evidence for claims about the world.

The second, 'causal' condition is more difficult to spell out. Some sort of causal relationship between the percept and percipient is necessary, otherwise an experience such as my hypnotically induced vision of Jones when Jones happens to be present would be a veridical perception. This causal relationship must also be an "appropriate" one, so that cases such as the perception of a hologram of a table are rejected as perceptions of the original table, though the original table is causally related to the hologram. Because of the difficulty of specifying a causal relationship which both maintains the logical possibility that telepathy and clairvoyance yield perceptions and allows for the complex causal chains by which such things as microscopes mediate perceptions, I will continue to use the vague word "appropriate" until Chapter VIII.3, where the religious application of the causal condition is discussed.

Religious experiences are often said to be "a matter of interpretation". There are so many ways in which experiences can be said to be 'interpreted', though, that the final task of this section must be to clarify the different uses of the term.

When it is claimed that religious experiences are ordinary experiences on which an unwarranted religious interpretation has been imposed, the term is usually being used in the 'derogatory' sense: "it is *merely* a matter of interpretation". Proponents of such a view often claim that though percepts such as tables and chairs can be 'given' in an experience, a divine presence must be 'interpreted'. More will be said on this misguided view of perceptual experience in Chapter VI.

A second, more important sense of 'interpretation' is that of 'retrospective interpretation',[43] used when an experience is under-

---

[43] The terms 'retrospective', 'incorporated', and 'reflexive interpretation' are borrowed from Peter Moore, "Mystical Experience, Mystical Doctrine, Mystical Technique", in Stephen Katz (ed.), *Mysticism and Philosophical Analysis* (London: Sheldon Press, 1978), pp. 101–31. I use them somewhat differently from Moore, since he applies them only to aspects of mystical experience.

stood in the light of subsequent reflection or new information. I may have the experience of its seeming to me that a duck is quacking, but if I look out of the window and see a person blowing a duck-call, I will retrospectively interpret that experience as the experience of hearing a duck-call being blown. My internal auto-description will remain the same—I cannot change the way things *seemed* to me to be at the time—but I would assert a different external description. There is a danger that such retrospective interpretation may become incorporated into our memory of our experiences, which then makes the experiences falsely appear to have been good evidence for certain claims. This danger is especially apparent when we are dealing with highly ramified descriptions of religious experiences.

This is not to say that retrospective interpretations should be avoided or that retrospectively interpreted experiences are eviden-tially useless. The second duck-call experience enabled the subject to understand her first experience *better*; and the two experiences together were excellent evidence for the claim that she heard a duck-call being blown before she looked out of the window. Religious experiences are often retrospectively interpreted in the light of other religious experiences, in which case the experiences can work together as evidence in an argument from religious experience alone. Often, however—like many of our experi-ences—their true significance is only brought out after reflection based on other types of experiences, beliefs, and so on. Many religious experiences are more like particularly insightful or efficacious moments within a continuing process of psychological, religious, and cognitive development than like one-off visions or ecstasies, and context is very important to their evaluation. We will see, in fact, that most types of religious experience best support religious claims when they are taken in conjunction with other types of evidence. Hidden retrospective interpretation is only a danger if one believes religious experiences on their own ought to be able to confirm highly ramified claims.

There is a sense in which *all* experiences are 'matters of interpretation'. This third, crucial sense, 'incorporated interpret-ation', is interpretation we perform unconsciously to transform the stimuli with which we are constantly bombarded into intelligible experiences of recognizable percepts. It is incorporated without our awareness into an experience and is thus inseparable from it; it is what makes us have *that* experience, see things *that* way. Far from being 'mere interpretation', it is necessary to all perception. Neither tables nor divine beings are 'given' as such to a passive recipient. This kind of interpretation is described more fully in Chapter VI.

A fourth category, 'reflexive interpretation', is like incorporated interpretation in that it is not arrived at by conscious inference or reflection; however, it is formed immediately after the experience, and not incorporated into the experience itself. Often this is because the experience is of such brief duration, as when one hears a sharp sound and reflexively interprets it as a gunshot. This sense of 'interpretation' will prove important in the case of mystical experiences, where the experiences themselves are said to be so overwhelming and so empty of all thoughts and distinctions that interpretation is impossible during the experience, but the auto-descriptions given on emerging from the experience (e.g. "union with God") are nevertheless often spontaneous rather than the result of reflection.

With some of the philosophical groundwork out of the way, let us now turn to the 'data' themselves, the reports of religious experiences.

2

RELIGIOUS EXPERIENCE

I. WHAT COUNTS AS A 'RELIGIOUS EXPERIENCE'?

Proponents of arguments from religious experience often succumb to the demand to provide a brief, precise definition of 'religious experience'. Such definitions can do more harm than good, however. If one restricts the term to experiences in accordance with the doctrines of one tradition, then any argument from religious experiences to those doctrines begs the question.[1] On the other hand, to widen the definition to include all experiences referred to as 'religious' would be foolhardy, since people often use terms such as 'religious' and 'mystical' metaphorically, to refer to any experience which is overwhelming, extraordinary, thrilling, or sublime. A brief definition such as "experiences of God", though plausible, excludes the many religious experiences of theists which are not "of God" as such, as well as experiences from atheistic mystical traditions such as 'cosmic consciousness' and Buddhism. Definitions involving the term "God" are difficult to work with in any case, since the term admits of such a variety of interpretations.

Because there are so many religious traditions and so many types of experience within those traditions, I look upon the quest for a neat, precise definition of 'religious experience'—even a definition 'for the purposes of this study'—as fruitless. Most people have a workable idea of what counts as a religious experience, based on the many uncontroversial examples available. What I shall do in this and the following sections is to sharpen up that idea with a few guidelines, comparisons with borderline experiences which I do not count as 'religious', and an extensive survey of different types of religious experience. Such a procedure should provide us with a much better understanding of religious experiences than a short definition ever could.

---

[1] Such experiences would nevertheless have some small evidential force, since it could have been the case that no experiences ever occurred which were in accordance with that tradition's doctrines.

It is the auto-description to which one must normally turn to determine the religiousness of an experience. A believer may give a hetero-description such as "that was the Holy Spirit working in you" of another's experience of new hope or peace, but such an experience would only be a 'religious experience' if the subject himself saw it in a religious light. Experiences such as ecstasy, being in love, deliverance from danger or despair, aesthetic experiences, and inspiration must all be given a religious incorporated or reflexive interpretation if they are to count as 'religious experiences'.

Some experiences are seen as religious by the subject because of their religious content or context—for instance, a vision or revelation with religious content, or a feeling of peace while praying or taking communion. However, not all experiences in a religious context are 'religious experiences'—an itch during communion is unlikely to be, for instance! Similarly, the perception of religious texts and works of art and the participation in religious rituals, though experiences with religious content, do not in themselves constitute 'religious experiences'. Thoughts with religious content will be religious if they seem to the subjects to have been the result of divine inspiration rather than produced by their own powers of reasoning. Again, though, not all 'flashes of insight' are religious experiences; suddenly seeing the solution to a mathematical problem, even if it seems to have 'come out of the blue', is usually not a religious experience, though it may be referred to metaphorically as such by an overjoyed mathematician.

The line dividing secular experiences from their religious counterparts is often difficult to draw, and rightly so. Sometimes, for instance, a subject may come to see things in religious terms over the course of a sustained experience which began non-religiously. In the aesthetic realm, works of art and the act of creating works of art can often trigger religious experiences, and aesthetic experiences sometimes merge into religious experiences with no clear moment of transition. Some artists, musicians and writers even see their activity as a religious exercise, though many may be using the word metaphorically.

Some religious experiences are what I call 'intrinsically religious'. Such experiences involve at least one of those 'other-worldly' factors which are missing in quasi-religions such as Marxism and humanism: the sense of the presence or activity of a non-physical holy being or power; apprehension of an 'ultimate reality' beyond the mundane world of physical bodies, physical processes, and narrow centres of consciousness; and the sense of achievement of (or being on the way to) man's *summum bonum*, an ultimate bliss, liberation, salvation, or 'true self' which is not attainable through the things of 'this world'. These are very general categories, and they include experiences as diverse as the sense of the presence of the risen Christ and the 'discovery' that the universe is guided by love. Unlike experiences of peace, joy, and so on, it is impossible for this type of experience not to be religious.

People occasionally describe an experience in religious terms such as 'holy presence' and 'ultimate reality', and yet refuse to apply the word 'religious' to it. This usually occurs where people restrict their application of the term 'religious' to things associated with institutional religion or to experiences which conform to a narrow set of doctrines. Since I am not restricting the scope of the term in this way, I count such experiences as religious, even though the word 'religious' could not appear in the auto-description. (In fact, one rarely finds the *word* 'religious' in auto-descriptions, but it would normally be legitimate to use it.)

Generally, then, religious experiences are experiences which the subjects themselves describe in religious terms or which are intrinsically religious.

The characteristics outlined above do not presuppose any form of intervention on the part of a conscious deity, although they do exclude the extreme form of deism according to which 'the transcendent' is in *no* way 'immanent'. Some religious experiences are described in a way that suggests divine intervention; others suggest that God is working through natural causes or that the world and human nature are so constituted that with suitable effort, we can attain salvation on our own. At the moment, while I am still taking religious experiences at their face value, I am assuming neither interventionism nor non-interventionism. The issue is important, however, and it will resurface in Chapter VIII, where a case will be made for a "non-crude interventionism".

Before I go on to describe the different types of religious experience, a note on my sources would be in order. Mystics and ordinary believers from non-Christian religious traditions have generally been reluctant to give the world autobiographical accounts of their experiences, and as a result, pure, straightforward auto-descriptions are rare. They must be distilled from biographies (and hagiographies), manuals, treatises, hymns, poems, and other religious works—rather like learning of Hebrew religious experiences through the Psalms and the Prophets. This can be done, but much care must be taken: retrospective interpretation is probably included; the original experience may have been edited or embellished to fit doctrines more closely or to make an astonishing or edifying story; and much information about the subject's psychological make-up and the conditions under which he or she had the experience is lacking. With those caveats, I shall nevertheless cite texts such as passages from the *Bhagavad Gita* as examples of religious experiences.

In the West, autobiographical material is much more abundant, and many great mystics have provided us with detailed and sensitive accounts of themselves, their lives and experiences. Contemporary auto-descriptions of religious experiences are also readily available in the West; some of these are particularly useful because the subjects are not adherents of a religious tradition and so attempt to describe their experiences without using either the standard metephors or the 'formulae' (e.g. "I accepted Christ as my personal saviour") characteristic of the auto-descriptions of many people deeply immersed in one tradition. A useful collection of such contemporary experiences can be found in Alister Hardy's book *The Spiritual Nature of Man*. Unfortunately, Hardy provides little information about the subjects' background beliefs, psychological state, and so on, and so the evidential value of any individual experience is difficult to assess; however, the sheer number and variety of independent reports helps to overcome this problem.

There certainly is an abundance of material to be *considered* as the basis of an argument from religious experience. Further discussion of the reliability of reports of religious experiences will be found in Chapter V, when various challenges to the use of religious experience as evidence are considered.

Let us turn now to the experiences themselves, to get an idea of the range and nature of 'the data'. I have divided the experiences into six categories: interpretive, quasi-sensory, revelatory, regenerative, numinous, and mystical. This is by no means the only possible classification of religious experiences. I have chosen it partly because many religious experiences seem 'naturally' to fall into certain categories, but its main function is to facilitate an orderly overview of the kinds of experiences we will consider as possible evidence for religious claims. The categories are not intended to be exclusive, since an experience may exhibit the characteristics of several categories at once. Indeed, they could be presented as six different aspects of religious experiences: how they are seen by the subject to fit into a larger religious pattern, the quasi-sensory element, the alleged knowledge gained in the experience, the 'affective' aspect and immediate 'fruits' of the experience, the 'holy' element, and the 'unitive' element. This approach might be misleading, however, since few religious experiences have all six of these features. Bearing these remarks in mind, then, let us proceed to the first type of religious experience.

2. INTERPRETIVE EXPERIENCES

Sometimes a subject sees an experience as religious not because of any unusual features of the experience itself, but because it is viewed in the light of a prior religious interpretive framework. Common examples of such experiences are seeing a misfortune as the result of sins in a previous life, going through an illness with joy because it is a chance to 'participate in Christ's suffering', experiencing love for all things of this world because of the belief that they are permeated by the divine, seeing an event as 'God's will', and taking an event to be the answer to a prayer. Some people are such fervent believers that they see all they do and experience as in some way religiously significant, whether fortunes or misfortunes, great works or just daily chores. I am reminded of John Donne's "Hymne to Christ, at the Authors Last Going Into Germany":

> In what torne ship soever I embarke,
> That ship shall be my embleme of thy Arke;
> What sea soever swallow mee, that flood
> Shall be to mee an embleme of thy blood. . .

Experiences which are seen as the answer to a prayer often make fragile evidence, since the subjects themselves are usually willing to admit that things could have turned out just as they did without any divine aid.[2] In particular, sceptics can have a field day with

[2] See Vincent Brümmer's study of prayer, *What are we doing when we pray? A Philosophical Inquiry* (London: SCM, 1984).

subjects who treat God as an invisible business partner or "meat purveyor", ready to intervene in response to materialistic prayers. William James gives a good example of such "primitive religious thought" in a footnote. An English sailor, prisoner on a French ship in 1689, is fighting his captors:

. . . and looking about again to see anything to strike them withal, but seeing nothing, I said, 'Lord! what shall I do now?' And then it pleased God to put me in mind of my knife in my pocket. And although two of the men had hold of my right arm, yet God Almighty strengthened me so that I put my right hand into my right pocket, drew out the knife and sheath . . . and then cut the man's throat . . .[3]

However, not all 'answers to prayers' use such a crude model of divine intervention. We will see in section 5 that many regenerative experiences such as renewed hope are seen as answers to prayers, and such experiences will play an important part in the 'fruits' argument of Chapter IX.3.

Paranormal experiences with no specifically religious content come into the 'interpretive' category when they are seen by the subject as due to some divine agency. I quote a clairvoyant experience from Hardy's collection at some length, to show how the religious interpretation seems to be 'tacked on' at the end:

I was a young married woman with a 6 month old baby daughter. My husband and I got an evening off to see a film at K—— about 6 miles away. One of the hotel staff had volunteered to baby sit . . . We had not been long seated in the cinema when a terrible uneasiness overcame me. I could distinctly smell burning. . . . eventually I told my husband I was leaving. He followed me reluctantly, muttering something derogatory about women.

. . . At last we were sprinting down the lane leading to the cottage. The smell of burning was now very definite to me though my husband could not smell a thing. We reached the door which I literally burst in. As I did so the dense smoke poured out and a chair by the fire burst into flames. I rushed through to the bedroom and got the baby out while my husband dragged out the unconscious girl. She had fallen asleep in the armchair and dropped her lighted cigarette into the chair which had smouldered for hours. Yes, God sent me home to save my baby. God was with me telling me to hurry home; of that I am convinced and also my husband.[4]

---

[3] James, pp. 450–1 n.
[4] In Hardy, p. 46.

There is no evidence that the woman sensed a divine presence guiding her. Up to the last two sentences, the experience could have been described by an atheist.

These examples are extreme, but they still show typical features of interpretive religious experiences in which a remarkable or beneficial event with no specifically religious characteristics is attributed to a divine source by a person with prior religious beliefs. Such religious experiences have little evidential force on their own (as later arguments will show), since they are so clearly the product of a prior interpretive framework. That interpretive framework may well be the right one to use, but the experiences themselves cannot tell us that. This is not to say, however, that interpretive religious experiences have no value at all as evidence: Chapter IX will describe how they can be combined with other sources of evidence to support religious claims. For instance, a preponderance of unexpected beneficial events might lead a person to suspect that there is a benevolent deity; but then it is no longer an argument from religious experience, rather an argument from providence or miracles. Ordinary events and feelings might be seen by a person to "make sense" only when interpreted within some religious model; crises and difficult moral decisions might be dealt with better if interpreted religiously. Paranormal experiences which the subjects do not consider 'religious' may nevertheless lead them to religious beliefs: for instance, an out-of-body experience could convince someone that human beings have a soul which is distinct from and separable from the body; and even a paranormal experience as mundane as the clairvoyant experience of 'seeing' a hidden object could shake a person out of a materialistic world-view.

Perhaps many interpretive experiences should not strictly be called 'religious experiences'; however, they form such an important aspect of the lives of deeply religious people that they ought not to be ignored.

3. QUASI-SENSORY EXPERIENCES

Religious experiences in which the primary element is a physical sensation or whose alleged percept is of a type normally apprehended by one of the five sense modalities are 'quasi-sensory' experiences. These include visions and dreams, voices and other sounds, smells, tastes, the feeling of being touched, heat, pain, and the sensation of rising up (levitation).

The most frequently discussed type of quasi-sensory religious experience is the apparent vision of a spiritual being who gives the subject advice. Unfortunately, this has led to the common view that quasi-sensory religious experiences are 'all-or-nothing' affairs: either a supernatural being really was present in some form, or these experiences are hallucinations and of no value at all. However, this is a false dichotomy; quasi-sensory experiences can be 'veridical' in several different ways.

(i) In the type of quasi-sensory religious experience already mentioned, the quasi-sensory elements are taken to be representations of a spiritual entity which is actually present. The experience can then only be veridical if the alleged percept is actually present as it appears to the subject to be. This type of experience is not in fact the most common—even visions of saints are often placed by subjects in category (ii) (to be discussed below), and the conviction that a divine being is truly there often comes through a non-physical 'sense of a presence' rather than through quasi-sensory features[5]—but they certainly do occur. A good example of one such is the conversion experience of Sadhu Sundar Singh in 1904.[6] Sundar could find no satisfaction in his own religion (Sikhism) but was violently opposed to Christianity; he finally decided that if he got no answer from God about the right path, he would kill himself. He took his usual cold morning bath and then began to pray fervently.

At 4.30 A.M. I saw something of which I had no idea at all previously. In the room where I was praying I saw a great light. I thought the place was on fire. I looked round, but could find nothing. Then the thought came to me that this might be an answer that God had sent me. Then as I prayed and looked into the light, I saw the form of the Lord Jesus Christ. It had such an appearance of glory and love. If it had been some Hindu incarnation I would have prostrated myself before it. But it was the Lord Jesus Christ whom I had been insulting a few days before. I felt that a

[5] See the last chapter of Timothy Beardsworth, *A Sense of Presence* (Oxford: RERU, 1977).
[6] Described in B. H. Streeter and A. J. Appasamy, *The Sadhu* (London: Macmillan, 1921), pp. 5–7. A more familiar example is St Paul's experience on the road to Damascus, which Sundar's vision echoes. Psychological accounts of such experiences will be discussed in Chapter VIII.

vision like this could not come out of my own imagination. I heard a voice saying in Hindustani, 'How long will you persecute me? I have come to save you; you were praying to know the right way. Why do you not take it?' The thought then came to me, 'Jesus Christ is not dead but living and it must be He Himself.' So I fell at His feet and got this wonderful Peace which I could not get anywhere else.

Sundar claimed after this experience "that some new power from outside entered into his life from that moment, and that it was Christ Himself who appeared and spoke to him".[7]

The disciples' post-resurrection experiences of Christ, if reliably recorded, would certainly come into this first category. They are particularly interesting, as they are less like hallucinations than are most experiences of apparitions.[8] Generally apparitions appear and disappear suddenly, do not leave physical traces, and do not interact with the subjects, although they may utter a message—as Sundar's Christ vision did. Whether this peculiarity supports the theory that Christ was actually present to the disciples or whether it provides further evidence for a demythologized view of their experiences, I cannot venture to say; such a question is beyond the scope of this book.

(ii) More often, the quasi-sensory elements of a religious experience are considered by subjects to be like 'pictures', 'sent' by a divine being and requiring a certain amount of interpretation. As such, they are 'hallucinatory'—i.e. they are not veridical sensory perceptions—but they are nevertheless considered to be valid sources of religious insight. One does not say that the experience of looking at a film with the knowledge that it is a film is unveridical just because one's field of vision contains 'images' rather than real people or actually occurring events; and one can acquire true beliefs even from fiction. Where quasi-sensory elements in the form of a religious symbol, a divine being, or even a whole spiritual drama are thus seen (in the auto-description) as 'pictures' shown the subject by a divine being for the subject's edification, the experience will be veridical if the quasi-sensory elements were actually brought about by that divine being (perhaps through telepathy). The fact that the contents of the vision were not physically present would only make such experiences unveridical if one forced them into the mould of sense perception.

---

[7] *The Sadhu*, p. 8.
[8] See the study by G. N. M. Tyrrell, *Apparitions* (London: Duckworth, 1953).

Examples of this attitude to visions can be found in the mystical works of all religious traditions. Julian of Norwich, for instance, describes in detail a vision she had of a lord and his servant when she wanted to understand how we could sin so much and yet never be blamed by God.[9] She says she did not fully understand this vision until twenty years had passed, when she analysed it as a detailed allegory. There is never any suggestion that the vision was veridical in the sense that she saw a really existing lord and servant; it was regarded as a divinely produced 'picture' from which she was able to derive valuable religious knowledge. Similarly, the author of *The Cloud of Unknowing* says that visions are generally sent to demonstrate religious truths to those who would have difficulty grasping them in any other way, so that St Stephen's vision in martyrdom of Christ standing in heaven was as if Christ had said to him, "I am standing by you spiritually"—not to show the actual posture of the heavenly Christ.[10]

(iii) In the third type of quasi-sensory experience, the quasi-sensory elements have no religious significance themselves and convey no religious insight. Light is by far the most common quasi-sensory element in this category, but one also finds reports of beautiful music, bells, sweet odours, and heat. Where these elements accompany a non-sensory or more complex religious experience, they are taken to be an indication that the experience was of special significance or originated from a spiritual realm—see, for instance, the 'flame-coloured cloud' of R. M. Bucke's experience, quoted in section 4, below, and the 'great light' of Sundar Singh's experience, both of which were so vivid that the subjects' first thoughts were of a real, immense fire. Where these quasi-sensory elements occur alone, they are only seen as religious because they occur during an exercise in meditation (when they are often accompanied by great joy), or because the subject has been taught to expect such experiences as 'favours' from God or as signs of progress. In other circumstances, an experience such as a sudden vision of flashing lights would be unlikely to make the subject think of God, rather more likely to send him off to the doctor.

Experiences where a non-religious quasi-sensory element predominates are regarded with somewhat more favour in the East

---

[9] Julian of Norwich, *Revelations of Divine Love*, tr. Clifton Wolters (Harmondsworth: Penguin Books, 1966), ch. 51.
[10] *The Cloud of Unknowing*, tr. Clifton Wolters (Harmondsworth: Penguin Books, 1961), ch. 58.

than in the West, and Indian mystics have drawn up elaborate classifications of the types of sounds, colours, smells, and so on that meditators may experience, giving each of them a religious 'meaning'.[11] Nevertheless, the different traditions are remarkably unanimous regarding the ultimate value and role of this third type of quasi-sensory experience. Such experiences may be rewards for the beginner, but they are generally trivial and can even be obstacles to spiritual advancement. The general consensus is that they should be disregarded: they are particularly suspect, as 'diabolical' and pathological states can bring them on much more easily than they can the more intrinsically religious experiences; they can be coveted, or seen as a source of pride, which would undo much of the subject's training in renunciation and purification; and there is a danger that they may be mistaken for the end of the path, so that salvation is never attained. The same can be said of the psychic powers allegedly attained by many mystics, especially those of Indian traditions; subjects are specifically enjoined to pay them no heed and never to exercise them.

Quasi-sensory religious experiences, perhaps more than any other type, acquire their specific form largely from the subject's own store of religious ideas. People have visions of saints and deities as they are portrayed in the pictures and sculptures of their community—examples of this are legion. Even the *type* of quasi-sensory experience can be conditioned by background beliefs; David Brown points out that Protestants, Jews, and Muslims, who are very averse to any kind of 'graven image', tend to hear voices, while Roman Catholics and Hindus see visions.[12] Such conditioning need not imply that the experience was entirely determined by the subject's background, however, as we shall see in later chapters.

4. REVELATORY EXPERIENCES

Religious experiences of this category comprise what their subjects may call sudden convictions, inspiration, revelation, enlightenment, 'the mystical vision', and flashes of insight. They may seem to descend upon the subject out of the blue, unaccompanied by any other feature which would make the experience religious, in which

[11] See Swami Sivananda, *Concentration and Meditation* (Rikhikesh: The Sivananda Publication League, 1945), ch. IX.

[12] David Brown, *The Divine Trinity* (London: Duckworth, 1985), ch. I.

case it is their religious content which makes them 'religious experiences'; or, more frequently, they are the 'revelatory' element in a more complex religious experience, very often a mystical experience. These experiences have distinctive features: (i) they are usually sudden and of short duration, though the after-effects may last a lifetime (especially in the case of conversion experiences); (ii) the alleged new knowledge seems to the subject to have been acquired immediately rather than through reasoning or sense perception; (iii) the alleged new knowledge usually seems to the subject to have been 'poured into' or 'showered upon' him (metaphors abound) by an external agency; (iv) the 'revelations' carry with them utter conviction, somehow even more than that which attaches to sense perception; and (v) the insights gained are often claimed to be impossible to put into words.

In Eastern religious traditions, though purity of soul is required, it is ignorance which is generally regarded as the greatest hindrance to liberation or salvation. 'Enlightenment experiences' are often seen as the goal of the mystical quest and the beginning of a new, 'true' life, particularly in atheistic traditions such as Buddhism. D. T. Suzuki describes the Zen Buddhist experience of satori thus:

Satori is the sudden flashing into consciousness of a new truth hitherto undreamed of. It is a sort of mental catastrophe taking place all at once, after much piling up of matters intellectual and demonstrative. The piling has reached a limit of stability and the whole edifice has come tumbling to the ground, when, behold, a new heaven is open to full survey. . . Religiously, it is a new birth; intellectually, it is the acquiring of a new viewpoint.[13]

Not all revelatory experiences are as cataclysmic as these mystical 'enlightenment experiences', but they do share the characteristics of immediacy and certainty. Philo reports that

Sometimes, when I have come to my work empty, I have suddenly become full; ideas being in an invisible manner showered upon me, and implanted in me from on high . . . for then I have been conscious of a richness of interpretation, an enjoyment of light, a most penetrating insight . . . having such effect on my mind as the clearest ocular demonstration would have on the eyes.[14]

---

[13] D. T. Suzuki, *An Introduction to Zen Buddhism* (London: Arrow Books, 1959), p. 95.
[14] Quoted in James, p. 460.

St Teresa also asserts emphatically that these insights are from an external divine source, are immediate, and are even *more* certain than "the clearest ocular demonstration":

The Lord is pleased that this knowledge should be so deeply engraven upon the understanding that one can no more doubt it than one can doubt the evidence of one's eyes—indeed, the latter is easier, for we sometimes suspect that we have imagined what we see, whereas here, though that suspicion may arise for a moment, there remains such complete certainty that the doubt has no force . . . The Lord introduces into the inmost part of the soul what he wishes that soul to understand . . . It is as if food has been introduced into the stomach without our having eaten it or knowing how it got there.[15]

It is "*knowing* in a quite different way from intellectual knowledge", says one of Hardy's respondents;[16] and the sentiment is echoed wherever there is religion. This sense of certainty is not restricted to revelatory experiences, of course; experiences of a holy presence, mystical experiences of 'oneness', and so on, are typically reported with the same sense of assurance, as we shall see in later sections.

Just what is claimed to be known in this utterly convincing manner varies. It may be a specific and easily articulable prophecy, revelation, or religious insight; it may be something so comprehensive and fundamental that the subject has extreme difficulty expressing it; it may be an obviously false claim to omniscience, as exhibited by one of Hardy's respondents who wrote, "I knew that I was capable of answering any question or problem put to me, no matter how abstruse".[17] Sometimes subjects may have the sense of 'having understood everything', and then devote much of their life to the struggle to spell out more specifically what they understood in that brief moment:

A great inward light seemed to illuminate my thoughts, I experienced a magnificent sensation of arrival. I was filled with joy as though I had just discovered the secret of world peace. I suddenly *knew*. The odd thing was that I did not know what I knew. From then on I set out to define it.[18]

---

[15] St Teresa of Avila, *Life*, from *The Complete Works of Saint Teresa of Jesus*, tr. and ed. E. Allison Peers (London: Sheed & Ward, 1946), vol. 1, p. 172.
[16] In Hardy, p. 109.
[17] Ibid. p. 56.
[18] Ibid. p. 110.

Others may never find the words to express their alleged knowledge—in which case there is no cognitive claim for which the experience could be used as evidence, and the experience is truly ineffable.

In most cases, however, the subject does make specific knowledge claims. In the simplest kind of case, the content of the 'insight' can be found in the sermon or religious text which suddenly struck the hearer as ineluctably true:

It was while listening to a sermon in St. Mary's, that I became convinced of the reality of God. Emotion was at a minimum . . . this sense of being convinced was not basically intellectual either. It was just that I knew the preacher was speaking the truth.[19]

Usually, however, the alleged knowledge is held to be revealed in some more interior way. These claims are often of a personal nature, and sometimes very specific, as when St Teresa says she received instructions and prophecies from the Lord regarding the founding of St Joseph's convent.[20] More typical are experiences in which some fairly general but articulable religious truths are alleged to have been apprehended, even in cases where the subject claims ineffability. These range from the highly ramified Christian claims of St Teresa and Julian of Norwich regarding the Trinity[21] to the more broadly religious claims of R. M. Bucke (see below), which are found in innumerable cases. Often subjects draw a distinction between the intellectual belief previously held and the way they now 'see' or 'know' the doctrine to be true (Newman's distinction between 'notional' and 'real' beliefs[22]): "Knowing with all my being what is meant by the concept God is Love";[23] "what we hold by faith [i.e. the Trinity] the soul may be said here to grasp by sight".[24]

Paradoxically, perhaps, these revelatory experiences, which inspire so much certainty, are also a type of experience spiritual authorities are very inclined to mistrust. Like secular 'intuitions', they are treated as unreliable sources of knowledge, guilty until

---

[19] In Hardy, p. 100.

[20] *Life*, ch. XXXIII.

[21] St Teresa, *Interior Castle*, 7. i; and Julian of Norwich, *Revelations*, ch. 58.

[22] Made in *The Grammar of Assent*; see the discussion in H. D. Lewis, *Our Experience of God* (London: Allen & Unwin, 1959), p. 25.

[23] In Hardy, p. 109.

[24] St Teresa, *Interior Castle*, 7. i.

proven innocent. There is a long tradition within the Roman Catholic church, for example, of subjecting alleged revelations to rigorous tests, many of which involve the same sort of criteria as we would apply to any perceptual claim (see Chapter III.3). Innocence is confirmed by such factors as consistency with (though not necessarily prior inclusion in) the teachings of the Church and the integrity, health, education, and spirituality of the subject.[25] Even then, private matters revealed through visions and voices are not accorded a high degree of trust. Meister Eckhart writes, for instance, that "private revelations" through angels or special illuminations can be deceptive, but there is a

second knowledge, which is incomparably better and more profitable and happens often to all who are perfect in their love . . . when a man, through the love and the intimacy that exist between his God and him, trusts in him so fully and is so certain of him that he cannot doubt.[26]

St Teresa of Avila, practical as always, writes that even if alleged revelations fulfil the criteria of agreement with Scripture and of increasing the soul's tranquillity, confidence, and devotion to God, if they are important, require action, or involve another person, then a wise confessor should be consulted.[27] Other religious traditions have similar reservations about revelatory experiences. Within Buddhism, for instance, the monk Mettānando Bhikkhu cautions that the insights which meditators think they obtain are more often wrong than not; such 'intuitions' are only accepted if the subject has reached a very advanced stage of meditation, and the intuition is shared by other meditators of high rank, or if the subject has had a gift for 'intuition' from childhood and so is known to be reliable.[28] Generally, revelations obtained during mystical experiences and the revelations of 'recognized' prophets and saints are accepted as valid religious insights within most traditions, while revelations conveyed by other means and trivial or mundane revelations are more suspect.

[25] See C. Wolters' introduction to *Revelations of Divine Love*, pp. 11–13, for a good account of the church's attitude towards alleged revelations.

[26] Meister Eckhart, *Counsels on Discernment* 15, tr. Edmund Colledge, from *Meister Eckhart: The Essential Sermons, Commentaries, Treatises, and Defense*, tr. and intro. Edmund Colledge and Bernard McGinn (London: SPCK, 1981), p. 264.

[27] *Interior Castle*, p. 144.

[28] Conversation with Mettānando Bhikkhu at Oriel College, Oxford, on 23 Feb. 1986.

Let me close by quoting an experience of R. M. Bucke which is particularly rich in alleged insights, and to which we shall have cause to refer many times:

All at once . . . I found myself wrapped in a flame-colored cloud. . . . Directly afterward there came upon me a sense of exultation, of immense joyousness accompanied or immediately followed by an intellectual illumination impossible to describe. Among other things, I did not merely come to believe, but I saw that the universe is not composed of dead matter, but is, on the contrary, a living Presence; I became conscious in myself of eternal life. It was not a conviction that I would have eternal life, but a consciousness that I possessed eternal life then; I saw that all men are immortal; that the cosmic order is such that without any peradventure all things work together for the good of each and all; that the foundation principle of the world, of all the worlds, is what we call love, and that the happinesss of each and all is in the long run absolutely certain. The vision lasted a few seconds and was gone but the memory of it and the sense of the reality of what it taught have remained during the quarter of a century which has since elapsed. I knew that what the vision showed was true.[29]

5. REGENERATIVE EXPERIENCES

Regenerative experiences are the most frequent type of religious experience among ordinary people—that is, people who are not mystics, ecstatics, prophets, or psychics. Most religious people find their faith sustained by such experiences; they are one of the features which make a 'living religion' more than the mere acceptance of a set of doctrines or the performance of certain rituals. Regenerative experiences, as their name suggests,[30] tend to renew the subject's faith and improve his spiritual, moral, physical, or psychological well-being; it is like, as a respondent in Michael Walker's study put it, having "my 'spiritual' batteries recharged".[31]

This category includes a wide range of experiences: experiences of new hope, strength, comfort, peace, security, and joy, seen as 'religious' because they are obtained during a religious activity such

[29] In James, p. 385.

[30] The term is from Peter Donovan, *Interpreting Religious Experience* (London: Sheldon Press, 1979), though what I include in the category differs slightly from what he includes.

[31] Reported in Hardy, p. 116.

as prayer, apparently brought about by a divine power, or accompanied by the sense of a divine presence; experiences of being guided, 'called', forgiven, and 'saved', usually by an external divine power; healing experiences; an apparently divinely aided increase in moral virtues and love for others; and the discovery of 'meaning' in life. These experiences may be mild or overwhelming, daily occurrences or extraordinary 'one-off' events, with or without other elements such as the quasi-sensory; they could be anything from a believer's vague feeling of peace during prayer to a combined vision, revelation, and 'sense of a holy presence' which converts and heals an alcoholic atheist.

It may be noticed that both the revelatory and regenerative categories have included 'conversion experiences'. Those who treat these as a distinct type of religious experience usually concentrate on the experience of being 'saved' at a revival meeting, but people can be converted by many different types of experience—e.g. visions (Sundar Singh), 'flashes of insight' (p. 42), and even nature mysticism. What makes these 'conversion experiences' is their effect on the subject. 'Senses of a presence' are likewise often put into a single category. I have chosen not to do so here, since one does not have just the sense of 'a presence', but the sense of some *kind* of presence (e.g. awesome, loving, guiding; individual, all-pervading) and of a certain relationship with the presence (e.g. devotion, union, feeling it at work within you); and these differences result in extremely diverse experiences. For some purposes, it can be useful to think of 'senses of a presence' as a separate category; later chapters will show that religious experiences which include a 'sense of presence' are of more value as evidence for the existence of a holy power than are experiences without it.

To return to regenerative experiences in general: one important type of regenerative experience, and a vital part of Christian tradition, is 'healing'. Although it is the physical effects which are considered most significant by the person looking for 'miracles' to convince unbelievers, those who have been healed and those who have done the healing very often stress other 'regenerative' effects, while still—importantly for this study—claiming that the experience was brought about by God. For instance, an elderly clergyman wrote of his healing ministry:

The one constant factor is a serenity of spirit that, as is commonly said, can almost be felt; it can be seen even in those whose physical ailment has not been healed . . . Death is not always defeated—I mean even temporarily, for of course death will always come—but people with cancer die without pain or drugs and in such serenity of mind and spirit that their passing is a triumph. It seems to me that it is impossible for one human being to do this for another unaided. I have comforted, and have been comforted, by another, but always the comfort waned. This awareness of a power, beyond us humans, remains and grows and wholeness or, if you like, righteousness, increases. . . . one woman . . . was healed, in a week, of a vast varicose ulcer; on being told by some friends that she seemed remarkably casual about it, she said: 'I'm not casual or ungrateful, but the much more important fact than my healed ulcer and the freedom from pain and discomfort is that whereas I was a worrier and built all my bridges before I came to them, now I pray and trust and have lost anxiety and fear.'[32]

A type of experience especially common in evangelical Protestant circles is the sense of being 'saved', especially through the forgiveness of sins. In John Wesley's Journal entry on 24 May 1738 we read:

In the evening I went very unwillingly to a society in Aldersgate-Street, where one was reading Luther's preface to the Epistle to the Romans. About a quarter before nine, while he was describing the change which God works in the heart through faith in Christ, I felt my heart strangely warmed. I felt I did trust in Christ, Christ alone, for salvation; and an assurance was given me, that He had taken away *my* sins, even *mine*, and saved *me* from the law of sin and death.[33]

The experience of being 'saved from the law of sin and death' is found in Eastern monistic religions as well, but there it usually takes the form of a mystical experience apparently liberating the subject from the round of rebirths and from the ignorant, sinful, precarious existence of the normal run of mankind.

Regenerative experiences often have dramatic results, lifting people out of depression, steering them through a crisis, starting them on a new, sounder path in life, even maintaining their will to live when all else has failed. Viktor Frankl, the psychiatrist who developed 'Logotherapy', described in *Man's Search for Meaning* how the assurance that there was meaning in life enabled him to

[32] In Hardy, p. 48.
[33] *The Journal of the Rev. John Wesley A.M.*, ed. Ernest Rhys, vol. 1 (London: J. M. Dent & Co.), p. 102.

survive a Nazi prison camp: "I sensed my spirit piercing through the enveloping gloom. I felt it transcend that hopeless, meaningless world, and from somewhere I heard a victorious 'Yes' in answer to my question of the existence of an ultimate purpose."[34]

The experience of being guided by a being or force beyond one's conscious self is also a common regenerative experience. Sometimes this may take the stronger form of being "called". Clergy, missionaries, and even social workers often express the opinion that they would not be doing what they are doing, had they not experienced an overwhelming conviction that this vocation was God's will for them and that he would give them the strength and the means to carry it out. "I now *am* a missionary", writes one of Hardy's respondents; "I know that nothing except a superhuman power could have got me out here, or having got me here could keep me here."[35] This same person writes that she derives "tremendous joy and satisfaction" from the work; like most people who have felt 'divine guidance', the action was one which she saw over time to be the best one for her. Occasionally, however, people have felt murders, purges, and other atrocities to be 'the will of God'. Such cases cannot be ignored, and they will reappear in the 'challenges' of later chapters.

Regenerative experiences are not always joyful affairs. They may be profoundly humbling, as when one becomes more aware of one's own failings when one sees oneself in the light of God's unconditional love.

Some regenerative experiences are so intense that they approach the mystical or the numinous. Experiences involving overwhelming love are particularly borderline, whether the love is one's own newly increased love directed towards other people or towards the deity, or the love of the 'presence' directed towards oneself. Leslie Weatherhead described an example of the former, when in a train in Vauxhall Station he suddenly "felt caught up into some tremendous sense of being within a loving, triumphant and shining purpose":

I loved everybody in that compartment. It sounds silly now, and indeed I blush to write it, but at that moment I think I would have died for any one of the people in that compartment. . . .[36]

---

[34] Viktor Frankl, *Man's Search for Meaning*, tr. Ilse Lasch (New York: Washington Square Press, 1963), pp. 63–4.
[35] In Hardy, p. 71.   [36] Ibid. p. 53.

At a less intense level, the experience of a loving, comforting presence can be an almost daily occurrence. Such an experience is aptly described in one of William James's examples as "the sense of a presence, strong, and at the same time soothing, which hovers over me. Sometimes it seems to enwrap me with sustaining arms."[37]

That people the world over do find comfort and strength in experiences of a divine power is reflected in the abundance of references to God as our 'refuge', 'home', 'rest', 'strength', and so on. "Even as the mighty winds rest in the vastness of the ethereal space, all beings have their rest in me. Know thou this truth", says the *Bhagavad Gita*;[38] and the Psalms declare, "God is our refuge and strength, a very present help in trouble."[39] The divine is experienced as that in which our souls can truly find rest, free from the uncertainties and petty cares of the world; it is always there, always the same, ready to sustain us; it is our 'true home'. Experiences of yearning for this 'true home' and of seeming to arrive at it are explored in the next two sections.

6. NUMINOUS EXPERIENCES

The previous section dealt in part with experiences of the divine in its loving, comforting, guiding aspects; in the experiences of this section, it is revealed in all its terrifying glory, its unapproachable 'holiness'. In *The Idea of the Holy*, Rudolf Otto describes 'the holy' as a combination of supreme moral goodness and something else, even more fundamental, which he calls 'the numinous'.[40] The 'feeling of the numinous' consists of 'creature-consciousness', that is, the feeling that mortal flesh is somehow despicable in the face of eternal majesty, and 'mysterium tremendum', which comprises (i) awe, dread, or terror before the numen, (ii) the sense of being completely overpowered in the presence of such majesty, (iii) an experience of intense, almost unbearable energy or urgency, (iv)

---

[37] In James, p. 86.

[38] 9: 6, tr. Juan Mascaró (Harmondsworth: Penguin Books, 1962). This is not the most reliable translation, but because of its eloquence I have used it where the translation is not inaccurate, as tested against the more reliable translations of R. C. Zaehner, Franklin Edgerton, and W. D. P. Hill. (The *Gita* 11: 18 says, "Thou art the ultimate resting-place of this universe" (tr. Edgerton) and many other passages talk of 'abiding', 'rest', 'refuge', etc.)

[39] 46: 1.

[40] Rudolf Otto, *The Idea of the Holy*, tr. J. W. Harvey (London: OUP, 1936).

the sense that the numen is "wholly other", and (v) a fascination with or attraction to the numen, and rapture upon contact with it.

A 'numinous experience' may exhibit only one of these features, or any combination of them. Let us begin with 'creature-consciousness': When faced with infinite goodness, might, and majesty, it is natural for a person to realize how puny and insignificant he is, how fragile his existence, even how imperfect and 'unclean' he is in comparison. "Woe is me!" he cries, "For I am lost; for I am a man of unclean lips . . . for my eyes have seen the King, the Lord of hosts!"[41] Julian of Norwich writes, after being shown how all will ultimately "be well":

The bliss and the fulfilment will be so vast in its immensity that the whole creation, wondering and astonished, will have for God a dread so great and reverent and beyond anything known before, that the very pillars of heaven will tremble and quake! But there will be no pain in this trembling and dread; it is wholly right that the worth and majesty of God should thus be seen by his creatures, who tremble in dread and quake in humble joy, as they marvel at the greatness of God their Maker, and the insignificance of all that is made. The consideration of all this makes the creature wonderfully meek and mild![42]

There are surprisingly few examples of creature-consciousness in Hardy's book, although there are plenty of numinous experiences. Perhaps this is due to the current attitude towards submission and to the belief that human beings are themselves 'sacred'. Modern man is reluctant to say, "We are not worthy to gather up the crumbs under Thy table"; though increased knowledge of the vastness of space has encouraged some to feel at least the degree of creature-consciousness expressed by Psalm 8: "When I consider thy heavens, the work of thy fingers, the moon and the stars, which thou hast ordained, What is man, that thou art mindful of him?"[43] Creature-consciousness should not be seen as something negative, however; it is not, as Otto points out, "impotent collapse and submission to a merely superior power", but rather a sign that one has recognized the 'mysterium tremendum' of the numinous presence.[44]

Certain things characteristically evoke this sense of 'mysterium

[41] Isaiah 6: 5.
[42] *Revelations*, ch. 75.
[43] See, for instance, the example in Hardy, p. 82.
[44] Otto, *The Holy*, p. 78.

tremendum'. It can be found, Otto writes, "in the lives of those around us, in sudden, strong ebullitions of personal piety . . . in the fixed and ordered solemnities of rites and liturgies, and again in the atmosphere that clings to old religious monuments and buildings, to temples and to churches." He continues:

The feeling of it may at times come sweeping like a gentle tide, pervading the mind with a tranquil mood of deepest worship. It may pass over into a more set and lasting attitude of the soul, continuing, as it were, thrillingly vibrant and resonant, until at last it dies away and the soul resumes its 'profane', non-religious mood of everyday experience. It may burst in sudden eruption up from the depths of the soul with spasms and convulsions, or lead to the strangest excitements, to intoxicated frenzy, to transport, and to ecstasy. It has its wild and demonic forms and can sink to an almost grisly horror and shuddering. It has its crude, barbaric antecedents and early manifestations, and again it may be developed into something beautiful and pure and glorious. It may become the hushed, trembling, and speechless humility of the creature in the presence of—whom or what? In the presence of that which is a *mystery* inexpressible and above all creatures.[45]

The awe involved in numinous experiences is no ordinary fear. It is the dread before the uncanny which makes our hair stand on end, terror before such grandeur that we feel compelled to kneel, incomprehension before such mystery that we are struck dumb. "Let all mortal flesh keep silence, and with fear and trembling stand", says the ancient Greek hymn; and the feeling is echoed in countless individual experiences.

. . . though the sight is the loveliest and the most delightful imaginable . . . because it so far exceeds all that our imagination and understanding can compass, its presence is of such exceeding majesty that it fills the soul with a great terror. It is unnecessary to ask here how, without being told, the soul knows Who it is, for He reveals Himself quite clearly as the Lord of Heaven and earth. This the kings of the earth never do: indeed, they would be thought very little of for what they are, but that they are acccompanied by their suites, or heralds proclaim them.[46]

If the "Holy, holy, holy" visions of Isaiah and Revelation are paradigm numinous experiences for Judaic religions, theistic Hindus can look to the *Bhagavad Gita*'s magnificent revelation of Krishna to Arjuna on the battlefield (chapter 11):

[45] Otto, *The Holy*, pp. 12–13.
[46] St Teresa, *Interior Castle*, p. 186.

12. If the light of a thousand suns suddenly arose in the sky, that splendour might be compared to the radiance of the Supreme Spirit.

14. Trembling with awe and wonder, Arjuna bowed his head, and joining his hands in adoration he thus spoke to his God.

17. I see the splendour of an infinite beauty which illumines the whole universe. It is thee! with thy crown and sceptre and circle. How difficult thou art to see! But I see thee: as fire, as the sun, blinding, incomprehensible.

20. Heaven and earth and all the infinite spaces are filled with thy Spirit; and before the wonder of thy fearful majesty the three worlds tremble.

24. When I see thy vast form, reaching the sky, burning with many colours, with wide open mouths, with vast flaming eyes, my heart shakes in terror: my power is gone and gone is my peace, O Vishnu!

25. Like the fire at the end of Time which burns all in the last day, I see thy vast mouths and thy terrible teeth. Where am I? Where is my shelter? Have mercy on me, God of gods, Refuge Supreme of the world![47]

Experiences of *evil* often involve a similar numinosity. In this example from Hardy's collection, the subject used a symbolic Christian act to dispel the evil and with it that paralysing terror peculiar to the numinous:

Suddenly I became aware of a sense of the uttermost evil, so much so that I became awake. I could feel this sense of evil enveloping me. I had the terrifying impression that this evil force or presence was bent upon taking possession of me. How does one describe evil? I only knew that I was enveloped by this revolting force, so vile and rotting I could almost taste the evil. I was in terror, so much so I could not call out or move. A part of my mind told me I must at all costs act or I would be lost. I recall that I managed by a great effort to stretch out my right hand and with my index finger I traced the shape of the Cross in the air. Immediately on my doing this the evil enveloping me fell away completely, and I felt a wonderful sense of peace and safety.[48]

The awe inspired by non–evil numina, unlike ordinary fear, does not drive the subject away. Subjects encountering the numen somehow realize that their ultimate bliss is to be found in the closest possible union with this awesome, mysterious power. This fascination or attraction is expressed in many ways, from

[47] Tr. Mascaró; see n. 38, above.

[48] In Hardy, p. 63. This book does not deal to any significant extent with the problem of alleged experiences of demonic or evil forces, but some of the remarks made in later chapters should prove relevant to the issue.

St Augustine's longing to be with God ("Thou hast made us for thyself and our hearts are restless till they rest in thee")[49] to the more ardent rapture and almost physical agony of many mystics, their "burning", and "being wounded with the dart of love"[50]—or, as Ramakrishna rather less elegantly put it, feeling "as if my heart were being squeezed like a wet towel".[51] But this painful yearning is in itself a blissful experience, for it is centred on God. For Gregory of Nyssa, for instance, ecstasy is "the intense experience of longing, desire, and love of which *epektasis*—following after God—is the fruit".[52] True satisfaction is an unceasing quest for God, for to seek him unendingly is to find him.

Otto attributes this anguish to the 'energy' or 'urgency' of the numen, the same energy as "the scorching and consuming wrath of God . . . only differently directed". It can be seen in the mysticism of love, in that "'consuming fire' of love whose burning strength the mystic can hardly bear, but begs that the heat that has scorched him may be mitigated, lest he be himself destroyed by it".[53] Such intense devotion to and yearning for the holy 'other' often leads to visions, ecstasies, and mystical experiences of apparent union with the numen. In the latter, which will be described further in the next section, the mystic gladly allows himself to be annihilated by the overwhelming 'other'. In the 'Spiritual Marriage' symbolism, he is the bride awaiting the embrace of the bridegroom, when they will become forever one.

That the experience of the 'scorching fire' can be unspeakably joyful is demonstrated by Pascal's famous experience, recorded on a piece of paper found sewn inside his doublet after his death:

> From about half past ten in the evening to
> about half an hour after midnight.
>   Fire.
> God of Abraham, God of Isaac, God of Jacob,
> Not the God of philosophers and scholars.

[49] St Augustine, *Confessions*, tr. R. S. Pine-Coffin (Harmondsworth: Penguin Books, 1961), I. 1.

[50] See, for example, Origen's *Commentary on the Song*, quoted in Andrew Louth, *The Origins of the Christian Mystical Tradition* (Oxford: Clarendon Press, 1981), p. 67; St Teresa, *Life*, ch. xxix; Richard Rolle, *The Fire of Love*; and many passages from St Catherine of Genoa (see Bibliography).

[51] *Life of Sri Ramakrishna* (Mayavati: Advaita Ashrama, 1948), p. 71.

[52] Louth, p. 97.

[53] Otto, *The Holy*, p. 24.

Absolute Certainty: Beyond reason. Joy. Peace.
Forgetfulness of the world and everything but God.
The world has not known thee, but I have known thee.
    Joy! joy! joy! tears of joy![54]

Not all numinous experiences are so overwhelming. One can apprehend the numen in a very mild manner, as a general sense of 'sacredness' in the world, a feeling of happy dependence upon or devotion to an 'other', or a gentle yearning for something, one knows not what—"a sort of homesickness", one of Hardy's respondents called it.[55]

Numinous experiences are often claimed to be ineffable. The numen is so different from and so far surpasses all ordinary percepts that the subject has difficulty describing it, and the experience itself is often so overwhelming that the subject is 'struck dumb'. However, as the examples in this section show, subjects can describe their experiences, albeit in a way that does not do justice to the numen—for how can one do justice to 'ultimate reality'? For our purposes, the important thing to notice is that however inarticulate the subjects may be, they all claim to have perceived *something* which is holy and external.

It may have been noticed that most of these examples of numinous experiences have come from theistic sources. Numinous experiences are characteristically dualistic; the subject seems to become aware of an 'other'. This will prove important in Chapter VII, when the evidence of apparently conflicting 'monistic' and 'theistic' experiences is compared. Not all numinous experiences are typical of a personal theism, however, as the following points will show: (i) The 'other' is not always described in personal terms—many of Hardy's respondents refer to it as 'It'; and a sense that the world is 'sacred' or 'imbued with a holy force' is consistent with deism. However, the former often occurs because personal terms seem anthropomorphic and crude, not because the numen is 'impersonal' in the sense of being inanimate, unconscious, or a mere 'principle'; and the latter types of experience are very mild and somewhat atypical examples of numinous experiences,

---

[54] Quoted in F. C. Happold, *Mysticism* (Harmondsworth: Penguin Books, 1970), p. 39.
[55] In Hardy, p. 60. C. S. Lewis's childhood experience of "Joy" seems to have been a somewhat more intense version of this type of experience; see his *Surprised by Joy* (London: Geoffrey Bles, 1955).

perhaps more akin to the nature mysticism of the next section. (ii) Numinous experiences often incline subjects to kneel or to sing praises at the time of the experience, but they certainly do not always lead them to worship in any regular manner. (iii) Many numinous experiences approach and sometimes even slip into the 'oneness' of mystical experiences, either because the yearning and love is so completely and intensely centred on the divine, or because the combination of creature-consciousness and awe leads to the feeling that one's own self has been annihilated and the numen is the sole reality. To see such experiences in their truly mystical form, let us turn to the next section.

7. MYSTICAL EXPERIENCES

Most discussions of mystical experience are full-fledged treatises on 'mysticism', but in this section I shall refer to doctrines, techniques, and so on only where necessary, and attempt to confine the discussion to mystical *experiences*. The term 'mystical' has been used to cover everything from the experiences of the great mystics of each religious tradition to mildly ecstatic, mysterious, or occult experiences. I shall restrict it—not rigorously, for the purpose of these categories is mainly to provide an orderly account of 'the data'—to experiences with the following characteristics: (i) the sense of having apprehended an ultimate reality; (ii) the sense of freedom from the limitations of time, space, and the individual ego; (iii) a sense of 'oneness'; and (iv) bliss or serenity. 'Ineffability' is often included in lists of characteristics of mystical experiences, but since it is a problem encountered in most categories of religious experience (i.e. it is not really a 'distinguishing mark' of *mystical* experience), and since it was discussed at length in Chapter I, I shall not include it here. The most paradigmatic mystical experiences have all four characteristics—not surprisingly, since, as will be shown below, they are closely interrelated.

Stace makes a useful distinction between 'extrovertive' and 'introvertive' mystical experiences.[56] In an extrovertive experience, the multiplicity of external objects is seen as somehow unified and divine. 'Nature mysticism' is typically of this type, as we shall see later. Introvertive experiences, usually obtained through the

[56] Stace, ch. 2.

practice of an 'introspective' meditative technique, are 'unitary' rather than 'unifying'; subjects shut out all external and internal diversity and dive deep within themselves to discover 'the One'. Both introvertive and extrovertive experiences can have the four 'mystical characteristics'.

(i) *The sense of 'ultimate reality'*. Mystical experiences are usually considered the pinnacle of the spiritual journey, the closest one may come in this life to seeing divine reality face to face. Even religions such as Judaism and Islam which stress the gulf between creator and creature have their mystics, their Sufis and their Kabbalah—though they often sit uneasily on the fringes of orthodoxy. When that yearning for union with the numen mentioned in the last section is consummated, the subject seems to apprehend something both more 'real' than and more 'ultimate' than the percepts of ordinary life. It seems to theistic mystics that the 'transcendent' reality of their numinous experiences has become 'immanent', to monistic mystics that they are now one with 'the Absolute', to nature mystics that they have glimpsed something fundamental underlying the apparently disparate things of this world. Normal objects of sense perception and all mundane matters are seen as in some way 'unreal' in comparison with the overwhelming reality of the divine, and are described as 'insignificant', 'a dream', 'a veil', 'a shadow', or 'illusion'. This is one foundation of the mystic's traditional ability to renounce the things of this world.

Insights gained during mystical experiences are similarly 'ultimate', never trivial matters: mystics feel they have penetrated to the very heart of things, that what has been revealed to them is eternally and universally true, that they now realize the true nature of human beings, the world, and their relationship to the divine. While the 'flashes of insight' described in section 4 are not always so fundamental, the remarks there on the sense of utter conviction and on the 'immediate' manner of acquisition of these insights apply just as well to this feature of mystical experience.

(ii) *The sense of freedom*. In this category I include the apparent transcendence of space and time, the sense that the boundaries of the individual ego have been dissolved, and the loss of concern for all worldly matters which so characterizes the mystic.

The transcendence of spatial limitations is usually explicitly mentioned only in accounts of extrovertive experiences, where subjects feel they are no longer limited by the physical boundaries of their bodies but are "part of something Other/Bigger/Wider",[57] part of the unity underlying the whole external world. In introvertive experiences, space is not felt as a limitation to be transcended; it simply does not exist for the mystic at all.

Though mystical experiences are usually transient, sometimes lasting only a few seconds, their subjects often report a feeling of 'timelessness'. This sense of 'eternity' is more than the 'losing all sense of time' common during extreme concentration; combined with the loss of the everyday sense of identity and the sense that one has been suffused with some divine essence, it often takes the form of a conviction that one is immortal. Thus Bucke claims to have become 'conscious that he possessed eternal life' (see section 4), and Tennyson writes of his "waking trances":

This has come upon me through repeating my own name to myself silently, till all at once, as it were out of the intensity of the consciousness of individuality, individuality itself seemed to dissolve and fade away into boundless being, and this not a confused state but the clearest, the surest of the surest, utterly beyond words—where death was an almost laughable impossibility—the loss of personality (if so it were) seeming no extinction, but the only true life.[58]

Tennyson's last line is typical of descriptions of the sense that one has escaped the narrow prison of the individual ego. This "boundless" state may be experienced in different ways, ranging from the isolation of the pure self or consciousness, through varying degrees of dissolution of the subject–object distinction, to the complete annihilation or absorption of the self. In Christian mysticism it is usually interpreted as a total surrender to God, a 'dying to oneself' so that God can take over. As Boehme writes:

The soul here saith, *I have nothing*, for I am utterly stripped and naked; *I can do nothing*, for I have no manner of power, but am as water poured out; *I am nothing*, for all that I am is no more than an Image of Being, and only God is to me I AM; and so, sitting down in my own Nothingness, I give glory to the Eternal Being, and *will nothing* of myself, that so God may *will all* in me, being unto me my God and All Things.[59]

From an agnostic tradition, Zen Buddhism, comes a different account of the dissolution of individuality:

---

[57] In Hardy, p. 89.
[58] Quoted by James, p. 370 n.
[59] Jacob Boehme (or Behmen), *Dialogues on the Supersensual Life*, tr. and ed. Bernard Holland (London: Methuen, 1901), p. 74.

The individual shell in which my personality is so solidly encased explodes at the moment of satori. Not necessarily that I get unified with a being greater than myself or absorbed in it, but that my individuality, which I found rigidly held together and definitely kept separate from other individual existences . . . melts away into something indescribable, something which is of quite a different order from what I am accustomed to.[60]

Metaphors of 'melting', 'dissolving', 'sinking', and so on can be found in descriptions of this experience from all traditions. The Hindu *Brihadaranyaka Upanishad*, for instance, uses the following analogy to describe the merging of the self with the Absolute:

. . . as a lump of salt cast in water would dissolve right into the water . . . so, lo, verily, this great Being *(bhuta)*, infinite, limitless, is just a mass of knowledge. Arising out of these elements *(bhuta)*, into them also one vanishes away. . .

For where there is a duality, as it were, there one sees another. . . Where, verily, everything has become just one's own self . . . then whereby and whom would one see?[61]

Whether the loss of the sense of 'I' is seen as a merging into something 'wider' or merely as the transcendence of a human limitation, it is normally connected with renunciation—of worldly things, of all desires, of the very ideas of 'me' and 'mine'. 'Dying to oneself' is encouraged by all mystical traditions, whether it is seen as a prerequisite for the unitive experience or as a consequence of it. Hence the paradoxical passage in the Gospel of St John: "He who loves his life loses it, and he who hates his life in this world will keep it for eternal life."[62]

In Indian traditions this renunciation tends to take the extreme form of refraining from action and of indifference even to good and bad states of mind—'attachment' to *anything* is supposed to be a hindrance to ultimate liberation. Indian mystics are thus often accused of indifference to the suffering of fellow humans and of feeling themselves to be beyond the distinctions of good and evil. Though this may be true of some cases, it is largely unjustified. It is clear from the biographies of Indian mystics that they see their prayer and purity as themselves working to help mankind, through

---

[60] D. T. Suzuki, *Essays in Zen Buddhism*, 2nd series (London: Luzac & Co., 1933), p. 18.
[61] The *Brihadaranyaka Upanishad* 2.4.12 and 14, from Robert E. Hume, tr., *The Thirteen Principal Upanishads*, 2nd edn. (London: OUP, 1931).
[62] 12: 25.

'spiritual vibrations', as it were;[63] and a major goal of Buddhist training is the cultivation of compassion and loving-kindness (*mettā*).[64] Nor is activity in the community shunned: the Rama-krishna Mission established schools, hospitals, and other charitable institutions, despite its strictly monistic mystical philosophy,[65] and even 'hermit' monks offer forms of assistance such as teaching and lending the prestige of their name to a worthy project in order to gain it backers.[66]

(iii) *The sense of 'oneness'.* This may take four forms: (a) nature mysticism and other extrovertive mystical experiences; (b) integration or isolation; (c) introvertive monistic mysticism; and (d) introvertive theistic mysticism.

(a) In the simplest kind of extrovertive experience of unity, all things are seen as intimately related, and the subject feels an extraordinary kinship with them:

I heard a voice saying: 'All men are brothers! Every land is home,' And I felt quite stunned with joy.[67]

The experiences known as 'nature mysticism' involve the transfiguration of external things, as if they have suddenly been imbued with deep meaning or with a living force; they also often involve the sense that everything is guided by Love or some inherently good power. R. M. Bucke's experience (section 4) is a good example of this, but a more paradigmatic example, since it deals with external objects, is this one from Hardy's collection:

One day I was sweeping the stairs down in the house in which I was working, when suddenly I was overcome, overwhelmed, saturated, no word is adequate, with a sense of most sublime and living LOVE. It not only affected me, but seemed to bring everything around me to LIFE. The brush in my hand, my dustpan, the stairs, seemed to come alive with love. I seemed no longer me, with my petty troubles and trials, but part of this infinite power of love, so utterly and overwhelmingly wonderful that one knew at once what the saints had grasped. It could only have been a minute or two, yet for that brief particle of time it seemed eternity.[68]

---

[63] See Winston L. King, *Buddhism and Christianity* (London: Allen & Unwin, 1962); this was also maintained by Mettānando Bhikkhu, in conversation.

[64] See Happold, ch. 5 (anthology); and Michael Carrithers, *The Forest Monks of Sri Lanka* (Delhi: OUP, 1983), ch. 13.

[65] See Geoffrey Parrinder, *Mysticism in the World's Religions* (London: Sheldon Press, 1976), p. 42.

[66] See Carrithers, ch. 13.   [67] In Hardy, p. 113.   [68] Ibid. p. 89.

William Blake's lines, "To see a world in a grain of sand / And a heaven in a wild flower . . ." give concise expression to that mystical sense of the immanence of divinity in nature, so magnificently described in Wordsworth's *Tintern Abbey*:

> . . . And I have felt
> A presence that disturbs me with the joy
> Of elevated thoughts; a sense sublime
> Of something far more deeply interfused,
> Whose dwelling is the light of setting suns,
> And the round ocean and the living air,
> And the blue sky, and in the mind of man:
> A motion and a spirit, that impels
> All thinking things, all objects of all thought,
> And rolls through all things.

Scenes of natural beauty very often trigger these spontaneous extrovertive mystical experiences in Westerners out hiking:

. . . the setting sun blazed out turning the whole world crimson and gold, there was a gust of wind, and I felt as if I had been swept into the very heart of all that glory and colour, taken over by something outside myself of which I was yet a part.[69]

Michael Carrithers reports that there is little 'nature mysticism' in India because 'nature' is so much more dangerous than in the West, and tends to be avoided by villagers;[70] but nature mysticism is not a purely Western phenomenon. Oriental landscape paintings show a deep sense of harmony with nature, and Taoism glorified nature and the spirit within it.[71]

It is within Indian cultures that extrovertive mystical experiences of the most radical type are found—the alleged apprehension of a complete identity between external objects. This is the territory of the famous *tat tvam asi* (thou art that) of the Upanishads:

Whatever they are, whether tiger, lion, wolf, boar, worm, fly, gnat, or mosquito, they all become that (the ultimate reality). That which is the subtlest of the subtle, the whole world has it as its self. That is reality. That is the self, and that art thou.[72]

---

[69] Ibid. p. 72.
[70] Carrithers, ch. 2.
[71] See Parrinder, p. 71.
[72] *Chandogya Upanishad* 6.10, tr. R. C. Zaehner, quoted in his *Mysticism Sacred and Profane* (Oxford: Clarendon Press, 1957), p. 139. The refrain, "That which is the

In its context in the Upanishads, this passage describes a doctrine rather than an experience; it is very probable, however, that Hindu mystics do have experiences of "seeing" all things as Brahman, the supreme, hidden 'self' of the universe and all beings.

Nature mysticism and other extrovertive experiences are often associated with pantheism, but there is nothing to prevent other types of theists from having such experiences. The difference is that whereas pantheists feel that what they have seen in nature is the *whole* of the divine, monotheists (or pan-en-theists) believe that the divine has transcendent aspects as well as immanent ones.

(b) Introvertive mystical experiences are usually attained during the practice of a meditative technique which enables subjects to shut out all physical and mental distractions and to 'peel off' all the layers of the ego until they have—so mystics say—transcended the superficial, 'empirical' ego and arrived at a state in which there is no multiplicity, only pure 'unity'. In this state one loses all sense of 'oneself' as a separate being, as a subject observing objects from a distance. In its monistic form this is the experience of apparent identity with or complete absorption into the Absolute, the recognition that our 'true self' (as opposed to the empirical ego) is divine. In its theistic form it is the experience of apparent intimate union with but not identity with God, expressed by metaphors such as 'indwelling' and 'marriage'. In the experiences of this section, however, there is no union with anything, but simply an attainment of *internal* 'oneness'. This may take the form of 'personal integration', the realization of a 'self' in which all the elements are in such perfect harmony that it appears to be a unity. William James describes something of the sort in his account of his experiences with nitrous oxide:

> . . . they all converge towards a kind of insight to which I cannot help ascribing some metaphysical significance. The keynote of it is invariably a reconciliation. It is as if the opposites of the world, whose contradictoriness and conflict make all our difficulties and troubles, were melted into unity.[73]

In the Theravada Buddhist mystical tradition (as opposed to many Mahayana Buddhist traditions, which are often close to

subtlest of the subtle . . . that art thou" is repeated frequently throughout this Upanishad. R. E. Hume has, "That which is the finest essence—this whole world has that as its soul"; the remainder is the same.

[73] James, p. 374.

theism), the subject claims to have arrived at a permanent, blissful state in which all external and internal multiplicity has been transcended. The sense of freedom from all attachments and limitations, as described in section (ii), is the primary thing; the subject sees it as the sign of release from the cycle of rebirth and suffering. By training themselves to regard everything, even their own states of mind, as inherently transient and imperfect, and by practising meditation, Theravada Buddhists strive to attain the supreme, enduring state of nirvana. Metaphysical questions about God, the form of 'existence' in nirvana, and so on are regarded in this agnostic tradition as distractions on the path to liberation, and subjects are therefore reluctant to "ontologize the contents of their mystical experiences".[74]

Somewhat similar to Buddhist experiences, but with the explicit assertion of the reality of the isolated, unified self, are experiences of the adherents of Yoga, whose doctrine Ninian Smart sums up as follows:

That there is an infinite number of eternal selves, who through Yoga can attain isolation or liberation, a state in which the soul exists by itself, no longer implicated in nature and in the round of rebirth.[75]

(c) In the monistic mystical experience the subject feels himself (his 'Atman') to be identical with the One, the world-soul, or 'cosmic consciousness' ('Brahman'); in this state of pure unity he is "a centre coincident with another centre" (Plotinus).[76] This is the experience sought by followers of Shankara's non–dualistic version of Hinduism, the Advaita Vedanta, whose doctrine Smart (once again) summarizes thus:

That there is but one Self, which individuals can realize, and which is identical with Brahman as the ground of being (which at a lower level of truth manifests itself as a personal Lord and Creator)—such a realization bringing about a cessation of the otherwise continuously reborn individual.[77]

Even theists may have an experience of apparent identity with the 'ground of being', though they usually try to wriggle out of it somehow. Meister Eckhart tries to explain here how the soul can

---

[74] R. M. Gimello, "Mysticism and Meditation", in Katz (ed.), p. 193.
[75] "Interpretation and Mystical Experience", p. 83.
[76] Ennead VI.9 |9| 10, from *The Essential Plotinus*, tr. Elmer O'Brien (1964).
[77] "Interpretation and Mystical Experience", p. 83.

be absorbed and yet remain an individual soul separate from the
Godhead:

In this exalted state she [the soul] has lost her proper self and is flowing full-
flood into the unity of the divine nature. But what, you may ask, is the fate
of this lost soul: does she find herself or not?. . . it seems to me that . . .
though she sink all sinking in the oneness of divinity she never touches
bottom. Wherefore God has left her one little point from which to get back
to herself and find herself and know herself as creature.[78]

The 'God-intoxicated' Sufis of Islam are especially prone to express
their experiences in terms of identity:

In that Presence, says the Sufi mystic [Shabistari], "I" and "thou" have
ceased to exist, they have become one: the Quest and the Way and the
Seeker are one.[79]

Al-Ghazali tried to account for these 'blasphemous' Sufi utterances
by dismissing them as "the words of lovers when in a state of
drunkenness". In their sober moments, he claims, the mystics
"know that this was not actual identity, but that it resembled
identity"—for they were "drowned in pure solitude" and "no
longer had the capacity to recollect aught but God".[80] (This passage
is quoted more fully in Chapter VII.)

(d) Theistic mystics usually regard their type of mystical
experience as the 'highest' type: other experiences may show that
the subjects have attained, by their own efforts, absolute purity of
soul and the kind of self-naughting required before union with God
is possible, but to rest in them would be to miss out on the 'Beatific
Vision', for which God's help (grace) is required. Many models
have been used to describe this experience of near perfect union,
just short of actual identity: 'Spiritual Marriage', which stresses
intimacy, love, the indissolubility of the bond, the 'oneness' created
by the act of consummating the marriage, and the sense of losing
oneself completely in surrender to and rapt contemplation of the
beloved; 'Indwelling' (sometimes called 'deification'), which implies that there is in human beings a 'divine spark' which the mystic

---

[78] Franz Pfeiffer, *Meister Eckhart* (Leipzig, 1857), tr. C. de B. Evans (London:
Watkins, 1956), vol. i, Tractates II ("The Nobility of the Soul"), p. 282.
[79] Margaret Smith, *The Way of the Mystics* (London: Sheldon Press, 1931, 1976),
p. 9.
[80] From al-Ghazali's *Mishkāt al-Anwār*, Zaehner tr., quoted in Zaehner, pp. 157–8.

has uncovered, or that the mystic has been transformed by a 'new birth', the birth of Christ or the spirit of God within him; and 'Absorption', which refers to the way the mystic feels entirely engulfed by the divine.

Mystics are not bound by one particular model. Even St Teresa, who generally uses the very personal imagery of marriage, sometimes describes her experience in the impersonal terms of absorption:

. . . it is like rain falling from the heavens into a river or a spring; there is nothing but water there and it is impossible to divide or separate the water belonging to the river from that which fell from the heavens.[81]

Descriptions of 'indwelling' are particularly frequent: "it is no longer I who live, but Christ who lives in me" (Galatians 2: 20); "I used unexpectedly to experience a consciousness of the presence of God, of such a kind that I could not possibly doubt that He was within me or that I was wholly engulfed in Him";[82] "those who with devotion worship me abide in me, and I also in them";[83] and, from sources as diverse as Sadhu Sundar Singh and Jacob Boehme,[84] the analogy of red–hot iron:

The iron is in the fire and the fire is in the iron, and yet the iron is not the fire and the fire is not the iron. In the same way we live in Christ and He lives in us and yet we do not become gods.[85]

(iv) The fourth characteristic of mystical experiences is what R. M. Gimello calls "an extraordinarily strong affective tone":[86] exaltation, rapture, bliss, sublime serenity, the 'peace which passeth all understanding', and burning love. "Might but one little drop of what I feel fall into Hell, Hell would be transformed into a Paradise," declared St Catherine of Genoa.[87] And Viktor Frankl, talking of his realization that "the salvation of man is through love and in love", wrote, "For the first time in my life I was able to

---

[81] *Interior Castle*, 7. II.

[82] St Teresa, *Life*, ch. x.

[83] *Bhagavad Gita* 9: 29, tr. W. D. P. Hill (London: OUP, 1928).

[84] Reported by Evelyn Underhill in her *Mysticism* (London: Methuen, 1911), ch. x.

[85] Streeter and Appasamy, pp. 66–7.

[86] "Mysticism and Meditation".

[87] *Vita* p. 94c (see Baron von Hügel, *The Mystical Element of Religion*, vol. 1, London: Dent, 1909, p. 159), quoted by Otto, *The Holy*, p. 38.

understand the meaning of the words, 'The angels are lost in perpetual contemplation of an infinite glory.'"[88]

There are many indications that both the profound peace and the 'unspeakable rapture' are intimately bound up with the sense of freedom described in section (ii). They are not a peace or a joy for the faint-hearted or for those who find security in material things and familiar, narrow boundaries. Peace can come through such thoroughgoing renunciation that one thinks neither about one's reputation nor about one's next meal; and great joy can attend the sense of freedom from such intransigent human limitations as death and the boundaries of the individual ego. D. T. Suzuki suggests that the source of the bliss accompanying 'satori' is "the breaking-up of the restriction imposed on one as an individual being . . . an infinite expansion of the individual".[89] J. A. Symonds, quoted by William James, actually disliked his experience of the dissolution of his conscious self, and wrote of his "return from the abyss", "At last I felt myself once more a human being . . . I was thankful for . . . this deliverance from so awful an initiation into the mysteries of scepticism."[90] This is the reverse of the Buddhist attitude, where the goal is precisely to plunge into that abyss! Just as some find skiing down a mountainside at top speed exhilarating, while others hate the sense of loss of control and prefer to stay at the bottom, so Symonds was like the majority of mankind, clinging to his everyday sense of identity rather than surrendering himself completely to receive a new and wider 'self'.

How the different doctrines alluded to in this section influence the subject's experience, and how different goals, methods, traditional exemplars, and cultural background all interact in mystical traditions, are questions for Chapters VI and VII. Chapter VII in particular will show to what extent mystical experiences from different traditions can be seen as consistent, when the culture-bound or metaphorical descriptions are understood at a deeper level. It should be pointed out here, though, that there is a remarkable degree of agreement between vastly different traditions regarding method and stages of progress. Most have something approaching the triadic Dionysian scheme of 'purgation', 'illumination', and 'union', and agree that without adequate preparation the subject's mind may become so unstable and confused that the journey to enlightenment takes the terrifying route through

---

[88] Frankl, p. 59.   [89] *Essays*, p. 20.   [90] In James, p. 372.

madness. Guidance must be given by a confessor, yogi, or similar experienced person; the subject must be trained to transcend the cares and complexities of this world and his own self; and the final stage is regarded as not just one experience among others but as a continuing state of liberation or 'God-consciousness', and not just one end among others but a human being's *summum bonum*.

3
ARGUMENTS FROM
RELIGIOUS EXPERIENCE

I. INTRODUCTION

In this chapter I will look at several 'arguments from religious experience' which have had wide appeal. Some of them, to be fair, were not originally intended as 'arguments from religious experience' in the full sense, but they can profitably be treated as such, for they represent common lines of argument about religious experience. It will be seen that most of them have the following shortcomings:

(i) They are all arguments for the existence of (or for the reasonableness of belief in the existence of) the Judaeo-Christian God. Rather than taking the chance that the data of religious experience might actually point to a different conception of God or to no God at all, these philosophers argue with only one purpose in mind: the defence of the Christian faith. There is nothing wrong with this approach, so long as they spell out somewhere what that faith consists in and why they feel that other religious alternatives are not worth considering. Unfortunately, this is rarely done.

(ii) These arguments tend to take the empirical research for granted, which can seriously weaken their case. (a) Their proponents often assume that religious experience is all of one kind, usually defining it with some brief phrase such as "an experience which the subject takes to be an experience of God or some supernatural thing".[1] They thus leave out many types of religious experience, both those which actually support their conclusion but do not fit into the mould of their argument and those which a sceptic could cite as apparent counter-evidence to their conclusion. (b) Reductionist explanations of religious experience are often given short shrift. Philosophers frequently consider only the

[1] William L. Rowe, "Religious Experience and the Principle of Credulity", *Int. J. Phil. Rel.*, 13 (1982), 85–92.

Freudian version of the reductionist challenge, a version which certainly does not do justice to the sceptic's case.

(iii) Many proponents of arguments from religious experience appear to demand too much of religious experience. They often employ one narrow method of argument (e.g. an analogy with personal encounters) without realizing how severely it limits the evidential force of which religious experiences are capable; and they often attempt to argue from religious experiences alone to a highly ramified system such as Christian theism. It will be seen that a more complex, 'cumulative' style of argument, drawing on many types of evidence, is required if religious experiences are to be considered good evidence for such highly ramified claims.

In this chapter, the following arguments from religious experience will be examined: the analogy with aesthetic and moral experience; the analogy with sense perception; the 'sense of a personal encounter' argument; the 'all experience is experiencing-as' argument; and an argument using the concept of basic beliefs. Swinburne's argument from the 'principle of credulity' and my own 'cumulative case' will be presented in the next chapter.

2. ARGUMENTS FROM ANALOGY

The most basic premiss in any argument from religious experience is that a great many people have had experiences in which it seemed to them that they were apprehending a divine reality. But it must be admitted that a great many people have never experienced intimations of such a reality. Are the former imagining things, or are the latter missing out on something?

The first claim would be maintained by those who hold that all experiences putatively yielding knowledge of an external reality must satisfy the criteria used in testing the sensory perception of a physical object, since this is usually considered the paradigm of the way we acquire knowledge about external realities. Certain disanalogies with the sensory perception of physical objects make religious experience appear to fail normal tests for veridicality, and challenges to religious experience are often based on these disanalogies. For instance, sensory perceptual experiences are universal—a human being with absolutely no sensory experience of the outside world would be a 'vegetable', unable to develop into a person; and we have sensory experiences almost constantly, escaping them only when we are unconscious (and not dreaming) or immersed in nonsensory mental activity. Religious experiences, on the other hand, are relatively infrequent even for those who have had them, and atheism is a practical possibility, unlike solipsism. Moreover, some people seem inexplicably unable to have experiences of God, no matter how diligently they pray (etc.), while all persons with the relevant physical and mental faculties are able to see tables and chairs. Some proponents of arguments from religious experience have attempted to show that such disanalogies are irrelevant by developing analogies between religious experience and certain familiar, relatively uncontroversial types of perceptual experience which exhibit similar disanalogies.

Two analogies which have remained popular with the general public, the analogies with aesthetic and moral experience, can be found in A. E. Taylor's "The Vindication of Religion", though they form only a small part of his argument:

A man with the artist's eye, we very rightly say, "sees beauty" everywhere, while a man without it goes through life not seeing beauty anywhere, or at best seeing it only occasionally, where it is too prominent to be missed. . . . however truly beauty may pervade the whole of things, there are special regions where its presence is most manifest and obvious. What is characteristic of the artist is that he makes just these elements of experience a key to unlock the meaning of the rest. So the religious man, no doubt, means the man who sees the whole of reality under the light of a specific illumination, but he has come to see all things in that light by taking certain arresting pieces or phases of his experience as the key to the meaning of the rest.[2]

Taylor continues with the moral analogy: "if a man has no direct perception of what 'ought' means, it is impossible to convey that meaning to him",[3] but the vast majority of people, not being psychopaths, can come to have more accurate and discriminating moral experiences by learning from those who are especially alive to situations with moral significance.

C. D. Broad argues in a similar vein that the capacity for having religious experiences is like having 'an ear for music':

---

[2] A. E. Taylor, excerpt from his essay "The Vindication of Religion", in Hick (ed.), *The Existence of God*, pp. 153–64.
[3] Ibid. p. 155.

Let us, then, compare tone-deaf persons to those who have no recognizable religious experience at all; the ordinary followers of a religion to men who have some taste for music but can neither appreciate the more difficult kinds nor compose; highly religious men and saints to persons with an exceptionally fine ear for music who may yet be unable to compose it; and the founders of religions to great musical composers, such as Bach and Beethoven.[4]

Other popular analogies shade into the area of sense perception, in which the non-universality of the experience can be ascribed to a deficiency in or lack of training of the relevant sense organs: wine-tasting, perfume-smelling, colour-blindness, and the form of tone-deafness which is not so much an inability to appreciate music as an inability to recognize such 'objectively demonstrable' things as recurring patterns of notes or that an instrument is out of tune. The effectiveness of this sort of analogy will be discussed in the next section on sense perception.

It can be seen that these analogies are all designed to show that it is the people who have never had religious experiences who are deficient in some way, in contrast to the proponents of reductionist challenges, who argue that those who have had religious experiences are intellectually or psychologically defective. Often the proponents of these analogies do not go into the reasons for unbelievers' 'spiritual blindness', but when they do, it is usually alleged to be the result of 'sin', broadly understood. This means that people with certain physical defects (such as the colour blind) are a less appropriate analogy to the 'spiritually blind' than are those who have no inkling of aesthetic or moral sensibility. But here we run into a problem, for it is precisely the latter types of experiences which are highly controversial as examples of veridical perception. Many scholars maintain that aesthetic and moral judgements are not the sort of thing which can be true or false. In order for these analogies to work, then, aesthetic and moral objectivism must be shown to be true. (I believe there are good arguments in favour of moral objectivism, but this is not the place to discuss them.)

In any case, all such analogies can hope to show on their own is that the fact that a type of experience is not available to all does not entail that it is a nonperceptual type of experience; there are in fact

---

[4] C. D. Broad, *Religion, Philosophy and Psychical Research* (London: Routledge & Kegan Paul, 1953), p. 190.

non-universal types of experience which yield veridical percep-tions. This does not of course show that religious experience is of that type, but anything which shows that the epistemological problems of religious experience are not unique to the religious case helps the theist.[5] Analogies can give theists some comfort in the face of hostile sceptics, then, but to justify the further conclusion that religious experience yields veridical perceptions, a full-fledged argument from religious experience is required. How well some versions of this work, we shall see over the next few sections.

3. THE ANALOGY WITH SENSE PERCEPTION

In "Mysticism and Sense Perception", William Wainwright argues for the cognitive value of mystical experiences as follows.[6] Sense perception is accepted as the paradigm of a cognitive type of experience. If the analogy between mystical experience and sense perception is very close, then mystical experience is probably cognitive. Both mystical experience and sense perception are noetic experiences—that is, they have an intentional object and typically involve the belief that that object really exists externally; both give rise to corrigible and independently checkable claims about external states of affairs; and in both cases there are checking procedures to determine whether or not the intentional object is real and whether or not the experience constitutes a genuine perception of that object. The analogy between mystical experience and sense perception is therefore close enough to warrant the claim that mystical experience not only *probably* is cognitive but *actually* is cognitive, "provided that we have independent reasons for believ-ing mystics' claims to have experienced a transcendent reality". Natural theology and the sanity, sanctity, and intelligence of mystics provide us with such reasons, and so we can conclude that mystical experience is a source of knowledge of divine reality.

Wainwright's last clause, which turns the argument into a

---

[5] I have used the word 'theist' in this book rather loosely to refer to 'the religious person' (as opposed to 'the sceptic'), even though many religious people (e.g. many Buddhists and Hindus) are not, strictly speaking, theists. The most common alternative, "the believer", could have carried overtones of gullibility.

[6] William J. Wainwright, "Mysticism and Sense Perception", *Rel. Stud.*, 9 (1973), 257–78; see also ch. 3 of his book, *Mysticism* (Brighton: Harvester, 1981).

cumulative argument, is thrown in without much defence. We will concentrate therefore on his claim that mystical experience is probably cognitive, based entirely on the analogy with sense perception.

Wainwright realizes that the first, most obvious challenge to his argument will be the claim that the disanalogies between mystical experience and sense perception outweigh the analogies. That is a challenge worth looking at in some detail, since the issues it raises will prove relevant in later chapters.

Disanalogies are particularly evident when we compare 'checking procedures'. Even sense experiences may be delusive at times, and so criteria of veridicality have been established along the following lines: (i) people of similar competence under similar conditions report similar experiences (the 'unanimity' criterion); (ii) predictions based on the experience are borne out; (iii) the claim is corroborated by the other senses (I know that I'm seeing double if my 'two pens' *feel* like one); (iv) the claim is corroborated by man-made equipment such as cameras; (v) The alleged percept remains the same on a 'closer look'; (vi) the subject's claim is consistent with background knowledge; and (vii) the subject's physical and psychological state and the conditions under which the experience occurred are not of a type which normally leads to false perceptual claims (e.g. intoxication).

Criteria for distinguishing genuine mystical experiences from delusive ones have also been proposed; indeed, 'spiritual authorities' such as the classical mystics are remarkably unanimous in their choice of criteria. A survey of the 'checking procedures' used by mystics yields four broad classes of criteria: (i) internal and external consistency, (ii) moral and spiritual fruits, (iii) consistency with orthodox doctrine, and (iv) evaluation of the subject's general psychological and mental condition.

(i) The criteria of internal and external consistency tend to be explicitly stated more in the writings of contemporary, Western-educated mystics than in classical works. They include such tests as the coherence of the concepts used in the auto-description, the internal consistency of that description, the way the experience fits into the pattern of other experiences, and consistency with non-religious background knowledge. J. Trevor, writing in 1897, provides an example of the use of such tests:

[These] experiences are proved real to their possessor, because they remain with him when brought closest into contact with the objective realities of life. Dreams cannot stand this test. We wake from them to find that they are but dreams. Wanderings of an overwrought brain do not stand this test. These highest experiences that I have had of God's presence have been rare and brief. . . But I find that, after every questioning and test, they stand out today as the most real experiences of my life, and experiences which have explained and justified and unified all past experiences and all past growth.[7]

(ii) 'Fruits' criteria are cited in all traditions, by all mystics. St Teresa of Avila is particularly insistent that although the devil can give some pleasures, only divinely produced experiences can leave the soul in such peace and tranquillity and with such eager devotion to God.[8] Wainwright's first two criteria come into this category (he does not propose criteria from the first category): "(i) The consequences of the experience must be good for the mystic, in the sense of leading to or producing a new life marked by virtues such as wisdom, humility and goodness of life" and "(ii) The effects of the experience must be such as tend to build up the community rather than destroy it."

(iii) The 'consistency with doctrine' criteria vary more from tradition to tradition, since they are bound up with particular doctrines. The disparity need not be as great as one might at first think, however, since mystical revelations must only be consistent with—i.e. not conflict with—orthodox doctrines; they need not repeat those doctrines or have any relationship of entailment with them. Insights gained during mystical experiences are often consistent with the doctrines of a great many traditions.

The last three criteria offered by Wainwright could be placed in this third category: "(iv) What is said on the basis of the experience ought to agree with orthodox doctrine", "(v) Resemblance of the experience to paradigm cases within the religious tradition will help establish its validity", and "(vi) The judgement of spiritual authorities about the experience should be taken into account."

(iv) The fourth type of test is important, though often not explicitly stated (it does not appear in Wainwright's list) and difficult to apply. However radical modern psychologists may think they are being when they point out that certain people can be

---

[7] Quoted in James, p. 387.
[8] *Interior Castle*, 6. ii and iii.

induced to have religious experiences through the power of suggestion, this possibility was certainly recognized in more ancient times. St Teresa writes, for instance, that in subjects who are "melancholy" or "have feeble imaginations", the hearing of voices is probably "fancy",[9] and mystics of Eastern and Western traditions alike constantly admonish disciples not to strain too hard, as this can give rise to illusory experiences.[10] Religious experiences occurring to subjects who are highly suggestible or known to be mentally ill or defective are thus usually discounted— though it is true that this criterion is not always very rigorously applied. After all, it is possible that God can get through to the mentally abnormal more easily than he can to those of us who are 'properly' oriented towards mundane realities. The analogy with the test for defective sense organs (etc.—test (vii)) is thus far from perfect.

Wainwright suggests a further plausible criterion which does not fit into the above four categories: "(iii) The depth, profundity and the 'sweetness' (Jonathan Edwards) of what the believer says on the basis of the experience count in favour of the genuineness of that experience." When the alleged percept is something as majestic and fundamental as God, "one would not expect a vision of him to lead to twaddle".

Let us assume that mystical experiences generally do satisfy these criteria; the question still remains whether these criteria actually pick out veridical experiences. Sceptics are quick to claim that the criteria presuppose the validity of religious doctrines and that they conspicuously omit the two sorts of criteria usually considered most important in the case of sense perception: corroboration by other percipients, other senses, and machines; and successful prediction.

Is it true that criteria of the 'genuineness' of a religious experience are bound to be viciously circular? (a) The tests of category (i) and (iv) do not presuppose any religious doctrines; they apply to any type of experience which is alleged to provide veridical perceptions. (b) The tests of category (ii) and Wainwright's 'profundity' criterion presuppose only that *if* God exists, then he is good, concerned for the welfare of his creation, and so on, so that we

---

[9] Ibid. 6.III.
[10] See, for instance, Carrithers, ch. 11, and, for a delightful account, *The Cloud of Unknowing*, chs. 45, 46, and 52.

would expect genuine perceptions of him to be beneficial to the subject and to the community. They do not therefore presuppose actual belief in God (though what counts as 'beneficial' may depend to some extent on religious doctrines). (c) It is only the third type of test which presupposes religious doctrines or accepts certain people as "spiritual authorities"; but even in this case, as was pointed out above, a great diversity of experiences can still be accepted. It should be remembered, moreover, that even judgements about sense perception are not immune from the influence of prevailing dogma—the test of consistency with background knowledge ensures that. We may laugh now at those churchmen who refused to look through Galileo's telescope, but they believed that experience mediated by a man-made instrument could never be as sure as metaphysical doctrines, in this case the doctrine of the perfection of heavenly bodies. Nowadays, in contrast, we place so much faith in technology that it is sometimes made the ultimate arbiter in matters of sense perception—"the camera doesn't lie!" (d) Even the criteria of sense perception are 'viciously circular' in one sense: they are designed to test individual experiences, and presuppose the reliability of sense experience in general. It would be impossible to demonstrate the veridicality of a sense experience without appealing at some point to other sense experiences, whether they are one's own experiences, those of other people, or experiences of and mediated by machines. Attempts to justify our confidence in sense perception *in general* have been notoriously unsuccessful.

What of the criteria of prediction and of corroboration by instruments, other people, and other senses? It should be pointed out first of all that these criteria are by no means sufficient for a veridical perception. Nonperceptual experiences may satisfy many of them (e.g. I can predict on the basis of my feeling of nausea that I will throw up), and many types of perceptual experience which are known to be illusory also satisfy them (e.g. all people rightly situated with functioning sense organs will see a mirage). But are they necessary to a veridical perception? And to the extent that they are necessary, do religious experiences satisfy them?

Some amount of agreement with other people is, indeed, necessary if the alleged percept is also alleged to be an aspect of the world we all live in and to be perceptible in principle by all human beings, however blind some may be to it. (It is logically possible that there should be an entity perceptible only to one person with a unique set of characteristics, but the divine reality is not claimed to be of this sort.) But it is arguable that religious experiences do satisfy the criterion of agreement to some extent (see Chapter VII for a detailed argument), and that good reasons can be given for the comparative lack of unanimity or universality. Perceptual experiences are only fully repeatable where the object exhibits known regularities and where we know something about the conditions required for perception. For instance, tables exist without discontinuity and stay where they are put; if I seem to see a table in a certain place, I expect every person with the concept of a table and with eyes in good working order who looks at that spot also to have the experience of seeming to see a table. There are good reasons why it cannot be so with the divine. God, as theists frequently point out, is not an automaton, to be called up every time we cry "Lord, Lord"; he can choose when, where, how, and to whom to reveal himself. If he appeared to everyone and in perfect clarity, we would have no choice but to believe in and worship him; but God, theists argue, values our freely given love, and therefore makes his manifestations somewhat rare and ambiguous.[11] In non-theistic traditions, too, religious experiences are by no means automatic upon the performance of rituals or meditative techniques; the subject must have the difficult-to-measure qualities of sincerity and purity, and may even then be barred from the transcendental realms by the sins of a past life.

It is these features of the divine which make prediction, too, a largely inappropriate criterion in the case of religious experience. It may be satisfied to some extent, however: (i) Some religious claims may be verifiable in an afterlife. (ii) C. D. Broad suggests that subjects of religious experiences might be able to predict in the sense of making "actual ethical discoveries which others can afterwards recognize to be true", introducing "many ideals of conduct and ways of life, which we can all recognize now to be good and useful".[12] (iii) Gary Gutting has put forward an argument claiming that experiences apparently of a very good and powerful

---

[11] Some may object here that if God believed our salvation to be as important as our survival in this world, he would have made atheism a practical impossibility in the same way solipsism is—but there are arguments against this, into which I cannot go here.

[12] Broad, p. 196.

being concerned about us are corroborated by the fulfilment of predictions based on those experiences, namely: that the subject will have further such experiences, that others will have similar experiences, and that the subject will be aided in the endeavour to lead a morally better life.[13] (iv) The 'fruits' criteria in effect involve the fulfilment of predictions regarding the subject's expected personality and behaviour if he has been in contact with God. (v) There is such a thing as a 'devotional experiment', in which agnostics who believe religious doctrines are plausible but who lack the evidence of personal experience sincerely attempt to 'open themselves to the divine' by praying, talking with believers, and so on.[14] These tests are, however, much less precisely formulated and less rigorously applied than their sensory counterparts.

The test of corroboration by the other senses is clearly inappropriate in the case of nonsensory religious experiences (though Wainwright suggests that numinous experiences might corroborate mystical experiences in the same way that tactile experience corroborates visual experience.) Corroboration by scientific instruments is also impossible. Though the use of such instruments is relevant to some aspects of religious experience— questionnaires may measure fear of death and EEGs record 'relaxed' brain wave patterns—they cannot detect the presence of God in the way that, say, a photoelectric 'eye' detects the presence of an opaque body. The divine is not a *physical* entity or force.

It should also be remembered that many quasi-sensory religious experiences are considered by their subjects to be veridical in the sense of being 'pictures' (etc.) shown to them by a divine being for their edification or encouragement; the quasi-sensory elements themselves need not correspond to any external reality. These experiences would thus fail the tests of veridicality for sense perception outright, being classed as hallucinations.

We are led to conclude, then, that the specific 'checking procedures' of sense perception are for the most part simply inappropriate to religious experience, and that the analogy is not very close. But we should also notice that religious experience is not alone in this. The concentration on the visual perception of a material object has led philosophers to ignore the widely varying

[13] Gary Gutting, *Religious Belief and Religious Scepticism* (Notre Dame: Univ. of Notre Dame Press, 1982), ch. 5.

[14] See my article, "The Devotional Experiment", *Rel. Stud.*, 22 (1986), 15–28.

criteria we use to test such things as the perception of other people's emotions and character, causality, the passage of time, and the meaning of words and signs. These facts should be borne in mind when we come to deal with challenges to religious experience, among which are the sceptical claims made on p. 73 above.

The most serious criticism of Wainwright's argument, however, is the following: the criteria of veridicality for sense perception cannot themselves be inductively justified, for one must appeal in the inductive process to the very sorts of experience one is trying to show to be veridical (see also point (d), above). Confronted by a sceptic who doubts the reliability of sense experience as a whole, it will not suffice for us to show that most sense experiences satisfy certain criteria of veridicality; no one has ever been able to justify our confidence in our sense experiences that way. To escape from this "sceptical bog", one must show that there is good reason to treat sense experiences as *prima facie* veridical, innocent until proven guilty. Similarly, if someone doubts the reliability of religious experience as a whole, then it will not do to show that they satisfy certain religious criteria of veridicality, however analogous these are to the criteria used for sense perception. What is needed is an argument which treats religious experience not as analogous to some 'uncontroversial' type of experience but as one type of perceptual experience among others, and which recognizes that all perceptual experiences are *prima facie* evidence for experiential claims. Then, and only then, can an argument be constructed to show that the religious case does not possess features which destroy that *prima facie* evidential force (many of the points made in this section will be useful to such an argument). There will then be no need to become entangled in discussions of the circularity of the criteria of veridicality. Such an argument, however, must wait until Chapter IV; other popular versions of the argument from religious experience need to be examined first.

4. RELIGIOUS EXPERIENCE AS A PERSONAL ENCOUNTER

One way theists have attempted to do justice to the 'immediacy' of their alleged knowledge of God in religious experience is through the analogy with personal encounters with other people. Countless theistic philosophers of religion have stressed that their knowledge of God is a knowledge by acquaintance, as uninferred, intuitive, and inexpressible as our knowledge of those who are close to us. The analogy with sense perception, they feel, obscures the immediate and intimate nature of these encounters. As J. Cook Wilson says in an oft-quoted passage, "If we think of the existence of our friends; it is the 'direct knowledge' that we want . . . We don't want merely inferred friends. Could we possibly be satisfied with an inferred God?"[15] John Baillie, in *Our Knowledge of God*, heartily concurs: "it is not as the result of an inference of any kind . . . that the knowledge of God's reality comes to us. It comes through our direct personal encounter with him in the Person of Jesus Christ his Son our Lord".[16] Baillie supports his contention with quotations from other prominent theists such as Martin Buber, whose well-known *I and Thou* expounds the claim that God is "the *Thou* that by its nature cannot become *It*": "Something else is not 'given' and God then elicited from it; but God is the Being that is directly, most nearly, and lastingly, over against us, that may properly only be addressed, not expressed."[17]

This analogy is certainly attractive to those who believe in a personal creator-God. To regard God as an object of scientific enquiry or as the product of a logical argument is not only verging on blasphemy; it does not lead to the infinite, incomprehensible, living God of Abraham, Isaac, and Jacob: "By love may he be gotten and holden; but by thought never".[18] And the Christian's experience of God is in many respects similar to our experience of other persons:

(i) We do not arrive at the knowledge that our friends exist through a process of inference, but rather through direct encounter.

(ii) We feel we know 'intuitively' that the persons we meet are conscious subjects and agents—we do not consciously base that belief on other beliefs (however much philosophers may try to tell us that we base that belief on some argument from analogy).

(iii) Many features of an 'I-Thou' relationship and many aspects of the 'Thou' which we apprehend in that relationship are practically impossible to put into words. As C. E. Raven wrote:

---

[15] J. Cook Wilson, *Statement and Inference*, II (Oxford: OUP, 1926), p. 853.

[16] John Baillie, *Our Knowledge of God* (London: OUP, 1939), p. 143.

[17] Martin Buber, *I and Thou*, tr. R. G. Smith (Edinburgh: T. & T. Clark, 1937), pp. 80–1.

[18] *The Cloud of Unknowing*, ch. 6.

As soon as we treat a human being not as a thing but as a person we discover in him elements that we can apprehend but not describe. It is only on the surface that we can define one another; even when, as we say, we know our friends through and through, share their impulses and react to their every mood, yet such knowledge when we try to express it remains ultimately mysterious: 'I know but cannot tell'.[19]

Persons trained in psychology might be able to do better than the rest at 'telling', but even they would admit that their verbal descriptions could never be adequate.

(iv) Just as humans reveal something of themselves through behaviour, speech, and other external signs, so God is said to reveal himself through the created world, through the effects of the holy spirit in individuals, and so on. 'Getting to know' a person is not some mysterious telepathic penetration into the person's 'essence', even in the case of a non-physical person. But it also is not—as the personal encounter analogy stresses—a matter of collecting facts about a person. Theists generally rate experience *of* God far above knowledge *about* him.

The personal encounter analogy has the added advantage, from the theistic point of view, that it allows 'faith' to be spelled out as a response of trust to the overwhelming Being encountered, rather than as the assent to theological doctrines on insufficient evidence or even in spite of evidence.

It might be objected that the personal encounter analogy is too 'parochial', in that it presupposes a conception of God as the sort of being who can be addressed, encountered, and interacted with. Might not subjects of religious experiences from other traditions say that apparent personal encounters must be illusory, since the divine is impersonal? Well, yes, they might; but theists can point out that the personal encounter analogy allows for the validity of other types of religious experience, since God is supposed to reveal himself in other ways and to reveal other aspects of himself than the 'personal', even within theistic traditions. It is therefore the non-theists who are being parochial. (This is, of course, not the end of the matter, and the whole of Chapter VII is devoted to apparently conflicting claims based on religious experience.)

The personal encounter analogy may well be appropriate—and it does fit most of the experiences in Chapter II well—but can it be

---

[19] C. E. Raven, *Natural Religion and Christian Theology*, vol. II (Cambridge: CUP, 1953), p. 47.

pushed far enough to provide grounds for the claim that the subject of such an apparent encounter really is apprehending a divine power? The argument would have to look something like this: our beliefs about other humans *qua* persons are things for which we cannot give grounds and which we often cannot articulate; and they seem to be generated directly by personal encounters—yet we accept them uncontroversially as knowledge. Many experiences of God are apparent personal encounters, and subjects should not therefore be required to give grounds for their belief in God or to describe the object of their experiences before they can be said to 'know' God. (This is a species of argument from 'basic beliefs', which, when it is not tied down to a particular analogy, is a somewhat more effective argument, as we shall see later.)

However, although we do not and ought not to treat our friends as objects of scientific inquiry, and our primary aim is not to gather information about them, nevertheless a certain amount of factual knowledge of our friends is presupposed in any relationship. I would have very odd friendships indeed if I (being a competent language user) could give no verbally articulated information about my friends—e.g. "a woman", "tall", "generous", "laughs a lot"— the description does not have to be adequate, by any means. The same goes for knowledge of cities, etc.: all knowledge *of* knowledge by acquaintance) involves a certain amount of knowledge *that* (factual knowledge). Fortunately, the inexpressibility of personal encounters is not radical in either the human or the divine case; subjects of religious experiences can usually cite analogous 'facts' about the object of their encounter—e.g. "very powerful" or "loving"—even if these are expressed by means of metaphors. But many theists seem to think that if we have personal encounters with people and God, all 'factual' questions regarding the nature and existence of those beings are irrelevant—we have direct experience of those persons, and that is the end of the matter. John Hick writes, for instance, that

it would be as sensible for a husband to desire a philosophical proof of the existence of the wife and family who contribute so much to the meaning in his life as for the man of faith to seek a proof of the existence of the God within whose purpose he is conscious that he lives and moves and has his being.[20]

---

[20] John Hick, *Philosophy of Religion* (Englewood Cliffs, NJ: Prentice-Hall, 1963), p. 61.

If by "philosophical proof" Hick means a deductive argument, then he is right, simply because it would never be sensible to desire such a proof of the existence of anything. If, however, he is implying that the beliefs that the wife, family, and God exist are immune from philosophical inquiry when the subject is so 'conscious' of their existence, then he is forgetting two things: even such 'obviously true' beliefs may be mistaken (see (i) below); and a husband would never argue for his wife's existence only because it is normally such uncontroversial knowledge that it would be ridiculously pedantic to do other than tacitly assume it in ordinary conversation (see (ii) below). In a case in which the wife's existence was controversial—for instance, if the husband were claiming to have personal encounters with her after her death—arguments would be far from irrelevant.

There are, moreover, serious disanalogies between encounters with humans and apparent encounters with God:

(i) Just as we may feel certain about something and yet not be right, so we may think we are having an 'I-Thou' encounter with a person when we are not—the 'Thou' may not be aware of us, may not be present, or may not even exist. We may also think we know a person thoroughly on the basis of a personal relationship, and be completely mistaken. Such situations provide ample fodder for fictional plots. In the case of human persons, there are accepted means of showing that the 'sense of encounter' was mistaken—observation by a third party that the 'Thou' had put down the telephone receiver and was no longer listening to the 'I'; the confession of a person who had been posing as a friend for some ulterior motive. In the religious case, we can weed out experiences which are likely to be illusory by applying 'subject-related challenges' (as I shall call them later), claims that the subject was in a state or situation which we know generally leads to illusory experiences; but there is nothing analogous to the conclusive 'object-related challenges' available in the human case. Granted, God is supposed never to deceive us, but we can nevertheless be mistaken, and without the possibility of independent access to the object of a person's religious experience, assessments of the veridicality of putative encounters with God must appeal to very different factors than assessments in the human realm. This disanalogy is recognized even by a mystic as unphilosophical as St Teresa, who writes of her sense of God's presence:

It is as if a person were to feel that another is close beside her; and though, because of the darkness, he cannot be seen, she knows for certain that he is there. This, however, is not an exact comparison, for the person who is in the dark knows that the other is there, if not already aware of the fact, either by hearing a sound or by having seen him there previously. But in this case nothing of that kind happens: though not a word can be heard, either exteriorly or interiorly, the soul knows with perfect clearness who is there, where he is and sometimes what is signified by his presence. Whence he comes, and how, she cannot tell, but so it is, and for as long as it lasts she cannot cease to be aware of the fact.[21]

(ii) The most crucial disanalogy, however, is the following: the tests which enable us to pick out illusory experiences of apparent human encounters are designed to show whether individual experiences are veridical or not; they cannot show that such experiences are veridical in general. For that, one must appeal to some more general principle of rationality such as Swinburne's principle of credulity (see Chapter IV). Since proponents of this analogy do not take this further step, their argument rests on the fact that our experiences of other human persons are uncontroversially and universally taken to be *prima facie* veridical (i.e. veridical unless good reason can be given to reject them). But experiences apparently of God are not thus believed by all to be *prima facie* veridical—that is one of the points at issue! Like the analogy with sense perception, then, the analogy with personal encounters is only of use within the framework of an argument from religious experience resting on more basic premises.

5. RELIGIOUS EXPERIENCE AS EXPERIENCING-AS

When the theist considers his experiences, I. M. Crombie argues,

All that is necessary is that he should be honestly convinced that, in interpreting them, as he does, theistically, he is in some sense facing them more honestly, bringing out more of what they contain or involve than could be done by interpreting them in any other way. . . . There is a partial parallel to this in historical judgment. Where you and I differ in our interpretation of a series of events, there is nothing outside the events in question which can over-rule either of us . . .[22]

---

[21] *Life*, p. 326.
[22] I. M. Crombie, in the "Theology and Falsification" debate in A. Flew and A. MacIntyre (eds.), *New Essays in Philosophical Theology* (London: SCM, 1955), p. 112.

Theists such as Crombie, beleaguered by demands for 'experimental evidence', have attempted to defend belief in theism by showing that it is one of those cases in which the disputing parties agree about 'the facts' or 'the data', but disagree about their significance, internal organization, relation to other events, and so forth. Theists cannot produce any 'evidence' which is different from the atheists', they argue, and they do not use different principles of inference, for God is not consciously inferred from 'the facts'; but they may nevertheless be able to show by various subtle arguments that their *interpretation* of the facts is the right one.

John Wisdom's paper "Gods" expresses at length this idea that belief in God is a matter of seeing 'in a different light' the very same 'facts' which the sceptic sees, as when a painting looks beautiful to one person but not to another.[23] Although his paper is by no means an 'argument from religious experience', it is relevant to one, since it attempts to show how theists could interpret their experiences of the world theistically, and possibly be right, without there being any different, uniquely religious 'facts' for them to experience. Wisdom's 'Invisible Gardener' parable from that paper, now so well known that it needs no retelling, shows how the sceptic and the person who believes in the gardener have exactly the same knowledge of untended gardens and of this particular garden, and yet see different patterns in the data, see different things as particularly significant. The puzzling signs of cultivation in this long-neglected garden lead the believer to one interpretation; the fact that no gardener is ever seen leads the sceptic to another.

Substantially the same argument was proposed by (the early) John Hick when he compared the difference between theists and atheists to the switch in visual gestalt when one is presented with an ambiguous figure such as Wittgenstein's duck-rabbit.[24] (Actually, it should be pointed out that Hick presents his account as "an epistemological analysis of religious faith, not an argument for the validity of that faith", and so in treating what he says here as an argument from religious experience, we are not being entirely fair. His account should nevertheless be considered here, since it does constitute a fairly plausible argument from religious experience, and it forms the basis of the sort of argument Hick would propose

---

[23] John Wisdom, "Gods", in his *Philosophy and Psychoanalysis* (Berkeley: Univ. of California Press, 1969), ch. x.

[24] John Hick, "Religious Faith as Experiencing-As", in Schedler (ed.), *Philosophy of Religion*, pp. 278–90.

for the existence of God.) According to Hick, the believer experiences God by interpreting in a religious manner the same 'facts' as those with which the atheist is faced. The argument begins with a description of 'experiencing-as' in the case of puzzle-pictures: although we can experience Wittgenstein's figure as a duck or as a rabbit, it is clear that the lines on the page—the 'facts'—remain unchanged. He then moves to

experiencing-as in real life—for example, seeing the tuft of grass over there in the field as a rabbit, or the shadows in the corner of the room as someone standing there. And the analogy to be explored is with two contrasting ways of experiencing the events of our lives and of human history, on the one hand as purely natural events and on the other hand as mediating the presence and activity of God. For there is a sense in which the religious man and the atheist both live in the same world and another sense in which they live consciously in different worlds. They inhabit the same physical environment and are confronted by the same changes occurring within it. But in its actual concrete character in their respective 'streams of consciousness' it has for each a different nature and quality, a different meaning and significance; for one does and the other does not experience life as a continual interaction with the transcendent God.[25]

Hick anticipates an objection that in order to see a tuft of grass as a rabbit, we must previously have seen real rabbits, whereas it would beg the question to assume that believers had had previous experiences of real acts of God before they could experience an event as an act of God. He attempts to meet this objection by pointing to his earlier claim that *all* experience is experiencing-as. Interpretation in terms of prior concepts and theories is required even to recognize something as familiar and uncontroversial as a table fork, which a "Stone-Age savage" could not experience *as* a table fork.

The considerations adduced by Wisdom, Hick, and the others do not, however, amount to a very successful argument from religious experience, for the following four reasons:

(i) The proponents of these arguments use the terms 'fact' and 'event' as if they were neutral, 'untainted' things to which we can gain access, about which we all agree, and upon which we impose interpretations. The notion of experiencing-as similarly suggests that there is some 'raw datum' which rivals realize they are interpreting *as* A or B. As I shall show in Chapter VI, however,

[25] Hick, "Religious Faith as Experiencing-As", p. 281.

there are no such things as 'neutral experiences' or 'bare facts', for facts and experiences are only neutral relative to a body of conventions and theories accepted by both parties, and always involve a certain amount of interpretation. In Wisdom's gardener parable, for instance, it is assumed that both men have the same idea about what counts as a weed, what as a garden plant, what, indeed, as a garden, and this is what makes it seem so obvious that they are in agreement about all the facts. In the religious case, most experiences are 'private'; they tend to be described using heavily theory-laden terms and culturally influenced imagery; and even on a very moderated description the atheist simply does not have certain experiences which the theist claims to have (e.g. a sense of being forgiven, a sense of a holy presence). These features entail that though there are many areas of agreement between theists and atheists, the putative 'bare facts underlying religious experiences' cannot be considered one of them.

(ii) As their arguments stand, Wisdom and Hick do not do justice to the case for theism. In Wisdom's gardener parable, in particular, many distinctive forms of experience have been left out which, had the believer experienced them, would have meant that the two men were not in such agreement over the facts after all. It has been suggested that Wisdom's parable should be amended to include the believer's "claim to have been vividly aware of the presence of the gardener"[26] and a sense of being guided, making him "better than his partner at discovering new things about the garden, explaining the point of the weeds, and so on".[27] It is only by leaving out such experiences—both experiences of apparent immediate awareness of a divine power, as in numinous and mystical experiences, and experiences which can only occur when one holds a theistic world-view, such as being forgiven or having one's prayers answered—that Wisdom and Hick can make it seem plausible that the theist and the non-theist are in agreement over the facts.

(iii) The argument presented here suggests that there are only two rival interpretations to consider: theistic and atheistic. But there are many forms of religious belief, many forms of theism, and many forms of atheism. Much, much more is needed to show that any particular interpretation is more warranted than another.

[26] Basil Mitchell, *The Justification of Religious Belief* (New York: OUP, 1981), p. 114.

[27] Donovan, p. 77.

(iv) The final objection is directed towards Hick's 'escape-clause' that all experience is experiencing-as. It is true that all experience involves interpretation ('incorporated interpretation'—see Chapter I.4, and, for a fuller account, Chapter VI), and this fact does help to defuse the 'vicious circle objection' that we must know religious doctrines to be true before we can justifiably interpret experiences in terms of them (see Chapter VI). But it is misleading to think of incorporated interpretation as the equivalent of 'experiencing-as'. The latter term is usually reserved for permanently ambiguous figures such as the duck-rabbit, which has no 'privileged' interpretation, and for cases in which an object or event is mistakenly experienced as something other than it really is. The term derives its usefulness from the contrast with cases of normal, veridical perception and is parasitic upon an understanding of normal perception. Assimilating all experiencing to experiencing-as obscures this distinction. Hick's use of the term 'experiencing-as' makes it possible for him to present religious experiences as interpretations of permanently ambiguous events about which the theist is nevertheless ultimately correct—an attempt to have his cake and eat it, too.

6. THE ARGUMENT FROM 'BASIC BELIEFS'

It may have been noticed that the last two arguments from religious experience had in common a desire to show that belief in God could be rational while preserving its 'immediacy', ensuring that God was not treated as an 'inferred entity'. The proponents of these arguments recognized, albeit in an inchoate form, an objection based on the epistemological doctrine usually called 'classical (or 'strong') foundationalism': the doctrine that to be rational, a belief must either be inferred from other beliefs considered rational, or be self-evident (e.g. "$1+1=2$"), incorrigible (e.g. "I am in pain"), or evident to the senses (e.g. "I see a tree"). The last three are the only types of belief classical foundationalists accept as 'properly basic beliefs', beliefs which are considered *prima facie* justified. Since belief in God is not properly basic according to these criteria, classical foundationalists pronounce it irrational unless a convincing argument based on 'rational beliefs' can be found for God's existence—and, they claim, no such argument exists.

The arguments from religious experience so far considered have attempted to deal with this objection by showing that religious experience is analogous to uncontroversial types of perceptual experience which also yield beliefs that are 'irrational' according to the classical foundationalists' criteria. Alvin Plantinga, the author of the argument considered in this section, attacks the problem in a more philosophically sophisticated way.[28] First of all, he shows that classical foundationalism is self-referentially inconsistent: it is itself neither inferred from rational beliefs (at least, no good argument for it has ever been put forward), self-evident, incorrigible, or evident to the senses, hence by its own criteria it is not a rational belief. He then attempts to give a better account of 'proper basicality' and to show that belief in God can be considered 'properly basic'.

I should point out here that though Plantinga's argument is not generally considered an argument from religious experience, it actually is one, for belief in God turns out to be properly basic only because it is generated by experiences—religious experiences—which there is no good reason to think delusive. Let us see how the argument proceeds, and whether it is the right approach to take.

With the foundationalist criteria rejected, Plantinga must tell us what he counts as a properly basic belief, and justify his choice. He maintains that most explicit criteria of proper basicality turn out to be self-referentially inconsistent (as classical foundationalism did), and so the best approach is to look at a broad range of uncontroversial cases, and eventually build up inductive criteria. As uncontroversial cases, Plantinga cites not only the self-evident, incorrigible, and sensory types of belief accepted by classical foundationalists, but also types of belief which they would (absurdly) have had to reject, such as beliefs about other persons and memories. Unfortunately, though, Plantinga never supplies us with the required 'inductive criteria'—yet he still cites belief in God as an example of a properly basic belief. It is not surprising, then, that critics have asked, "But how can we know that theistic belief is properly basic? Isn't that the whole issue?" and "Doesn't Plantinga's approach legitimize any belief a person might hold, such as the belief that the Great Pumpkin returns every Hallowe'en?"[29]

---

[28] See Alvin Plantinga, "Reason and Belief in God", in Plantinga and Wolterstorff (eds.), *Faith and Rationality* (Univ. of Notre Dame Press, 1983), pp. 16–93.

[29] Plantinga's example, drawn from the "Peanuts" cartoon.

Plantinga's answer is twofold:

(i) Being properly basic does not entail either that a belief is incorrigible or that it is groundless; to think otherwise is to misunderstand the term. It only means that, rather than being inferred from other beliefs, a properly basic belief arises in us spontaneously under certain conditions yet to be specified (see (ii)). For instance, if I have an experience of its seeming to me that there is a tree in front of me, then my 'natural disposition' to believe what my sense experiences reveal to me generates my belief that there is a tree in front of me. I do not infer that belief from the belief that "I am being appeared to treely", but it is not groundless, since, if challenged, I could cite my experience as a "justification-conferring condition"; nor is it incorrigible, since successful counter-arguments could make me give up the belief—Plantinga suggests, whimsically, that "I might know, for example, that I suffer from the dreaded dendrological disorder, whose victims are appeared to treely only when there are no trees present."[30] Basic beliefs are only *prima facie* justified; they can be overridden. A belief in the Great Pumpkin could easily be defeated, but theistic belief is much more resilient. Plantinga does not attempt to meet challenges to theistic belief in this article, but he has elsewhere, for instance, in his 'free will defence' against the problem of evil.[31]

(ii) Answer (i) is certainly not sufficient. Plantinga does not want to say that belief in the Great Pumpkin is properly basic but untenable; he does not want to allow it to be *properly* basic at all. He therefore makes an attempt at a rough criterion of proper basicality by bringing in the notion, already alluded to, of a 'natural disposition to believe' in certain circumstances. "The Reformed epistemologist may concur with Calvin in holding that God has implanted in us a natural tendency to see his hand in the world around us;" writes Plantinga, but "the same cannot be said for the Great Pumpkin, there being no Great Pumpkin and no natural tendency to accept beliefs about the Great Pumpkin."[32] He then illustrates the natural disposition to believe in God with some examples from religious experience:

. . . there is in us a disposition to believe propositions of the sort *this flower was created by God* or *this vast and intricate universe was created by God* when

---

[30] Plantinga, "Reason and Belief", p. 83.

[31] See, for instance, ch. IX of his *The Nature of Necessity* (Oxford: Clarendon Press, 1974).

[32] "Reason and Belief", p. 78.

we contemplate the flower or behold the starry heavens or think about the vast reaches of the universe . . . Upon reading the Bible, one may be impressed with a deep sense that God is speaking to him. Upon having done what I know is cheap, or wrong, or wicked, I may feel guilty in God's sight and form the belief *God disapproves of what I have done*. Upon confession and repentance I may feel forgiven, forming the belief *God forgives me for what I have done*. A person in grave danger may turn to God, asking for his protection and help; and of course he or she then has the belief that God is indeed able to hear and help if he sees fit. When life is sweet and satisfying, a spontaneous sense of gratitude may well up within the soul; someone in this position may thank and praise the Lord for his goodness, and will of course have the accompanying belief that indeed the Lord is to be thanked and praised.[33]

None of these is the belief "God exists"; Plantinga admits that, strictly speaking, it is only particular beliefs such as the above which are basic, and the belief "God exists" is entailed by them. In the same way, we believe that 'there are trees' and 'there are persons' because they are entailed by particular basic beliefs such as "I see a tree" and "that person is pleased". He continues to refer to the more general beliefs as basic, however, recognizing that he is "speaking loosely".

Not just any disposition to believe qualifies a belief as properly basic; the disposition must be triggered in "justification-conferring conditions" and be a "reliable" disposition. It is here that the argument from basic beliefs begins to run into real difficulties. Plantinga does not seem to be able to give a good, non-question-begging account of these conditions.

There are dispositions to believe which are very natural and thoroughly *un*reliable. Nicholas Wolterstorff mentions, for instance, the dispositions to believe what we wish were true and to believe that everything a person towards whom we are hostile says is false;[34] we could also add the disposition to believe statements which are continually and forcefully repeated. All sane adults know that these dispositions are unreliable, and it is this which prevents just any capricious belief from being properly basic: believing "what one takes a fancy to" is known to be an unreliable means of arriving at beliefs. How do we know that the disposition to believe that "this flower was created by God" is not unreliable? Nowhere

[33] Ibid., p. 80.
[34] "Can Belief in God be Rational if it has no Foundations?" in Plantinga and Wolterstorff (eds.), pp. 135–86.

does Plantinga respond to possible alternative explanations of the religious experiences which trigger such beliefs, explanations which might show the belief tendency to be unreliable.[35]

Plantinga does have the following in his favour: we could not show that a belief-generating mechanism was *reliable* without at some point relying on a disposition to believe the judgements employed in that argument (believing inferences requires dispositions too). Either the argument would be viciously circular or it would have to pronounce some arbitrary set of dispositions (such as the one favoured by classical foundationalists) reliable and base the rest on those. Dispositions, like basic beliefs, must therefore be considered innocent until proven guilty. But a sceptic would say of the alleged disposition to believe in God just what Plantinga said of belief in the Great Pumpkin: 'there is no God and no natural tendency to accept beliefs about God.' Unbelievers certainly seem to have no natural tendency to believe in God. Plantinga, following Calvin, would reply that in such people the natural disposition has been suppressed through sin. This response seems both *ad hoc* and condescending; moreover, it does not explain why in every other field of properly basic belief cited by Plantinga—sense perception, other persons, testimony, memories, etc.—the disposition to believe is not suppressed in any sane person. Because of this, Plantinga ultimately concedes that his argument is not "polemically useful". The believer will include theistic beliefs in his list of accepted properly basic beliefs; the sceptic will not; and that is that.

Plantinga's argument suffers from several further defects:

(i) He talks as if the only religious disposition to believe were the disposition to believe in the God of Christianity, and that if that disposition were suppressed, the subject would automatically be an atheist. Are adherents of other religions all suffering from suppressed and/or unreliable dispositions to believe, then, and from sin?

(ii) Plantinga does not distinguish between experiences in which God (or the holy spirit, etc.) is felt somehow to be present, and experiences which the subject merely has a 'natural disposition' to believe were caused by or are best explained by the divine

[35] Plantinga has since refined his account somewhat. In his article "Justification and Theism", *Faith and Philosophy*, 4 (1987), 403–26, for instance, he discusses the 'proper working of the cognitive faculties within an appropriate environment' However, this account still leaves most of the questions of this section unanswered.

('interpretive' religious experiences). The former are much more important evidentially than the latter, and should not be confused with them.

(iii) An account which rests on the notion of natural dispositions to believe such general things as "our sense experiences" and "our memories" is far too simplistic. As very young children we may have dispositions to believe such things universally, but we gradually learn both that our dispositions are not to be trusted under certain circumstances and that they are always confirmed under others. They gradually become "restrained and modified" and "more finely articulated" (Wolterstorff); under certain circumstances, a disposition may disappear altogether. The idea that a disposition should be considered reliable unless we know it to be unreliable becomes very difficult to elucidate: with what degree of specificity should the disposition be characterized? All belief dispositions are known to be unreliable under many circumstances. If we say that the dispositions in question are reliable under "justification-conferring conditions", then those conditions remain to be spelled out—and Plantinga has not done so. If all dispositions are really dispositions to believe such specific things as "this flower was created by God" and "that person is pleased", then mention of these conditions is even more important. But then one ends up with a world overpopulated with specific dispositions to believe. (An argument based on something similar to Plantinga's 'natural tendencies to believe', but which manages to avoid most of the pitfalls of his argument, is discussed in the next chapter.)

(iv) Plantinga's argument was not an attempt to persuade atheists or agnostics that theism is highly probable; his aim was merely to show that a person who could provide no justification for his religious beliefs might nevertheless be rational (in the weak sense of 'not irrational') in maintaining them. To show that religious beliefs are rational in a stronger sense, i.e. that there is good reason to believe them, requires a much more complex and extensive argument. In such an argument, religious experiences would be treated not just as triggers of a 'disposition to believe' which is already considered reliable, but as evidence in their own right.

The argument from basic beliefs does exhibit a fundamental insight which will soon prove important, viz. the insight that experiential claims should be treated as 'innocent until proven guilty'. The next chapter will show how that discovery is used in

Richard Swinburne's argument from religious experience, and how that argument can be developed further to give religious experience a crucial role within a 'cumulative case'.

4

A CUMULATIVE CASE

One of the most recent attempts to use religious experiences as evidence for theism is Richard Swinburne's argument in *The Existence of God*. Unlike Plantinga, Swinburne aims to show not only that it is rational to maintain a current religious belief but also that "theism is more probable than not".[1] He recognizes that religious experience on its own cannot yield such an ambitious conclusion; it does, however, play a crucial role in a cumulative argument for the existence of God. In this chapter I will look closely at Swinburne's argument, suggest some modifications, and provide the guidelines for the most crucial part of this book, the response to sceptical challenges.

Swinburne's first move is to discuss what he counts as a 'religious experience', a step many other authors of arguments from religious experience have—rather surprisingly—omitted. For the purposes of Swinburne's argument, a religious experience is "an experience which seems (epistemically)[2] to the subject to be an experience of God (either of his just being there, or doing or bringing about something) or of some other supernatural thing".[3] He then expounds and defends the 'principle of credulity', a principle which, I believe, must form the ultimate underpinning of any successful argument from religious experience. Rather than tying his principle to experiences with a particular type of percept, to a host of 'dispositions to believe', or to viciously circular criteria of veridicality, Swinburne conceives of a principle so fundamental that even religious experiences are subsumed under it:

it is a principle of rationality that (in the absence of special considerations) if it seems (epistemically) to a subject that x is present, then probably x is present; what one seems to perceive is probably so.[4]

---

[1] Swinburne, p. 291.
[2] See Ch. I.4.
[3] Swinburne, p. 246.
[4] Ibid., p. 254.

Though no experience entails the existence of its apparent percept (and here Swinburne is in agreement with other proponents of arguments from religious experience, in contrast to those mythical champions of 'self-authenticating experiences' so richly berated by Antony Flew[5]), experiences must nevertheless be regarded as *prima facie* evidence for the alleged percept. Failure to accept this principle of credulity lands us in "the sceptical bog" hinted at in previous sections, and discussed further below.

After dealing with two objections to the use of the principle of credulity in the case of religious experience, Swinburne describes the four sorts of "special considerations which limit the principle of credulity". Although an experience is *prima facie* evidence for its object, it is only *ultima facie* evidence in the absence of successful challenges. These challenges can be formulated as follows: One may show that the experience was the sort of experience which has in the past proved to yield unreliable perceptions, by (i) showing that the conditions under which the alleged perception was made generally lead to unveridical experiences or that the subject himself is generally unreliable, or (ii) showing that the subject could not make reliable perceptions in similar circumstances on other occasions or that he has not had the training necessary to make reliable perceptions of that sort; or, looking now at the apparent object of the perception, one may (iii) show that the alleged percept was not actually present or (iv) show that even if the alleged percept was present, it was not a cause of the subject's experience of seeming to perceive it. Swinburne claims that these challenges have very limited application in the case of experiences apparently of God.

To complete the argument, Swinburne moves from individual cases to a general argument by invoking another "fundamental principle of rationality", the principle of testimony. This, too, appears to me to be basically correct: it is impossible even in principle to check everything we are told; our very understanding of the words used depends "on the assumption that other people normally tell the truth".[6] In the absence of special considerations, then, it is reasonable to believe that "the experiences of others are (probably) as they report them";[7] combined with the principle of

---

[5] See Flew's *God and Philosophy* (London: Hutchinson, 1966), pp. 132–3.
[6] Swinburne, p. 271.
[7] Ibid., p. 272.

credulity, this yields the principle that "other things being equal, we think that what others tell us that they perceived, probably happened".[8] Corroborating reports of similar experiences can thus often overcome a challenge (such as improbability on background evidence) which would defeat an individual experiential claim. Since, Swinburne continues, there is in general no reason to doubt subjects' reports of their religious experiences—most subjects of such experiences are not habitual liars or given to exaggeration or misremembering—we can conclude that the "combined weight of testimony" in the religious case will only be insufficient to show the existence of God more probable than not if the prior probability of God's existence is "very low indeed". But the arguments put forward in the rest of Swinburne's book—from consciousness, providence, and so on—show that the prior probability of theism is not very low, though it is not very high either. The evidence of religious experience is enough to tip the balance and make theism "more probable than not".

Though this argument deals with the problems facing religious experience better than previous arguments, it is, as will be seen below, inadequate in many respects, and I cannot agree with it on every point. However, it does provide a very effective framework for a general argument from religious experience. In the paragraphs which follow, I shall elaborate upon some important points of Swinburne's argument (particularly the principle of credulity), discuss both its virtues and shortcomings, and attempt to remedy any defects with suggestions of my own, providing the groundwork for the remaining chapters—the response to challenges, and the outline of a cumulative case.

Before we move on to the sections dealing with the principle of credulity, the challenges to religious experience, and the nature of cumulative arguments, a word should be said about Swinburne's conception of religious experience. His definition effectively rules out many experiences of nature mysticism, integration and isolation of the 'purified soul', Theravada Buddhism, and monism. This consequence is defended in a footnote: "Only religious experiences of the kind which my definition picks out have apparent evidential value in pointing towards the existence of God, and that is why I am concerned with them alone."[9] We shall see

---

[8] Ibid., p. 271.
[9] Ibid., p. 247.

later, however, that this leaves out experiences which support the case for theism in an indirect way, as part of a cumulative argument—for instance, by their 'fruits', or by being evidence not for the existence of some supernatural entity but for some proposition which is generally believed by theists and not by atheists. (Chapter IX shows how such indirectly valuable experiences can be worked into a cumulative case.) It also leaves the theist open to the 'conflicting claims challenge' (see Chapter VII), since some of the experiences Swinburne ignores are *prima facie* counterevidence to the theistic case. If Buddhists and monists made no claims at all based on their experiences, described them only phenomenologically, and remained agnostic on the question whether they signified mental derangement, an interesting brainstate, or universal truth, then we could conveniently ignore them. But they apparently do make claims; and the theist must therefore show how such experiences can be reconciled with theism without making the *ad hoc* move of declaring them all illusory. In any case, since my argument is not in the first instance an argument towards Christian theism, I must investigate a much wider range of religious experiences than Swinburne does.

2. THE PRINCIPLE OF CREDULITY

Swinburne expresses the principle of credulity as follows:

It is a principle of rationality that (in the absence of special considerations) if it seems (epistemically) to a subject that x is present, then probably x is present; what one seems to perceive is probably so.[10]

It may not be entirely clear why this principle is a principle of rationality, what its limitations are, and just what role it plays in an argument from religious experience. The following paragraphs should shed some light on these matters.

(i) The above formulation of the principle of credulity is somewhat misleading. As the last clause indicates, the principle is intended to cover all perceptual experiences, not just those which would naturally be described by their subjects as the perception of the presence of some entity; and it is clear from later remarks that Swinburne also means it to apply to memory, which is not

---

[10] Swinburne, p. 254.

normally considered a form of 'perception'. One may use such words in a wider sense than their 'ordinary language' sense, however. Swinburne has explained, for instance,[11] that, as he is using the word 'present', it can 'seem to the subject that x is present' even when the subjects are only experiencing effects which seem to them to have been caused by an external source, so long as the belief about that cause was not a retrospective interpretation. And perceptual memories are believed to have been caused by something which was *once* a 'perception'. If we still feel dissatisfied with these 'stretched' senses, other formulations are possible: for instance, "What seems (epistemically) to a subject to be the case probably is the case, unless there are defeating conditions"; "Any experience in which it seems (epistemically) to a subject that an object is present, that an event is occurring, or that a certain state of affairs is the case, is *prima facie* evidence for the subject's corresponding external claim"; and many more. The main points such a formulation must bring out are (a) that experiences must in general be considered innocent until proven guilty; to make a general practice of accepting what seems to us to be the case as really being the case only after our experiences have satisfied certain 'criteria of veridicality' would land us in the "sceptical bog" (see (iii) below); (b) there is an evidential asymmetry between claims about the presence of something and claims about the absence of something (see (ii) below); and (c) the principle of credulity does not imply that all beliefs a person might happen to hold are justified, nor that all experiential beliefs are fully justified, but it gives experiential auto-descriptions an important initial credibility (see (iv) below).

(ii) One reason why Swinburne expressed his principle of credulity in terms of perceiving the presence of x was his belief that experiences of "how things seem not to be" are not *prima facie* evidence for how things really are; only "positive seemings" are such evidence. But this is a very strong claim, and it appears to go against some of our common-sense intuitions about experiential evidence. Michael Martin has objected,[12] for instance, that in ordinary life we do believe that an experience of the apparent absence of an object such as a chair gives us good grounds for

[11] In conversation.
[12] "The Principle of Credulity and Religious Experience", *Rel. Stud.*, 22 (1986), 79–93.

supposing that there is no chair there. I believe that Martin's claim is true, but that there are still good reasons for maintaining that experiences of an apparent absence are not *prima facie* evidence in as unqualified a way as are experiences of apparent presences. When modified, this aspect of the principle of credulity still expresses an important insight.[13]

Experiences of the apparent absence of an entity (non–occurrence of an event, etc.) are *prima facie* evidence, but only in a very limited respect: they are *prima facie* evidence only for the claim that an entity which is perceptible by the means the subject was using at the time (e.g. vision) was not present in the area to which the subject was directing his attention on that occasion. They are not *prima facie* evidence that the entity does not exist at all; for that, the claim must be added that there is very good reason to believe the subject would have perceived the entity there and then if it had existed anywhere, or that subjects have failed to perceive the entity at all times and places that it should have been perceptible to them if it had existed. Where the very existence of an entity is at issue, then, a failure to perceive it is not by itself *prima facie* evidence for its nonexistence, whereas an experience of its *presence* is itself *prima facie* evidence for the entity's existence. The chair example may have seemed a potent objection because one is not normally concerned with the question whether there are such things as chairs or even whether a particular chair exists, but only with the question of the presence or absence of a particular chair or of a chair in a particular spot. In the religious case, however, the main issue is the very existence of a divine reality. Granted, God is supposed to be omnipresent; but this does not entail that he is perceptible everywhere, always, or by all. (Where chairs are present, in contrast, they normally *are* perceptible.)

'Negative' 'flashes of insight' should also be regarded as *prima facie* evidence for "how things seem not to be". I can see no reason for dismissing a 'flash of insight' that something is not the case while accepting a belief acquired in the same way that something is

---

[13] In a recent article, Swinburne has revised his earlier views on 'negative seemings'. They are not "no evidence at all of how things are"; rather, "as such (in advance of detailed empirical evidence about them), negative 'seemings' on empirical matters give much shakier support to claims about how things are not than do positive 'seemings' to how things are." See "Does Theism need a Theodicy?" *Canadian Journal of Philosophy*, 18 (1988), 287–311, p. 294 n.

the case. 'Revelations' that there is no God[14] thus provide *prima facie* counter-evidence to the religious case. Many of these can be dealt with by the argument that revelatory experiences are considered generally unreliable, but some (e.g. some Buddhist experiences) are more difficult. Chapter VII will explore ways of dealing with this type of apparent counter-evidence.

One reason it appears so obvious that an experience of the apparent absence of a chair is good evidence for the absence of a chair is the fact that chairs are difficult things to miss. Many experiences of alleged absence are, however, open to the challenge that the disputed object might have been present but not perceived: perhaps it was a difficult thing to perceive, or could easily be overlooked, or was only fleetingly present. In the case of a divine reality, a multitude of factors, both hidden and expected, could prevent perception of the reality even though it was present. As was mentioned earlier, a personal God might even choose whether or not to reveal himself. Now, few people have "experiences of the absence of God" (such as 'revelations' that there is no God); rather more have an absence of experiences of God. (It should be noted in passing that many experiences which could be called "experiences of the absence of God" are the experiences Christian mystics refer to as "the dark night of the soul", when it seems that God's presence has been withdrawn. These experiences are not considered by their subjects to be evidence for the nonexistence of God!) When the failure to experience a divine reality is associated with a lack of any kind of attempt to perceive one, as in the case of many wholly secularly oriented people, the *prima facie* counter-evidence is outweighed; one would not expect such people to have religious experiences. There are, however, people who have sincerely striven for experiences of a divine reality by all known methods (e.g. prayer, a virtuous life) and have failed to achieve any perceptual awareness of one. Although we realize that no known techniques can guarantee a perception of divine reality, we do feel we are justified in having a mild expectation of success in certain cases. Where those expectations are disappointed, the degree of counter-evidence provided is by no means comparable to that provided by the failure to perceive a chair, but it must be taken into account. Although no data are available on the proportion of subjects sincerely seeking God who fail to find him, I suspect that it

---

[14] See e.g. Hardy, p. 113.

is relatively small. The counter-evidence provided by these subjects forms part of the 'cumulative challenge', which is discussed below.

Of course, evidence that an entity does not exist can come from many sources besides experiences of its apparent absence. Inferences from other experiences (e.g. "I saw it destroyed"), background knowledge, and authority can all contribute. Such sources will also be seen to form part of the cumulative challenge.

(iii) The principles of credulity and testimony are fundamental principles of rationality. (We could also add a 'principle of inference'—perhaps Swinburne includes this under the principle of credulity[15]—according to which my experience of it seeming to me that *q* follows from *p* is *prima facie* evidence for the validity of that inference.) No philosopher has yet managed to provide inductive justification for our confidence in our reasoning processes, experiences, memories, and the assertions of other persons, but that is no reason to succumb to scepticism or to regard the human race as 'irrational' (perhaps taking refuge, like Hume, in games of backgammon). If there are principles by which we find we must operate, and if we do consider ourselves rational beings, then let us call those 'principles of rationality'—but we must not expect an inductive proof of their reliability. As has been pointed out several times in this chapter, attempts at such a proof would inevitably be viciously circular, for they could not be carried out without presupposing the reliability of at least some of the experiences and processes in question.

It is with considerations such as the above that Swinburne meets the objection that the principle of credulity does not apply to religious experience, but applies only in ordinary cases, where the assumption that the experiences are *prima facie* veridical has proved to be successful. Since we have no inductive evidence to show that such an assumption is warranted in the religious case, the objection continues, we ought to regard religious experiences initially with suspicion rather than with credulity. Now, it is true that general trust in our sense experiences and memories *works*: we are enabled thereby to survive, to manipulate the environment, to fulfil our desires and purposes, to communicate, and to do whatever else

---

[15] In fact, on Swinburne's present view, the principle of credulity applies to *all* beliefs, though an understanding of the way we acquire belief leads us to regard all logically contingent nonperceptual beliefs as requiring justification. (Personal communication.)

might constitute 'success'. But none of this would have been possible if we had distrusted all our experiences from the moment of birth, for we could never have developed into rational human beings; we would have been trapped in a solipsistic shell. We could not at that point distinguish experiences which atheists would later reject from those which they would accept; the principle of credulity applied to all experiences which generated beliefs. We now know that there are good reasons to reject certain types of experience as unveridical—dreams, for instance, and hallucinations. But it remains to be shown that religious experiences can be rejected *en bloc* in the same way. The onus is squarely on the sceptic to show that religious experiences are *not* reliable perceptual experiences.

(iv) The principle of credulity is not an invitation to 'gullibilism', as some critics have feared.[16] The following remarks should help to clarify this matter.

In the first place, as was mentioned in the previous point, the challenges to certain types of experience (e.g. dreams) and to experiences of certain types of entities and phenomena (e.g. elves, 'auras') are so widely successful and so well known that claims based on such experiences have come to be regarded by adults initially with suspicion rather than with credulity. The principle does not force one to believe in wildly improbable entities which relatively few subjects claim to have seen or in phenomena which are so unequivocally rejected by the vast majority of adults that one assumes successful challenges must be available, even if one cannot formulate them oneself. Where successful challenges are not so obvious and many people take the claims seriously, perhaps it is not such a bad thing if the principle of credulity forces us to treat the claims as innocent until proven guilty. If we are required to find good reasons for rejecting or revising claims to have perceived controversial phenomena, at least it will prevent us from uncritically yielding to baseless cultural prejudices.

It should be noted that I am not saying that the principle of credulity does not *apply* to experiences such as dreams. It does apply initially; but since it is widely known that powerful challenges are available against the *prima facie* probability that such

---

[16] e.g. Michael Martin, who uses the word "gullibilism" in "The Principle of Credulity".

experiences are veridical, the onus of proof is automatically placed on the subject. If one begins to impose restrictions on the applicability of the principle of credulity—e.g. Martin's restriction that the principle only applies if we know under what conditions the alleged percept would appear if it existed—one ceases to treat it as a fundamental principle of rationality. There is a substantial difference between demanding that a type of experience be shown to satisfy requirements such as Martin's before taking experiences of that type to be *prima facie* probably veridical, and accepting a type of experience as *prima facie* probably veridical *unless* it is shown that it does *not* satisfy such requirements (i.e. employing the proposed restrictions as possible challenges).

A second and very important factor which prevents the principle of credulity from leading us into 'gullibilism' is the following: the principle of credulity does not by any means guarantee that the probability it confers on an experience will be sufficient for a rational person to believe strongly in that experience. Whether or not an experience can be considered *sufficient* evidence for a perceptual claim depends on many factors such as the importance of the claim; if one is making an important perceptual claim, the principle of credulity alone will not take one very far.

A mere absence of challenges does not make experiential claims highly probable. If we wish others to accept an important experiential claim, we must, like a scientist proposing a new theory, *anticipate* possible challenges. The principle of credulity does not entitle us to regard our claims as 'proven' just because no challenges have yet been issued. Where it is demanded by the nature of the claim, a thorough investigation must be carried out into possible sources of challenges. It would be a complete misuse of the principle of credulity to say, "The onus is on the sceptic to produce challenges and therefore I can completely trust all unchallenged religious experiences." That would be blind faith, not an argument from religious experience.

Swinburne's use of the word "probable" has perhaps obscured this point somewhat, making the principle of credulity appear to provide more support than it really does. He does not sufficiently emphasize that by phrases such as, "what one seems to perceive is probably so", he means only that experiential claims are (*prima facie*) "more probable than not"—not that they are 'very likely' or that they 'ought to be believed, though there is some room for

doubt' (both common interpretations of 'probable').[17] My knowledge that 51 per cent of babies born are male does not, for instance,
entitle me to claim in ordinary situations that "Mary's baby will
probably be a boy"; that would be misleading, although it is true
that it is more probable than not that the baby will be a boy.

The principle of credulity does not therefore guarantee that in the
absence of successful challenges, experiential claims are highly
probable or that one ought to believe them wholeheartedly. It does,
however, justify an *initial* attitude of credulity, ensuring that an
argument from religious experience does not founder in the
sceptical bog before it even gets started.

The probability of an experiential claim will rise as the quantity
and severity of defeated possible challenges rise, and the confidence
one has that the claim deserves a certain degree of belief will
increase with the care and completeness of the investigation, when
one asks whether any factors exist which might affect the
probability either way. What one considers 'sufficient' evidence
will vary according to the circumstances. Whether or not one saw a
rabbit in a field, for instance, is normally a trivial issue with very
minor consequences, and we may accept Jones's claim that he saw a
rabbit in the field without bothering to investigate further, without
checking whether there are any grounds for suspicion. If it
suddenly becomes very important to know whether or not there
was a rabbit in the field, however, we will subject Jones's claim to
many plausible challenges, to ensure that he is not lying, that he has
good vision, and so on. Jones's claim that the presence of the risen
Christ comforted him last night, if true, normally has more serious
consequences; accepting that claim commits us to a host of
fundamental doctrines about the nature of the world and man,
man's destiny, and the sort of life one ought to lead. It is
understandable, then, that religious sceptics should be so persistent,
and demand a full, careful inquiry into the nature and possible
causes of religious experience. They will not be satisfied with
arguments from religious experience which focus on a narrow
range of experiences, explore only a few challenges, appear to rely
on little empirical research, or employ a very limited line of

---

[17] Gary Gutting must have been misled in this way, for instance, when he accused
Swinburne of claiming that experiences are *prima facie* evidence in "too strong a
sense", since experiences are *prima facie* only "some", not "sufficient" evidence for
their claims. See Gutting, ch. 5.

argument—characteristics of so many of the arguments discussed in the previous chapter.

This is not to say that a high degree of probability is required before religious commitment is warranted, nor that those who already believe are being irrational if they do not carry out such an investigation. One must only be confident, if one wishes to show that there is good evidence for religious claims, that one has investigated with sufficient thoroughness and sensitivity for it to be unlikely that further argument and investigation would significantly alter the degree of probability attained. I shall not argue here for the rationality of committing oneself to a religious life even if one cannot show religious claims to be highly probable; such arguments can be found elsewhere.[18] Suffice it to say that there are times when no one option can be shown to have high probability, and yet some course of action is necessary, since the stakes are high and to do nothing is also to commit oneself to a course of action—and to one which would definitely *not* lead to the goal in question.

(v) A word on the relationship of the principle of credulity to some theories of epistemic justification is called for here. It may seem that the principle entails a covert foundationalist epistemology, but that would be to misconstrue my use of it. The principle does not provide 'secure foundations' for knowledge in the strong foundationalist's sense, in which a class of beliefs (such as sense-data statements), alleged to require no justification, are put forward as the proper terminus for justification. It must be remembered that the principle of credulity does not absolve beliefs from all need for justification; it only grants them a presumption of innocence. Experiential reports provide *prima facie*, defeasible evidence for claims about the world. Moreover, as this whole study will show, some perceptual beliefs can only be justified by a cumulative argument, in which the various pieces of evidence by no means all build upon the 'foundation' of the initial perceptual belief. Even on non-foundationalist theories of knowledge, the task of justifying a belief must begin and end *somewhere*, but this does not mean we begin or end with some special type of belief which is always beyond doubt, or that we proceed in a linear fashion from starting-point to end-point.

---

[18] See, for instance, William James, "The Will to Believe", in *The Will to Believe and Other Essays in Popular Philosophy* (New York: Longmans Green, 1902), pp. 1–31; and my "The Devotional Experiment".

By putting the initial onus of proof on the sceptic, the principle of credulity avoids many of the problems and paradoxes which have plagued attempts to formulate necessary and sufficient conditions for a belief being justified or an experience veridical.[19] In particular, it avoids the dangers of scepticism inherent in such theories as coherentism and reliabilism—for how can one judge coherence or reliability except against a body of beliefs which we already accept? The conditions demanded by these other theories function as potential *defeaters* in theories which use the principle of credulity: an experience loses its *prima facie* evidential force if it does not satisfy the traditional criteria for veridicality, appears not to cohere with background knowledge and other experiences, or was generated by a process known to be epistemically unreliable. For an outline of these and other possible challenges to perceptual experiences, let us turn to the next section.

3. THE CHALLENGES TO RELIGIOUS EXPERIENCE

Swinburne's anticipation of and response to challenges to religious experience are better than those of most previous authors, but they are still inadequate, doing justice to neither side of the dispute. He does recognize the strength of certain sceptical challenges, which leads him to claim that religious experiences are good evidence for the existence of God only if it can be shown on other grounds that the existence of God is not very improbable. It is this move which makes his argument a cumulative one (see the next section). As was mentioned above, however, one reason many other arguments from religious experience are so unconvincing to sceptics is their lack of empirical research, and even Swinburne's argument could have gone further in this direction. Admittedly, his argument is confined to only one chapter of a book, and so he lacks the space to undertake a full-scale defence. But since he does not acknowledge any limitations, one must take it that he believes himself to have effectively quashed the challenges he considers.

Specific shortcomings of Swinburne's (and others') responses to challenges to religious experience will be discussed in the relevant chapters; here I wish merely to give an overview of the challenges and to discuss some possible modifications to Swinburne's account.

[19] See, for instance, the discussion of criteria for veridicality in Chapter III.3.

My classification of challenges is similar to Swinburne's, but it is more comprehensive and applies both to the principle of credulity and to the principle of testimony—an important point in the case of religious experience, where most of the data are reports of experiences. There are three basic categories of challenge: (i) description-related challenges, (ii) subject-related challenges, and (iii) object-related challenges.

(i) Description-related challenges: these include Swinburne's briefly described considerations limiting the principle of testimony, "evidence that generally or in matters of a particular kind [the subject] misremembers or exaggerates or lies",[20] but they also include conceptual issues. Auto-descriptions of subjects' experiences may be rejected as evidence if the subjects are known to be pathological liars or to have an extremely poor memory regarding their own experiences; if the subjects' subsequent behaviour suggests that they gave an insincere or mistaken description of their experiences; if there is evidence that the subjects do not understand the terms they used to describe the experiences; if the descriptions are not self-consistent; if we have reason to believe we understand the subjects' terms in a different sense from the one they intend; or if the subjects have incorporated a highly ramified retrospective interpretation into their auto-descriptions.

If any of these challenges succeeds, it does not automatically mean that the experience, if there was one, was unveridical or unsuitable as evidence, but only that it was not veridical or cannot be used as evidence *under that description*. The subjects can be invited to redescribe their experiences, still attempting to describe 'the way things seemed to them to be at the time', but in a more coherent, accurate, sincere, or comprehensible way.

A person may describe an experience in many different ways. Each description can presuppose different beliefs and attitudes on the part of the subject and describe different propositions for which the experience could be evidence (with varying degrees of success). If there is reason to suspect the subject's description, then, we cannot even begin to evaluate the evidential force of the experience.

(ii) Subject-related challenges: Swinburne's first two special considerations limiting the principle of credulity come into this category, which consists of challenges that: the subject has been shown to be unreliable in the past; the subject was in a certain state

---

[20] Swinburne, p. 272.

or situation or had a 'set' (beliefs, expectations, personality, cultural background, etc.—see Chapter VI) such that experiences occurring under those conditions are usually unveridical, or such that it is very likely that the subject would have had the experience whether or not the alleged percept was there or caused the experience, or such that memories of experiences under such conditions are usually adversely affected; or the subject has not had the training normally required to have veridical experiences of that sort.

Successful subject-related challenges do not necessarily mean that the experience was unveridical—after all, people can and do have veridical perceptual experiences while intoxicated, hypnotized, psychotic, and so on—but they do mean that the experience cannot be used on its own as evidence for the subject's experiential claim. It may still form part of a cumulative argument, however, if there is strong independent evidence in its favour. Subject-related challenges are thus most damaging when we have no independent access to the putative object of the experience, as is largely the case with religious experience. The two most intractable challenges to the evidential force of religious experience, the conflicting claims challenge (Chapter VII) and the reductionist challenge (Chapter VIII), belong to this category.

(iii) Object-related challenges: these challenges include Swinburne's third and fourth special considerations, "that on background evidence it is probable that x was not present"[21] and that "whether or not x was there, x was probably not a cause of the experience of its seeming to me that x was there."[22] One may defeat an experiential claim by showing that on background evidence it is unlikely or even impossible for the alleged percept to exist or to be as the subject described it, that the alleged percept did not have the "appropriate causal connection" (see Chapter I.4) with the subject and his experience, or that a percept of the claimed type could not have been perceived at all or in the way claimed. The first of these challenges, though sometimes involving conceptual issues only, often appeals to empirical corroboration by other people and instruments, and it can thus appear very similar to the traditional criteria of veridicality for perceptual experiences, though 'in reverse': an experience is accepted unless it fails to satisfy the criteria, rather than being rejected until it satisfies them.

[21] Ibid., p. 261.
[22] Ibid., pp. 263–4.

Challenges, background evidence (including the subject's set), and different auto-descriptions must all be taken into account together when evaluating a perceptual experience. A challenge may be successful at defeating an experience under one description, for instance, but lose its power when the experience is redescribed. Or a challenge, though successful, may be overridden by some other piece of evidence—in which case the experience could become part of a cumulative argument. It will be seen that religious experience plays its main evidential role within such an argument, since the sceptic's objections cannot be decisively refuted in all cases.

A further sort of challenge to religious experience is possible. It does not seem to have been realized, even by philosophers who have recognized the importance of cumulative arguments, that, just as theists can combine evidence to make a cumulative case, sceptics can combine their challenges to religious experience. Swinburne, for example, attempts to show only that each challenge, when considered on its own, is insufficient to defeat the evidence of religious experiences; he does not consider a 'cumulative challenge'. An outline of such a challenge will be presented at the end of the next chapter; the nature of cumulative arguments in general is discussed in the next section.

In the next chapter some secular applications of these types of challenges will be described. Then we will tackle the crucial question: Are any of these challenges applicable to religious experience, and if so, can they be defeated?

4. CUMULATIVE ARGUMENTS

Challenges to a perceptual experience may be overcome in two ways: a prospective challenge may be *defeated*, or a successful challenge may be *outweighed* by other evidence in favour of the experience's veridicality. In the former case, the subject's perceptual claim remains more probable than not—if Smith was only pretending to be drunk, then the challenge that his perceptual claim is probably unreliable because he was drunk is defeated. In the latter case, the subject's perceptual claim is not more probable than not when taken on its own, but other evidence increases its probability to such an extent that it becomes more probable than not, in light of the total evidence. If Smith claims to have encountered a wallaby

on his way home at night from a country pub, the claim may be
defeated by the successful challenges that it was dark, he had had a
lot to drink, and the alleged percept is *a priori* very improbable. If,
however, it is learned that a wallaby has escaped from a nearby
wildlife park, then Smith's claim becomes very probable, despite
the challenges. Indeed, Smith's experiential report now becomes
important evidence in its turn for there having been a wallaby on
that road, evidence which may help people to track the animal
down. We now have a 'cumulative argument'. I shall explain in this
section how such arguments work, and give a brief outline—to be
filled in in later chapters—of the way they might be employed both
for and against religious experience.

Theistic philosophers of religion have only recently begun to
complain that critics such as Flew do not recognize the force of
cumulative arguments.[23] Such critics look at one-dimensional
arguments for the existence of God, find each of them flawed or
inadequate, and then reject them all. What they fail to see is that
these arguments can interact in such a way that their combined
weight overcomes individual inadequacies. "If one leaky bucket
will not hold water that is no reason to think that ten can," says
Flew;[24] but it might be possible to arrange the buckets inside each
other so that the holes do not overlap. Such an argument would be
a "synergism", in which (according to the *OED* definition) the
combined effect of the components exceeds the sum of their
individual effects.

A cumulative argument is not, therefore, merely an *accumulation*
of evidence.The whole is greater than the sum of the parts, and
these 'parts', though perhaps individually weak as evidence and
easily defeated, provide mutual support, like the members of an
athletic team. This means that the force of a cumulative argument
will not be appreciated if its elements are assessed in isolation or if
they are expected to build upon one another in a linear fashion, like
links in a deductive chain. Basil Mitchell gives a good example of
such an argument in *The Justification of Religious Belief*, which I
quote at length, since it will illustrate many of the comments which
follow:

In a ship at sea in stormy weather, the officer of the watch reports a
lighthouse on a certain bearing. The navigating officer says he cannot have

[23] See, for instance, Basil Mitchell, *The Justification of Religious Belief*, ch. 3.
[24] Flew, p. 63.

seen a lighthouse, because his reckoning puts him a hundred miles away from the nearest land. He must have seen a waterspout or a whale blowing or some other marine phenomenon which can be taken for a lighthouse. The officer of the watch is satisfied he must have made a mistake. Shortly afterwards, however, the lookout reports land on the starboard bow. The navigating officer, still confident in his working, says it must be cloud— and it is indeed very difficult to distinguish cloud from land in these conditions. But then a second cloud-looking-like-land or land-looking-like-cloud appears on another bearing. It really does begin to look as if the navigator might be out in his reckoning. He has, perhaps, underestimated the current, or his last star sight was not as good as he thought it was. The reported sightings are consistent with one another and indicate that he is approaching land.

. . . The question whether there was a lighthouse there and the question whether the officer of the watch saw it or saw something else, or just imagined that he saw it, can only be answered in relation to some overall appraisal of the situation. The navigator's original appraisal, based on his dead reckoning, led him to say there was no lighthouse and the officer of the watch did not see it; and this was reasonable enough at that stage. But the other reports, although their evidential value, taken singly, is as slight and as controversial as the first, do cumulatively amount to a convincing case for reading the whole situation differently.[25]

It is worth looking at this example in close detail. First of all, it should be pointed out that the elements of a cumulative case may be very varied. In Mitchell's example, they are all claims to have sighted distant land or an object on land, but they could well have included such items as close sightings of debris, a radio message from shore that the ship was now approaching a certain country and must obtain clearance before proceeding further, or evidence that the navigating officer was not very reliable. Cumulative cases do not have to consist of more and more similar experiences corroborating each other, but can appeal to a wide range of evidence.

It should also be noted that the original experience is not just shown to be probably veridical *by* the cumulative case; it forms *part of* the cumulative case. The navigator does not back down because of the evidence of the second and third sightings alone, but because the evidence of all three sightings together has made him doubt his calculations. The successful challenges (that the claim of the officer of the watch was very improbable on the navigator's evidence, that

[25] Mitchell, pp. 112–13.

the viewing conditions were poor) overcame the *prima facie* evidential force of the original experience, but they did not destroy its evidential force for all time. In the same way, religious experiences which succumb individually to a particular challenge (e.g. that the subject was highly suggestible) can still be useful evidence for religious claims if there is sufficient additional evidence to make a strong cumulative case.

In real life, so many factors are at work that a perceptual claim is rarely defeated by a single, straightforward challenge of the form, "You were drunk" or "Your companions did not hear it", even if those accusations are clearly true. On their own, these true accusations do shift the burden of proof to the shoulders of the claimant, but they would often be outweighed by factors favouring the claimant unless they were themselves supported by some sort of cumulative argument. Factors which interact to strengthen or weaken challenges to perceptual experiences are: (i) the 'intrinsic strength' of the challenge; (ii) the claimant's degree of conviction; (iii) the *a priori* probability of alternative causal explanations of the experience; and (iv) whether further challenges are available to reinforce this challenge in a 'cumulative challenge'.

(i) By 'intrinsic strength' of the challenge I refer to the degree to which, taken on its own, a successful challenge makes it improbable that the subject perceived the alleged percept accurately. For instance, a true charge of profound intoxication has much greater intrinsic strength than a true charge of mild intoxication; proof that the alleged percept is logically incoherent has much greater intrinsic strength than the true charge that it is highly unusual or unexpected; and—as Swinburne pointed out—the fact that the allegedly perceived man is dead has much greater intrinsic strength than the fact that that man normally spends his time in a different city from the one in which the subject seemed to see him. Challenges of little intrinsic strength will require bolstering by further challenges before they can overcome the evidential force of an experiential claim, unless the claimant is very unsure of his experience—factor (ii).

(ii) Although there are cases in which this does not hold true, we generally feel that the strength of a person's confidence in his experience reflects the clarity and force of that experience, or its unambiguous nature. If the officer of the watch had been absolutely convinced that he had seen a lighthouse, saying that he saw it so distinctly and for so long that he could not have been mistaken, then his perceptual claim would not have been so easily defeated by the navigator's challenge. Many religious experiences, particularly numinous and mystical ones, have this 'forceful' character; one need only return to those expressions of "absolute certainty" and "ultimate reality" in Chapter II.4, to see this. Challenges to religious experience must therefore either be strong enough to outweigh the force of this conviction or give a highly plausible explanation of why unveridical experiences should elicit such confidence. The reductionist challenges of Chapter VIII claim to do the latter; we shall see how successful they are there.

(iii) In many cases there is good reason to doubt the perceptual claim, but no evidence which directly supports a particular alternative explanation of why the subject had that perceptual experience. Where sceptics can offer plausible alternative explanations, their challenges are strengthened; where they cannot, they are weakened. If we accept that it is highly unlikely (or impossible) that a person could have a perceptual experience which was completely uncaused, then any challenge to the veridicality of a perceptual experience in effect claims that the experience was caused by something other than the presence of the alleged percept. Where alternative explanations are very implausible, the explanation which simply allows that the experience was caused by the percept as claimed will be the most probable explanation unless other evidence seriously undermines its probability. For instance, hallucinations are very rare in healthy, sane adults; if the only possible explanations of the officer of the watch's experience had been either that it was a hallucination or that there really was a lighthouse there, and there was no other evidence that it was a hallucination (he was not on drugs, etc.), then we would probably choose the latter alternative, despite the navigator's claims. Where many experiences are at stake, such implausible and unsupported explanations look even more *ad hoc*, and the counter-evidence has to be even more overwhelming before the simplest explanation (veridicality) is rejected. Were the implausible theory that religious experience is all a giant hoax the only alternative to taking it to be veridical, for instance, the sceptic would be in a very weak position.

(iv) Challenges of low intrinsic strength are usually easily overcome unless they form part of a cumulative challenge.

Evidence of a mild degree of intoxication, for instance, will only defeat a perceptual claim if it is backed up by evidence that the alleged percept is highly improbable (e.g. pink rats), if the others present fail to have similar perceptual experiences, or if perceiving that percept accurately normally requires a higher degree of sensitivity than we would expect a mildly intoxicated person to have (e.g. judging another person's intentions and emotions). In Mitchell's example, the experience of the officer of the watch was initially discounted not just because it conflicted with the navigator's reckoning, but because the conditions for perception were poor (stormy weather) and because several highly plausible alternative explanations of the experience were available. If the conditions had been excellent for long-distance viewing, the officer of the watch would not have been so ready to concede defeat; nor would he if it had been stormy weather, but his sighting had been consistent with the navigator's reckoning. Where challenges depend on the interaction of factors, as in this 'lighthouse' case, it would be unfair to assess the 'defeating power' of each element of the challenge in isolation from the rest, just as it would be unfair to an argument from religious experience to assess the evidential force of each individual experience without reference to the rest, as if it were the only religious experience on record.

Swinburne recognizes the importance of cumulative arguments in favour of theism, but does not pay adequate attention to the fact that they can be used by 'the other side' as well. He attempts to show only that each challenge, considered on its own, is far too weak to defeat the evidence of religious experiences. But sceptics can combine those challenges and present a cumulative case of their own, which is much more difficult to defeat. An outline of the cumulative challenge to religious experience will be presented at the end of the next chapter.

A brief outline of this first stage of my argument from religious experience runs very much like Swinburne's, then. What seems to a person to be the case in a perceptual experience, and what a person says seemed to him to be the case in a perceptual experience, probably is the case, in the absence of good grounds for challenges. (The use of nonperceptual experiences as evidence is discussed in the final chapter.) These principles of credulity and testimony are ultimate principles of rationality which apply to all types of perceptual experience, though there are some modes of experience which succumb as a whole to challenges (e.g. dreams). The task now is to see to what extent religious experience yields to challenges, individual and cumulative, what conclusions can be drawn from the data which remain undefeated, and what other factors besides the experiences themselves must be taken into account before those experiences can play their full evidential role.

If an adequate, well-grounded response is to be made to the diverse challenges which face religious experience, evidence from many disciplines must be considered. The remaining chapters will draw upon psychology and other human sciences, philosophy, theology, and religious studies. The cumulative nature of the argument will not, however, become very apparent until the final chapter; and that will inevitably be programmatic, since I can only hint at the vast and varied resources available to reinforce the argument from religious experience.

5

CHALLENGES TO RELIGIOUS EXPERIENCE

Arguments from religious experience must generally rely heavily on people's descriptions of their past experiences. Only rarely can the proponents of such arguments appeal to their own personal experiences, and they are seldom able to examine other subjects undergoing a religious experience. Religious experiences are not the sort of thing which can easily be produced for observation in a controlled setting; they are normally 'private' experiences to which the subject has privileged access, so that auto-descriptions are essential data; and reports of religious experiences are usually obtained some time after the experience occurred. Suspicion of the accuracy or sincerity of subjects' reports of their religious experiences will therefore have serious consequences for any argument from religious experience, for they are our 'data', our primary means of access to the experiences themselves. The task of this section is to show that description-related challenges are not generally successful, and that the theist has enough information about the way things seem to be to subjects of religious experiences to begin constructing an argument from religious experience.

We should remind ourselves first of all of the principle of testimony: it is a fundamental principle of rationality that, in the absence of good grounds for believing otherwise, subjects' descriptions of their experiences should be taken as probably revealing the way things appeared to them to be at the time. In both the religious and the secular spheres, we should consider a person's auto-description more probably than not to be a sincere and acccurate description of the experience, as it seemed to them at the time, unless there are grounds for suspicion.

The most common indicator that something is amiss is some kind of inconsistency, whether within the description itself or between the description and something else we consider true. These 'inconsistency' challenges may be defeated by showing that there is no real inconsistency or that the propositions with which the description is alleged to be inconsistent should themselves be rejected. Where they succeed, they often become the grounds for a further type of challenge, such as the challenge that the subject was lying. (They are not, however, the only grounds for such challenges.) The first three description-related challenges below are of this 'inconsistency' type.

(i) Obvious logical inconsistencies or incoherence within an auto-description are a clear indication that the description does not accurately reflect the way things seemed to the subject to be. It can seem to a person that something physically impossible is the case, and some logically impossible things can seem to be the case (e.g. a person may get a mathematical proof wrong), but how could a person seem to perceive the inconceivable? When faced with the claim to have seen a square circle, for instance, we should not accept that as a sincere and accurate auto-description, but probe further, if possible, to discover whether the subject was joking or mistaken, or whether he can defeat the challenge by explaining away the inconsistency. Perhaps the subject was speaking meta-phorically, or perhaps the inconsistency disappears when one understands the framework within which the auto-description is set.

Internal inconsistencies (whether logical or not) are often far from obvious, however. For instance, the sceptic may have to be very alert to realize that the subject claimed at one time to have been on the train at noon and at another to have received the registered letter at noon, and that this entails being in two places at once. (The eliciting of such inconsistencies is an accepted method of discrediting the testimony of witnesses in court cases—though studies have shown that such inconsistencies are often due to the innocent confusion of normally reliable witnesses under the stress of cross-examination.[1]) The incoherence of a concept of which the subject claims to have perceived an instantiation may also be subtly hidden.

Charges of internal inconsistency in the religious case are rare, but important. It has been argued, for instance, that the traditional

---

[1] Arne Trankell, *Reliability of Evidence* (Stockholm: Beckmans, 1972).

Judaeo-Christian concept of God is incoherent, since (it is alleged) omniscience is incompatible with immutability and free will, omnipotence is incompatible with lack of responsibility for sin, and it is logically impossible for persons to exist or to act in a disembodied state.[2] If successful, that last challenge would also vitiate claims to have encountered many lesser types of 'spirits' and persons enjoying an afterlife. I have not found these arguments convincing, however. Clearly there is not space to refute them here, but one very thorough defence can be found in Swinburne's book, *The Coherence of Theism*.[3]

It has also been claimed that the apparent self-contradictions within mystical auto-descriptions make them such nonsense that the subjects could not possibly have experienced what they say they experienced. However, as was pointed out in Chapter I ("The Ineffability of Religious Experiences") and will be shown in more detail in Chapter VII, once the purposes, background, and implications of apparently self-contradictory mystical utterances are understood, it can be seen that the God who is both personal and impersonal, transcendent and immanent, and subject and object, has a very different status from a square circle.

(ii) When an auto-description apparently conflicts with background knowledge, or is apparently rendered highly improbable by background knowledge, the fault could lie with the description, the experience, or with the beliefs taken to be background knowledge. Which type of challenge is initially seen as most plausible depends on many factors. For instance, if Mary, who has very keen eyesight, claims to have seen a dodo, we have good reasons for believing that it is more likely that she is lying or does not understand the term 'dodo' than that she misperceived something or that dodos are not extinct after all.

Most challenges that religious auto-descriptions are inconsistent with or rendered highly improbable by background knowledge are directed towards the veridicality of the experience rather than towards the sincerity and accuracy of the description. They will thus be discussed with the object-related challenges, below. There

---

[2] See, for instance, the arguments in Anthony Kenny, *The God of the Philosophers* (Oxford: Clarendon Press, 1979); Kai Nielsen, "In Defence of Atheism" in Schedler (ed.), pp. 251–78; and Nielsen's *Contemporary Critiques of Religion* (London: Macmillan, 1971), ch. 6.

[3] Oxford: Clarendon Press, 1977.

are some cases, however, to which a description-related challenge of this type might apply. Where a person claimed that he heard the voice of God telling him to do something evil and cruel which he very much wanted to do anyway, or where he claimed that it had been revealed to him that all people ought to worship him and send him money, we would suspect that the person was lying in order to lend the 'authority of divine revelation' to his self-seeking purposes. This challenge is only available in a very small number of cases, however.

(iii) Another type of inconsistency one may notice is that between the subjects' actual behaviour and the behaviour one would expect if they had had the claimed experience—"by their fruits ye shall know them" (Matt. 7: 20). If a man claims to see a cobra in the corner of the bedroom, then we would expect him to avoid that spot, show signs of fear, arrange to have the cobra removed, and so on, whether or not his experience was veridical. (It must be remembered that with description-related challenges, we are trying to uncover the way things *seemed* to the subject to be, rather than the way things actually were—that comes later.) If the man claiming to see a cobra calmly and nonchalantly walked to the corner of the room, we would conclude either that it does not really seem to him that there is a cobra there or that he has some as yet unknown reason for appearing unconcerned—perhaps he knows the cobra has been de-fanged or he is carrying out some foolhardy bet. In any case, his behaviour deprives his testimony of its initial probability.

Reports of religious experiences, too, arouse certain expectations. If one claims to have had an intense experience of the presence of God and then carries on as if nothing had happened, or if one claims to have had an overwhelming conviction of the truth of the gospel of Jesus Christ and then fails to become a Christian, one's testimony would rightly be suspected. But the vast majority of auto-descriptions of religious experience do not succumb to the challenge in this form; most people who claim to have had religious experiences do exhibit 'religious' behaviour and attitudes consistent with their reports. Even where they are not affiliated with an institutional religion—and there are many instances of profound religious experiences driving people away from their previous 'shallow' institutional religion—they react in the direction of greater 'genuine religiosity', showing a greater interest in spiritual questions, and so on.[4] There are also many cases, many of them well known, in which people have been inspired by their religious experiences to live lives of great sanctity, courage, hardship, and religious zeal. Such people might be suspected of some things, but insincerity in their religious auto-descriptions would not be one.

It might be objected that psychological studies have shown that religious people are less tolerant, loving, courageous, and helpful than non-religious people, and that this shows that people must generally be mistaken, exaggerating, or lying when they claim to have had a religious experience which one would expect to make the subject into a better person. In order for this to work as a description-related challenge, however, it would have to be shown that the sub-class of religious people who claimed to have had regenerative religious experiences is as intolerant (etc.) as the class of 'religious people' in general, and that when people claim that their experiences have made them better in certain ways, they are often proved wrong. Neither of these has been shown to be the case, and there is reason to believe that they are not the case. In the studies correlating religiosity with such characteristics as racial prejudice, for instance, it was found that the correlation was not the same for all types and degrees of religiosity, but that the more 'genuinely devout' were less prejudiced than those who attended church for social and other non-religious reasons. It is reasonable to suppose that subjects of religious experiences would be more likely to fall into the former category than into the latter. Other studies have shown that religious beliefs and experiences often do have the claimed 'fruits': they help people cope with fear of death, promote social integration, help people recover from such things as alcoholism and depression, and, again in the case of the 'genuinely devout' only, contribute to individual wellbeing, peace of mind, and personal adjustment. (Chapter VIII will discuss these issues from the psychology of religion in more detail.) As a challenge to the general sincerity or accuracy of auto-descriptions of religious experiences, then, this does not succeed, though it may be able to defeat some individual claims.[5]

---

[4] The term 'religiosity' is used throughout in its standard psychological sense, to mean simply 'religiousness' or 'the quality of being religious'; it does not connote fanatical or sentimental religion.

[5] One could also consider the argument that some forms of intolerance, e.g. of false beliefs and of sin, should be considered praiseworthy.

(iv) Evidence that the subject is a habitual liar or prone to exaggerate can constitute a challenge to an auto-description. Such a challenge may be overcome by independent evidence that what the liar says occurred really did occur or by evidence that the subject really believes the report to be a true description of the way things appeared to be. Fortunately, there is absolutely no evidence that most (or even a great number of) subjects of religious experience are habitual liars or are prone to exaggerate their auto-descriptions. One occasionally comes across the challenge that reports of religious experience are a giant hoax, but the initial implausibility of such a claim, together with the independence and number of subjects of religious experience and the 'fruits argument' advanced in point (iii), make such a challenge a laughing-stock.

(v) Another type of description-related challenge is the claim that the subjects have a very unreliable memory, especially regarding their own experiences. They may sincerely believe they are correctly reporting their experiences, but if a great many of their previous auto-descriptions have been shown to be inaccurate, this severely weakens the probability that the present auto-description is accurate. Once again, however, there is no evidence that subjects of religious experiences generally suffer from such a defect.

One might be able to show that people generally have inaccurate recall of their own experiences under certain circumstances, however; and then claim that religious experiences occur under those circumstances. But the studies on this issue are difficult to apply to religious experience, since a great many factors are at work, and none of the studies deals with religious experience directly. We know on the one hand that experiences which are very brief, not repeated, unfamiliar, and not easily codifiable (the subject has no readily accessible verbal label for it), tend to be difficult to remember and to report; and religious experiences are often of that sort. We also know that when such experiences are codified, the subject's memory of the experience tends to conform more and more closely over time to his 'mental model' of the situation, subtly changing the original features of the experience. Studies in cognitive psychology have shown that anomalous elements are often "normalized" or absent and that features which the subject would expect on the basis of his interpretation of the situation can be added. On the other hand, experiences which do not fit our mental models may be remembered better precisely because they are so anomalous;[6] experiences which are not highly complex can often be remembered well without being codified;[7] and experiences which are highly significant, vivid, and frequently 'relived' in the memory are remembered more accurately and for longer than insignificant experiences.[8] It is clear from subjects' reports that most of the religious experiences which are brief, rare, and not easily codifiable are also highly significant, vivid, unusual, and frequently recalled.

The evidence is thus too ambiguous to allow this description-related challenge to discredit religious auto-descriptions in general, but it should make us wary of auto-descriptions which consist of a traditional 'formula' (e.g. "Then I fell on my knees and accepted the Lord Jesus Christ as my personal Saviour"; "This Saguna meditation automatically turned into a Nirguna type. I felt perfect Santi for 10 minutes"[9]), and of auto-descriptions which conform closely to a paradigm when hints are given that this conformity is only due to some influence such as the intolerance of orthodox authorities (as is suspected in the case of Meister Eckhart, for instance). In such cases, more work must be done before we can arrive at 'the way things really seemed to the subject'. Since this further investigation often *can* be done, the success of this description-related challenge in certain cases by no means entails that the experiential claim must be rejected.

(vi) Where there is reason to believe that the claimants misunderstand some of the terms in their auto-descriptions or do not understand them in the way required for recognition of the alleged percept, their auto-descriptions cannot be taken to be an accurate description of the way things appeared to them. We may suspect that the terms are above the subjects' level of comprehension, for instance: a doctor faced with a patient untrained in medical terminology will be much more confident that the patient's account of his or her symptoms is accurate if the patient uses 'lay' terms rather than trying to impress by using jargon picked up from television. Alternatively, the terms may not be beyond the subjects' expected level of comprehension, but it may be clear from their

[6] See A. J. Sanford, *Cognition and Cognitive Psychology* (London: Weidenfeld and Nicolson, 1985), ch. 8.

[7] See Jerome Bruner, "Culture and cognitive growth", ch. 21 of his collection, *Beyond the Information Given* (New York: Norton, 1973), pp. 368–93.

[8] For further information on memory, see Chapter VI.4.

[9] Swami Sivananda, *Concentration and Meditation*, ch. IX, p. 363.

behaviour and other evidence that they are applying the terms incorrectly. I once read an account of a small boy who had been hospitalized for several days, complaining of a 'headache': many tests had been run, but to no avail, until one bright nurse asked the boy to point to his 'headache'—and he pointed to his stomach. In another type of case, we may know that the subjects have some understanding of a concept, but suspect that they do not have the sort of understanding which would enable them to recognize an instantiation of it—they may know only where a certain metal is in the periodic table, for instance, and so we would mistrust their claim to have recognized a lump of it in front of them.[10]

The challenge of misunderstanding is difficult to apply to the religious case, since terms such as 'God', 'ultimate reality', and 'holy power' can sustain such a rich variety of interpretations. There are recognized limits, however, and a person who used these terms in a highly inappropriate way, say, to refer to a pen, could be challenged on that point. Quasi-sensory religious experiences may be open to this type of challenge, too: the subject may claim to have had a vision of a certain religious symbol but prove unable to recognize that symbol in subsequent tests. And there may be cases in which the subject uses highly technical and probably misunderstood terminology to describe a religious experience—for instance, we would mistrust the auto-description of a person who claimed to have experienced "samadhi" but had learned nothing of Eastern religions. Such challenges, however, are only successful in a very limited number of cases.

It may be claimed that no understanding of the concept of 'God' could be sufficient for the recognition of a being qualitatively so different from all our other percepts—how could a human being recognize 'infinite wisdom', 'the creator and sustainer of the universe', or a 'non-physical person'? It is indeed difficult to see how one could recognize that a holy presence's wisdom was infinite, love unlimited, and so on (unless one was told that they were so in a revelatory experience). One suspects that words such as 'infinite' are frequently used either as descriptions of something recognized to be God and believed therefore to be infinite or as hyperbolical descriptions of characteristics seen as vastly superior to anything encountered elsewhere, overwhelming, and with no perceptible limits. As far as descriptions such as 'creator and

[10] I owe this example to Swinburne.

sustainer' are concerned, most have not been shown to be incoherent (though the debate continues); and that, together with the massed weight of claims to have encountered a non-physical person and a being on whom one feels utterly dependent, should be sufficient to outweigh any *a priori* improbability which the qualitative difference might have lent such descriptions. Theologians and philosophers may attempt to formulate precise definitions of God and discuss the respects in which his power is infinite or the manner in which he might create and sustain, and religious experiences might contribute to such theories within a cumulative argument (Chapter IX will suggest such a role for religious experiences), but these experiences ought not to be expected to reveal such niceties on their own. If one seriously maintained the hypothesis that there were many beings in the universe which were very, very similar to God and were easily mistaken for him, then the ability to recognize something like a creator 'ex nihilo' and 'infinite wisdom' would be important. As it is, however, descriptions as vague as "an overwhelming holy presence"—qualitatively different from everyday percepts, but surely recognizable—are usually accepted as sufficient indicators that the alleged percept was 'God'.

People often describe their religious experiences using terms and whole sentences which they admit they do not fully understand. Indeed, few religious people would claim to *fully* understand terms such as 'God'. But full understanding is not required even in the secular field. The discussion of metaphorical language in Chapter I.2 should have made it clear that successful reference is possible even when speakers have only the barest inkling of the nature of their intended referent (indeed, they could even be largely mistaken, as the Columbus example showed), as long as the terms used are grounded in experience, linguistic continuity within a community, and a communal network of concepts. What is necessary is that the nature and degree of the understanding be sufficient for correct application of the terms to the subject's experience. There is no evidence that subjects of religious experiences do not generally have this type of understanding of their auto-descriptions. (A challenge closely related to this one is discussed in section 2 (ii), below.)

(vii) When an auto-description is to be used as evidence, those assessing the claim must ensure that they have understood any ambiguous terms in the auto-description in the way the subject intends. Misunderstandings of this type can cause many problems in real life; a clear-cut example would be the case of the American tourist who says she saw the accident take place on the "pavement", meaning the area the cars use, while the British policeman takes her to mean the area the pedestrians use (American 'sidewalk'). In the religious case, a term such as 'God' can mean very different things to a Christian fundamentalist and a Hindu non-dualist, while a 'non-aligned' religious person may use the term to refer to the overwhelming holy power he claims to have apprehended, and say that he is still trying to discover who or what this power he calls "God" is. How far such different intentions behind the use of one term can be reconciled is a question for Chapter VII.

When applied to an argument from religious experience, this is not so much a challenge to the accuracy and sincerity of auto-descriptions as a claim that when subjects of religious experiences use the same terms in their auto-descriptions, what they mean by those terms may be more diverse than the proponents of most arguments from religious experience would have us believe. The latter can point out, however, that diversity does not necessarily mean conflict, and that the challenge that a person's testimony may not have been understood before being used as the basis for an argument can work both ways; it can be shown that sceptical claims are often based on a misunderstanding of religious auto-descriptions. Chapter VII will examine both sides of this argument in more detail.

(viii) When a retrospective interpretation has been incorporated into the subject's auto-description, that description no longer reflects the way things seemed to the subject to be at the time. Where there is good evidence that this has occurred, the subject's perceptual claim cannot always be taken immediately to be more probable than not, since it was based both on the way things appeared to the subject and on certain inferences. Such cases are difficult to pick out, but there can sometimes be good reason to believe that an interpretation as highly ramified as the one in the auto-description could not be incorporated into a perceptual experience, but must have been inferred from the experience or from background knowledge and reflection. When, for instance, Professor Higgins stated which area of London and, more incredibly, which street certain people came from, no one believed he could tell that from listening to the voices alone; they thought he must be basing his claims on information he had secretly obtained about them. Eventually he was able to defeat the challenge by showing that as a result of his skill and training in phonetics, such judgements were incorporated into his auditory perceptual experiences and were not consciously inferred, retrospective interpretations or independent beliefs.

Many elements of religious auto-descriptions have been claimed by sceptics to be retrospective interpretations contributed by the subject's beliefs rather than elements of perceptual experiences. The Christian Trinity, a God of infinite wisdom, power, and love, identity with Brahman, the immortality of the soul, and release from the cycle of rebirth are just a few of these alleged 'inferred percepts'.

Now, there are serious problems with claims to identity with Brahman, which will be discussed below; but they are not such as would preclude its *seeming* to subjects that they had become Brahman. Claims to have experienced immortality or release from the cycle of rebirth may be doubted because they are claims to have experienced, here and now, a state of affairs which is negative and in the future or of infinite duration (I will never die; I will never be reborn). However, they could well be 'revealed' in a revelatory experience; they do seem in practice often to be reflexive interpretations of feelings of 'timelessness', 'eternity', 'freedom', and so on (and reflexive interpretations are covered by the principle of credulity); and there seems to be no reason to doubt that expressions such as "death was an almost laughable impossibility"[11] reflect a real sense of having attained a state untouched by the frustrations and limitations of ordinary human existence.

In some cases, an alleged inference may simply be a term which has crept into the auto-description without being intended literally: perhaps the subject used "infinite" to emphasize the greatness of the holy power which overwhelmed him or because "infinite power" was such a familiar phrase.

Where the description of the subject's experience is second or third hand (as in many hagiographies), in a highly stylized form such as poetry, or part of a carefully argued treatise, it may be

---

[11] Tennyson, quoted in James, p. 370.

suspected of containing retrospective interpretation. As was pointed out in Chapter II.1, however, so much material is available that
the proponent of an argument from religious experience is able to
avoid such sources almost entirely. Where they must be used—for
instance, in Eastern religions where autobiographies are rare—
attention can be paid to the less ramified aspects of the experiences,
and they can be compared to whatever auto-descriptions *are*
available from those traditions.

A detailed study of the challenge that many alleged religious
percepts are too highly ramified to be likely to be incorporated into
perceptual experiences would show that most of the challenges are
not strong enough to defeat religious experiential reports. Regarding the Trinity, for instance, there are many Christians who claim
to have experienced different types of divine power which
correspond to the persons of the Trinity, and arguments that it is an
abstract theological doctrine only, never grounded in experience,
are unconvincing.[12]

Where it can be shown that an experiential report probably
contains retrospective interpretation, the report can often be
revised, perhaps to a moderated auto-description plus certain
background beliefs and inferences. It should, however, be noted
that one is not required to justify one's inferences unless there is
evidence that they do not follow from one's experiences and beliefs;
inferences, too, are innocent until proven guilty. Moreover, as was
pointed out in Chapter I.4, experiences as well as beliefs and
inferences may contribute to a retrospective interpretation; and
when such an interpretation is made in the light of other *religious*
experiences, it can still form part of an argument from religious
experience.

It should be pointed out here that challenge (viii) is not the same
as the general philosophical claim that we do not 'really hear' the
doorbell ringing, and so on, but merely infer that the sound we
heard was produced by the doorbell. Any inference involved in
such cases is entirely unconscious and as such is not *based on* the
experience but *part of* the experience; it simply 'seems to the subject'
that the doorbell is ringing. Unconscious inference will be
discussed further in Chapter VI.

[12] See David Brown, p. 207.

Even when description-related challenges do work—and they are by no means generally successful against religious auto-descriptions—it must be remembered that it is normally only the auto-description which has been discredited, and not the original experience (if any). Where one can investigate and revise the discredited description, an experience may emerge which is still useful to the proponent of an argument from religious experience.

2. SUBJECT-RELATED CHALLENGES

Subject-related challenges charge that some factor or set of factors associated with an individual subject or class of subjects makes it likely that the described experience was unveridical. Where such challenges are successful, it is still *possible* that the experience in question was veridical, and sometimes this veridicality can be shown by means of a cumulative argument (see Chapter IV). If a cumulative argument is not available to counteract a successful subject-related challenge, the possibility of veridicality remains, but it is not sufficient to maintain the *prima facie* evidential force of the experience. A religious experience which succumbs to a subject-related challenge may well be veridical, then, but it cannot be used as evidence in an argument from religious experience. Subject-related challenges may initially seem less damaging than the object-related challenges of the next section, which can often destroy any hope of veridicality, but they can do just as much damage to an argument from religious experience.

(i) A challenge which must be mentioned but which would be used very rarely in practice is the charge that this subject's perceptual claims are usually unreliable. (Specific charges of unreliability in certain areas, such as colour perception, come into category (iv).) Since the vast majority of subjects of religious experiences are as reliable as the rest of humanity in their general perceptual claims, this challenge is not successful against arguments from religious experience.

(ii) Evidence that the subject has not had the sort of training usually considered necessary to a veridical perceptual experience of the alleged type can drastically reduce the probability of the subject's claim. 'Training' is to be understood very broadly to mean any experience or experiences found in the past to be necessary before a person can have a veridical perceptual experience of a certain type. For instance, a person who has learned musical theory but has never heard music would be very unlikely to be able to perceive that a singer is out of tune; if I have never heard Smith speaking before, it is highly unlikely that I will be able to recognize his voice on the telephone; and—to adapt one of Swinburne's examples—if a person claims that he saw a Victorian table in the next room and knew it was a Victorian table just by looking at it, we can challenge his claim if we know that he has had no training in art history, antiques, or anything similar. As was noted above, it is still possible that the claimant's experience was veridical, but unless he can provide other evidence that it was (e.g. by demonstrating that he can recognize other Victorian tables by sight), the experience cannot be used as evidence for his perceptual claim.

It is difficult to apply this challenge to religious experience. We have little idea of the sort of training which might enable one to have veridical experiences of God or other spiritual forces, and the kind of training which might seem appropriate—theological training, engaging in religious rituals, the cultivation of virtues, and guidance in meditation by a spiritual master or guru—does not by any means guarantee that one will have experiences of God, if he exists. Theists agree that genuine religious experiences may occur spontaneously to theologically naïve and even irreligious subjects. Indeed, there are cases of subjects who had religious experiences as children and who only later, through their reading of mystical and other religious texts, discovered what it was they had apparently experienced. Edward Robinson cites examples of subjects who had a childhood relationship with something they called "It" but which they did not relate to their Sunday school image of God; only later, when they had acquired a more mature concept of God, did they connect the concept and the experiences.[13] On the other side of the problem, there are people who are highly trained in theology and are fine examples of virtue and brotherly love who have never experienced apparent contact with the divine. Moreover, it is a common religious belief that subjects of religious experiences can acquire knowledge 'directly', without having to go through the normal channels of experience, authority, or conscious inference.

---

[13] Edward Robinson, *The Original Vision* (Oxford: RERU, 1977). See also the discussion of childhood experiences in Chapter VI.4, below.

In such a situation, who can say that a particular subject has not had the right type of prior experience to be able to make religious claims?

There is, however, a version of this challenge which might defeat many claims to have acquired religious knowledge. Some types of experience are known to be generally unreliable routes to knowledge. Dreams and hallucinations come into this category, as do 'hunches' and 'intuitions'. When a knowledge claim is based on a type of experience against which challenges are so notoriously successful, it must be considered guilty until proven innocent. Indeed, this is the way many revelatory experiences are treated by religious authorities, as Chapter II.4 showed; and religious dreams are given the status of 'visions' only if there is reason to believe they were brought about by an external agency, unlike ordinary dreams. But if religious visions themselves are often considered by their subjects to be hallucinations—though divinely produced—how can they be considered reliable sources of knowledge?

A partial response to this challenge is possible at this point. There is evidence in the secular realm that dreams, visions, and 'flashes of insight' should not be dismissed out of hand, as many have proved to lead to knowledge. One famous example is that of Kekulé and the benzene ring.[14] One day, after Kekulé had been dwelling on the problem of the structure of the carbon atoms in benzene, he sank into a doze in front of his fire, and began to dream of atoms whirling around like snakes. Suddenly one of the snakes caught its tail in its mouth; Kekulé awoke, and began working out the revolutionary theory that the six carbon atoms in benzene are linked together in a circular chain. Another example comes from a 1963 study into hypnotism, in which subjects who had just awakened from hypnotic trances almost invariably gave correct answers to algebraic questions which could only have been worked out unconsciously—subjects said the answer simply entered their

---

[14] See the translation of Kekulé's description of his experience by O. Theodor Benfey, "August Kekule and the Birth of the Structural Theory of Organic Chemistry in 1858", *Journal of Chemical Education*, 35 (1958), 21–3. Arthur Koestler, in *The Act of Creation* (London: Hutchinson, 1964), describes this and other discoveries which seemed to depend more on creative insight than on discursive reasoning and sense perception; see also the excellent discussion in Margaret Yee, "The Validity of Theology as an Academic Discipline", D.Phil. thesis (Oxford University, 1987), sections 3.3 and 4.1.2, which shows that such creative processes are nevertheless rational and analysable.

mind as a "sudden flash of certain knowledge".[15] Such experiences are evidence that people are able, by some means not yet understood, to solve problems effectively by methods other than conscious reasoning and sense perception, and they thus raise the probability of the truth of insights acquired through religious revelatory experiences and visions.

This is not enough, however, to show that religious revelatory experiences and visions ought generally to be considered innocent until proven guilty. Just as Kekulé had to subject his "benzene ring" theory to scientific tests before he could be confident of its truth, subjects of visions and revelatory experiences must apply tests to check whether they have correctly interpreted their 'pictures' and 'messages', whether the alleged insights apply only to the subject's particular situation or are intended as universal truths, and so on. If, moreover, the "warrant" for the truth of the insights is their alleged divine source, one must show that there is no good reason to believe these experiences are products of the subject's own unconscious rather than of divine activity, and that the divine agent is trustworthy. This can best be done within a cumulative argument; and so a more complete response to this challenge will be found in the final chapter.

Sceptics sometimes make the further challenge that a person can only recognize God if he has had previous veridical experiences of God and been told that the percept was God—i.e. if he has inductive evidence that that 'interpretation' (God) is warranted for that 'experience'. That this 'vicious circle challenge' fails entirely, not just in the religious case, but in any case, will be explained in Chapter VI.

(iii) Where a great many people claim to have perceived some object or event, but give conflicting accounts of it, doubt is cast on all the accounts, even though there may be no reason to suspect any particular account when they are taken individually. This 'conflicting claims challenge' could have gone under many headings, since many factors could be at work—some claimants could be lying; some might have a poor memory; others might have misperceived the situation; still others might be imposing different interpretations on the events; and many could simply be describing different

---

[15] Reported by Stanley Krippner in "The Psychedelic State, the Hypnotic Trance, and the Creative Act", ch. 18 of Charles Tart (ed.), *Altered States of Consciousness* (New York: John Wiley & Sons, 1969).

aspects of the percept (in which case the challenge is defeated). I have chosen to put it with the subject-related challenges since it can be seen as a general claim that many, if not all of the subjects are 'unreliable'. Such a challenge could arise where there are many witnesses to an accident, many interpretations of a personal interaction (such as an argument), many descriptions of a city, and so forth.

The 'conflicting claims' challenge to religious experience runs as follows: so many religious claims are in conflict that a great many of them, if not all of them, must be false, and the experiences which they purport to describe must be either misinterpreted or straight-forwardly illusory. With such widespread epistemic failure, re-ligious experience generally would have to be considered an unreliable source of knowledge.

This challenge is an important one, and it requires much more than a sub-section of a chapter for its discussion. I will therefore devote all of Chapter VII to it, and say no more here.

(iv) The fourth type of subject-related challenge is by far the most complex, but also the most common: it is the challenge that factors relating to the subject at the time of the alleged experience were such that the experience was probably unveridical in some way. It is known, for instance, that nearly all perceptual experi-ences occurring while the subject is asleep or hypnotized are unveridical, that many perceptual experiences occurring while a subject is intoxicated or under the influence of a hallucinogenic drug are unveridical, and that certain physiological conditions (e.g. jaundice, fatigue, damage to perceptual organs), psychological states (e.g. hypersuggestibility, strong desires), and expectations (whether from beliefs or conditioning) can affect a person's ability to perceive accurately.

It is these types of factors which are most often cited in 'reductionist' challenges to religious experience, since their pres-ence is taken to be evidence that the subject probably would have had an experience of the alleged percept, whether or not that percept was actually there or caused the experience. Since these challenges will be dealt with in detail in Chapter VIII, only the barest outline will be presented here.

Though there is occasionally confusion as to whether a vision occurred while the subject was asleep or awake, the claim that the experience occurred while the subject was asleep or hypnotized is hardly generally true of religious experiences. The majority of religious experiences also do not occur under conditions of intoxication. It should be noted here that I am not saying that drug-induced religious experiences are not genuine religious experiences or are all illusory. It may well be that the hallucinogenic drugs many individuals have taken prior to profound religious experiences have made them receptive to a divine power to which they were partially or totally blind in their sober moments of mundane consciousness. But since intoxicants and hallucinogens are known generally to have an adverse effect on perception, this subject-related challenge does rob drug-induced experiences of their *prima facie* evidential force. Like other successfully challenged experiences, however, they may play a role in a cumulative case, and that is where arguments that drugs might actually enhance powers of spiritual perception could prove useful.

The strength of the challenge that the experience was induced by drugs or occurred during some other physiological state which might distort perception (e.g. fasting) will be discussed in more detail in Chapter VIII. All that needs to be noted at this point is that this challenge does not in fact apply to most religious experiences.

The final word on subject-related challenges will have to await the outcome of Chapters VII, "The Conflicting Claims Challenge", and VIII, "The Reductionist Challenge".

3. OBJECT-RELATED CHALLENGES

The challenges in this section support the charge that the perceptual experience was very probably unveridical by citing evidence related to the alleged percept. It may be highly improbable that the alleged percept was present (or that the percept corresponded exactly to the subject's description of it), highly improbable that the alleged percept was a cause of the subject's experience of seeming to perceive it, or highly improbable that anyone could have perceived such a percept in the manner claimed. (It should be remembered throughout that "the percept was present" is shorthand for "the percept was 'present' if it was an object, 'occurred' if it was an event, and 'obtained' if it was a state of affairs".) Unlike subject-related challenges, object-related challenges can sometimes show that it is logically or physically impossible for the alleged percept to have been present or to have caused the experience, and thus destroy any hope of showing the experience to be veridical, even by a cumulative argument. Most object-related challenges are not so strong, however, as we shall see.

(i) The challenge that, on background evidence, it is highly unlikely that the alleged percept was present as described, can take several forms: (a) deductive arguments that it is logically impossible for such a percept to exist, (b) inductive arguments that such a percept is improbable or that it is improbable that the alleged percept was exactly as claimed, though a somewhat revised claim might well be true, and (c) evidence that the percept probably was not present at the place and time of the claimed experience.

(a) The first type of challenge applies to such impossible percepts as square circles; its application to the religious case was discussed in the section on description-related challenges, above.

(b) The second type of challenge concerns entities whose existence is very improbable, such as green Martians and abominable snowmen, and occurrences which are regarded as physically very improbable or impossible in the light of our present scientific knowledge, such as telekinesis and levitation. Swinburne's remarks on challenges (b) and (c) are so sound and clearly expressed that I quote them at length:

Now I suggest that in this case it is not enough that the background evidence makes it more probable than not that x was not present. It has to make it very improbable that x was present if it is to outweigh the force of S's experience sufficiently for it to remain more probable than not that [x] was not present. For, after all, most of the things which we think that we see are on background evidence less probable than not. It may seem to me, when I go to London, that I see Jones walking along the other side of Charing Cross Road. I may believe *a priori* that it is more probable than not that he is in Dover where he lives; and that even if he is in London, the odds are against his being in Charing Cross Road at that particular moment. But my experience suffices to outweigh this background evidence. We would indeed be imprisoned within the circle of our existing beliefs, if experience did not normally have this force. However background evidence may make it very, very improbable that x is present—e.g. because it makes it very improbable that x exists at all, or very probable that he is somewhere else. If it is very probable on background evidence that John is dead, then it is very, very improbable that he is walking along the other side of Charing Cross Road at this moment; and my experience does not by itself suffice to push the latter into the category of the probable.[16]

It should be added that the degree of improbability on background evidence required to defeat the combined perceptual claims of many witnesses is far greater than the degree of improbability required to defeat an individual perceptual claim. Since arguments from religious experience are based not on a single experience but on the testimony of a great many subjects, it is important to bear such qualifications in mind.

To religious experience, then: it has certainly been claimed that the alleged percepts of many religious experiences are highly improbable. Some religious experiences are rejected by theists themselves—for instance, it is considered highly improbable that a good, wise God would command an individual to murder people, and so the "Yorkshire Ripper's" experiences allegedly of the voice of God are rejected as unveridical. Claims to have suddenly become omniscient, to be another Messiah, or to be God himself, are usually dealt with in the same way. In these cases, what makes the claim so improbable is the evidence that the claimant simply does not have the alleged properties. But relatively few religious experiences are rejected for this type of reason, and those which are thus rejected often involve psychotic individuals whose religious experiences would have been disallowed as evidence in any case.[17] One must be careful, however, to distinguish obviously improbable claims which are meant literally from similar claims which call for a deeper interpretation, such as those mystical claims to identity with God which are discussed below and in Chapter VII.

Where the charge of improbability has a potentially much wider application, the evidence for improbability is usually much more controversial. The 'problem of evil', for instance, has been cited by sceptics as proof that the existence of God is highly improbable or even impossible: God, being perfectly good and omnipotent, would prevent evil if he existed; but there is evil in the world; therefore there is no God.[18] But theists have proffered many solutions to this problem, and while some of them are unsatisfac-

---

[16] Swinburne, pp. 261–2.

[17] See, for instance, the cases of the "three Christs", Chapter VIII.2.3.

[18] See the arguments in J. L. Mackie, *The Miracle of Theism* (Oxford: Clarendon Press, 1982), ch. 9.

tory, most are very plausible and thought-provoking. I cannot even begin to deal adequately with the problem of evil in the space available here, but the interested reader might wish to refer to the books listed in the footnote below.[19] Suffice it to say that the evil in this world does count against God's existence, but the debate over whether the evil is excessive and wanton or justifiable remains sufficiently open to prevent the problem of evil from showing God's existence to be highly improbable. And, as was pointed out above, it is a *high* degree of improbability which the sceptic requires if he is to outweigh the evidence of the many claims to have experienced God.

Members of one religious tradition may claim that the alleged percepts of another tradition are improbable—alleged Roman Catholic encounters with the Virgin Mary and other saints are often scoffed at, for instance. But scoffing is not enough: the onus is on the sceptic to show that the alleged percept is very improbable. Where his evidence is inconclusive, or where he can only show a mild degree of improbability, his evidence may be outweighed by the degree of probability conferred on the percept by the many vivid and otherwise unimpeachable experiences apparently of the percept. There is not space here to show that most of these 'improbability' challenges are too weak or controversial to defeat religious experiences, but the fact that most alleged religious percepts are considered even by committed atheists to be worthy of serious discussion should be some indication that they are not 'highly improbable' on the background evidence generally available.

Claims to literal identity with the deity, such as those found frequently within Sufi and monist Hindu traditions, appear largely to succumb to the charge of high improbability. As Chapter VII will show, however, such claims are very often understood within these traditions themselves in a less literal way, as a 'partaking of the divine nature', or as an overly enthusiastic way of expressing the mystical sense of losing oneself in God. Adherents of those traditions also recognize severe problems with the doctrine that there is one God with whom all persons and things are fully

[19] See, for instance, Swinburne, ch. 11; Austin Farrer, *Love Almighty and Ills Unlimited* (Garden City, NY: Doubleday, 1961); John Hick, *Evil and the God of Love*, 2nd edn. (London: Macmillan, 1977); Nelson Pike (ed.), *God and Evil* (Englewood Cliffs, NJ: Prentice-Hall, 1964); and Alvin Plantinga, *The Nature of Necessity*, ch. IX.

identical. Moreover, the claimants generally do not exhibit divine attributes such as infinite or even outstanding wisdom, virtue, and powers (though they do say they are not supposed to exercise or display the latter). Chapter VII will describe some ways of interpreting claims to literal identity with God or Brahman so that they remain 'mystical' but are no longer so improbable.[20]

Some challenges that the alleged percept probably was not present do not damage the probability that some *other* percept was present, and the subject's auto-description can then be revised (usually moderated) to yield a perceptual claim which is probable on the principle of credulity. Suppose Jones claims to see a rabbit at the edge of the field: if there is good evidence that all the rabbits in this region have been exterminated, but also that there are many other animals around that could look like rabbits from a distance, then Jones's experience, though a misperception, still makes it probable that there was a rabbit-like animal at the edge of the field. Many successful charges of improbability in the religious sphere allow such revised claims. Experiences of alleged identity with the deity, for instance, can often be redescribed without sacrificing much evidential force, in a way which preserves important religious aspects of the experience (see Chapter VII): they are usually experiences of supreme elation, of being completely overwhelmed by a holy power, and of discovering a 'true', 'wider' self.

(c) The third version of this object-related challenge was the claim that the alleged percept probably was not present at the place and time it was alleged to have been perceived. In non-religious cases, this challenge is usually supported by evidence either that the alleged percept was somewhere else at the time or that other people who would have been expected to perceive the alleged percept if it were there did not have the experience of its seeming to them that the object was there.

The first of these is a very powerful challenge in non-religious cases, since physical objects cannot be in more than one place at a

---

[20] Some incarnational claims appear to resist the above challenges, but the onus is certainly on the claimant. Moreover, the less implausible incarnational claims are usually based on evidence other than the subject's own experiences of seeming to be God. See, for instance, the reference to Ramakrishna in Chapter VIII. 2.3, below; and E. P. Sanders, in *Jesus and Judaism* (London: SCM Press, 1985), pp. 240 and 273, maintains that though Jesus may occasionally have claimed to be speaking for God, he never himself claimed to *be* God.

time. However, there are no such restrictions on most objects of religious experiences. Religious 'percepts' such as profound insights, a comforting presence, an awe-inspiring holy power, ultimate reality, and God, are not supposed to be restricted by space and (perhaps) time, and it would be no evidence against a person's experience of one of these to point out that a person halfway across the globe was having an experience of the same alleged percept at the same time. The challenge would succeed in many cases of visions of saints and other 'lesser' spiritual beings if one took the view that these beings had to be present in some quasi-physical manner which prevented them from being present anywhere else simultaneously. Since I think it is far more likely that if such dis/unembodied beings do exist, they communicate via some form of mental telepathy in which the recipient contributes to the final quasi-physical appearance of the being,[21] I do not consider this a plausible challenge; there is no reason why a person could not mentally communicate with more than one person at a time. (It should be remembered that the disciples' experiences of the risen Christ do not conform to the general pattern of visions.)

The challenge that other people did not have corroborating experiences when they would have been expected to perceive the alleged percept if it were there is, like the previous challenge, powerful in many secular cases but fairly harmless to religious experience. In the secular realm, we can often specify the kind of sense-organs, training, mental set, and external conditions which will (almost) ensure that if a percept is there, the subject will perceive it. The absence of the perceptual experience with the presence of all the enabling conditions implies that the object probably was not present. Finicky Aunt Vera may claim to see crumbs on a well-lit, white tablecloth, but if other people with good eyesight, who know what crumbs look like, who are honest and not in a state which usually affects perception adversely, and who are told to scrutinize the tablecloth for crumbs, say they see no crumbs, then Aunt Vera's claim becomes improbable. Most real-life situations are not quite so clear-cut: we cannot always be sure that the other observers fulfilled all the necessary conditions (for instance, that they looked carefully enough), or, often, just what those necessary conditions are. The religious case is even less clear-cut; as was explained in Chapter III.3, the fact that people

[21] See Tyrrell, *Apparitions.*

apparently satisfying the same perceptual conditions do not have the same religious experiences does not count against the veridicality of a religious experience. Where the alleged percept may choose to whom to reveal himself, where we do not understand what makes one person 'receptive' to the presence of the divine and another not, and where many 'hidden' factors such as faith may be at work, we do not have good reason to suppose that all people in a certain situation should have an experience of the alleged religious percept, if it is there.

Although this challenge is inapplicable to religious experience, it does by its very inapplicability make an argument from religious experience slightly less strong than it could have been otherwise. As Swinburne points out, the fact that we do not know what other observers ought to be able to perceive if the alleged percept really is there means that "we cannot have the confirming evidence of failure to find evidence which counts against the claim. . . . If your claim could have been disconfirmed by certain phenomena, but the phenomena are shown not to occur, that very fact confirms the claim."[22] As was shown in Chapter IV.2, the probability of a perceptual experience's being veridical rises with the quantity and severity of defeated possible challenges. The nature of religious experience deprives it of the possibility of overcoming some challenges which are powerful tests in most secular situations.

(ii) An important type of object-related challenge to religious experience, since veridical experiences must have an "appropriate causal connection" with their percepts, is the claim that whether or not the alleged percept was present, it very probably was not an appropriate cause of the experience of its seeming to the subject that it was present. This challenge may take two forms: the claim that a causal explanation of the experience which does not involve the alleged percept is very probable, and the claim that, though the alleged percept may well have been a cause of the experience, it is very unlikely that it caused the experience in the manner required for veridical perception.

In the first type of case, there may be good evidence that the experience was caused by an imitation of the alleged percept—that the fruit the subject claimed to see was wax or that the violent argument he claimed to witness was the rehearsal of a scene from a play. Or there may be evidence that something very similar to and

<hr />

[22] Swinburne, p. 263.

easily mistaken for the alleged percept caused the experience—perhaps only Jim's twin brother John was in town the day it seemed to me that Jim was across the street. We may also be able to show that the subject was in such a state and in such a situation that he would very probably have had that perceptual experience, whether or not the alleged percept was present—he may have been hypnotized, for instance, and then told that the alleged percept was present (this is more a subject-related challenge, however; see section 2(iv) above).

In an example of the second type of case, it would be very improbable that the alleged percept caused the experience in the appropriate manner if a person claimed to have read the small print on a poster at a great distance; we may suspect that they were able to recognize the poster at that distance and already knew what it said, in the same way that small children often appear to be reading their favourite story aloud, but have actually memorized it.

The version of this challenge which appeals to an alternative causal explanation based on psychological factors such as hypnotism is a 'reductionist challenge' in the case of religious experience. It requires a great deal of discussion, and so will be reserved for Chapter VIII.

The challenge that it is highly improbable that the alleged percept caused the experience in an appropriate way must, to be different from challenge (i) above, allow that the alleged percept is perceptible in principle, though not under the conditions of the particular experience. Since, as was explained in section 2(ii) above, we do not know what conditions are necessary for the perception of religious percepts, this type of challenge does not pose a threat to arguments from religious experience.

The challenge that a religious experience was caused by something other than the alleged percept, when it is not a physiological-psychological reductionist challenge, may take two forms: the claim that the subject was deceived by a diabolical power, and the claim that the subject misperceived a public object or event. Though there is some evidence for the existence of evil non-physical centres of action, it is highly controversial; moreover, the types of religious experience which might earlier have been attributed to 'the devil' are now usually attributed to the kinds of natural factors mentioned in section 2(iv). Cases in which a religious experience arose because the subject misperceived a public object or event (for instance, if Mary believes she saw an angel at the foot of her bed one night, but discovers on subsequent nights that it was merely a repeatable pattern of shadows) are rare and so do not affect an argument from religious experience.

We must await the verdict of the final chapters before declaring victory over the challenge that religious experiences are probably caused by factors other than their alleged percepts. Claims that the presence of the alleged percept is highly improbable, while successful in a few cases, are generally too controversial to do much damage. They might carry more weight in a cumulative argument, however; and it is to that type of challenge that we must now turn.

4. THE CUMULATIVE CHALLENGE

Most of the arguments in the previous sections were designed to show that challenges to religious experience were clearly defeated in the vast majority of cases of religious experience, or that there was such controversy over the challenges that they could not be considered successful until much more overwhelming evidence had been produced. But while none of those challenges can destroy the evidential force of religious experience on its own, they can be combined into a cumulative argument of much greater strength. In such an argument, the challenges can interact with background knowledge and each other to overcome some of the weaknesses of individual challenges. Where background knowledge shows a religious claim to be very improbable, for instance, a challenge of only mild intrinsic strength may succeed; or if certain religious experiences have been shown to be of pathological origin, a sceptic may argue that similar experiences are defeated where there is only slight evidence of pathology. (It should be noted that the following outline of the cumulative challenge occasionally assumes conclusions which will be defended in later chapters.)

Some individual challenges are clearly incapable of overcoming the massed evidence of religious experiences on their own, since they so obviously fail in the majority of cases. These are the challenges that subjects of religious experiences behave in a way which is inconsistent with the truth of their auto-descriptions (though this is somewhat controversial); that they are liars, have an unreliable memory, or generally have unreliable perceptual experiences; that they were asleep, hypnotized, or under the influence of drugs or alcohol; and that they misperceived a public percept, taking it to be something of religious significance. It would be possible to construct a cumulative argument out of these challenges simply by claiming that most religious experiences succumb to at least one of them, and that this fact has been missed by examining each challenge separately. A brief survey of religious experiences would, however, show that the vast majority are not affected by *any* of the above challenges. This form of cumulative challenge does not therefore pose a threat to arguments from religious experience.

Challenges which do not apply (or which are difficult to apply) to religious experience because of special features of the religious case cannot be worked into a cumulative challenge, but they do deprive arguments from religious experience of a possible source of positive support, viz. the absence of counter-evidence which would have been expected to turn up if the experiences were unveridical. The challenges in this category are the claims that the subject lacks the conceptual understanding necessary to perceive the alleged percept, that the subject has not had the experiences usually found necessary to veridical perceptions of the claimed sort, that it is improbable that the subject could have had a veridical perception of the alleged percept under such conditions, and that other people of similar capacities who were similarly situated did not have an experience apparently of the alleged percept.

More likely to form part of a strong cumulative challenge are the challenges based on the interaction of controversial background beliefs and the 'conflicting claims' and 'reductionist' challenges. The sceptic may cite as 'background evidence' the sorts of considerations which might show that religious percepts are improbable: the problem of evil, the fact that many people who are apparently well equipped perceptually have no experiences of such things, and the fact that religious percepts are so different in kind from all our other percepts. To back up the more ambitious claim that it is highly improbable that religious experiences are veridical, he will add to this 'background evidence' the claim that subjects of religious experiences cannot agree on a single, coherent description of their alleged one supreme reality (the conflicting claims challenge) and the claim that religious experiences can be given highly probable causal explanations which leave out the alleged percept (the reductionist challenge). This last challenge could not succeed on its own; like the counter-claim that God "works through natural causes", it relies so heavily on 'hidden factors' that it can only succeed within a cumulative argument. One hidden factor in most reductionist explanations, for instance, is suggestibility; there is evidence that some subjects of religious experiences are highly suggestible, but these sceptics must assume that *most* subjects of religious experiences are, even those who are normal by all standard criteria. Explanations which rely on such hidden, postulated factors—factors for which the only available evidence is the plausibility of the explanation which posits them—must be made highly probable by other evidence if they are to escape the charge of being *ad hoc*. Sceptics argue that the religious reductionist challenge is made highly probable by the additional evidence.

This, then, is the cumulative challenge—though it requires a great deal of "fleshing out". There is not space here to discuss the background evidence—that would require several books!—but the remaining chapters will show that even if religious experiential claims are not always "more probable than not" on that background evidence, and even with the powerful support of the 'conflicting claims' and 'reductionist' challenges, the cumulative challenge is not as devastating as the sceptic hoped. It will be seen that certain types of religious experience provide good evidence on their own for very fundamental religious claims, and that religious experiences of all types can be worked into—and indeed, play a crucial role in—a strong cumulative case for more highly ramified religious claims.

6

EXPERIENCE AND INTERPRETATION

An extremely common challenge to arguments from religious experience—though not to the veridicality of religious experiences as such—is the claim that because religious experiences involve interpretation in terms of religious doctrines, any argument attempting to justify those doctrines by an appeal to religious experiences must be viciously circular. Despite its defects, this challenge is so frequently proposed and so influential in the debate about the evidential force of religious experience that I feel compelled to give it close attention. The discussion which follows will also prove important to Chapters VII and VIII, since they are based on the understanding presented here of the crucial role played by 'incorporated interpretation' in all perceptual experience.

According to proponents of the vicious circle challenge, only 'the given' is good evidence on its own; all 'interpretations' must be justified by evidence independent of the 'experience' before they can be accepted. Prior evidence that religious doctrines (e.g. that God exists) are probably true is required before a person is warranted in placing a religious 'interpretation' (e.g. "God is comforting me") on an 'experience'. And so, as Antony Flew puts it, "the whole argument from religious experience must collapse into an argument from whatever *other* credentials may be offered to authenticate the revelation supposedly mediated by such experience."[1]

Such a narrowly empiricist and foundationalist position is rarely found now outside discussions of religious experience. It is very frustrating for the philosopher of religion to come up time and again against the outdated assumptions which underlie the vicious circle challenge. This chapter will attempt to expose and correct those assumptions, which can be expressed as: (i) the idea that one can distinguish between 'the given' and 'interpretation', that the

---

[1] Flew, p. 139; emphasis mine.

former is the real 'experience', and that a religious experience is 'an interpretation of an experience' in a way that the sensory perception of material objects is not; (ii) a linear, foundationalist view of the relationship between beliefs and experiences, and a naïve 'associational' view of concept formation; (iii) a rigidly non-cumulative view of the justification of perceptual claims; and (iv) ignorance or neglect of the principle of credulity.

Points (iii) and (iv) can be dealt with quickly, since both cumulative arguments and the principle of credulity have been discussed at length above. Regarding (iii), Mitchell's 'lighthouse' example showed that a perceptual claim in need of verification may form part of the evidence in its own favour, without the least hint of vicious circularity, and—the other side of this coin—that an experience may be 'interpreted' in terms of the very doctrines (e.g. "the ship is near land") for which it constitutes part of the evidence. It is not necessary first to show that God probably exists, only then accepting some claims to have experienced him directly; religious experiences can work *in conjunction with* other types of evidence for religious claims.

Regarding (iv), the discussion of incorporated interpretation below will give some empirical grounds for treating unconscious interpretations as innocent until proven guilty: if they were not generally reliable, the human race would not have survived so long; and psychologists have to devise such complex, artificial situations to produce misperceptions through the misapplication of unconscious rules of inference that it is reasonable to believe that in ordinary, real-life situations these rules of inference generally lead to veridical perceptions. The *a priori* grounds for accepting incorporated interpretations as *prima facie* reliable are more important, though: if we were always required to provide independent evidence that the beliefs in terms of which we had unconsciously 'interpreted' a perceptual experience were probably true before we could take the perceptual experience to be probably veridical, we would be trapped in the same "sceptical bog" in which failure to recognize the principle of credulity lands us. Perceptual experiences must be regarded as probably (i.e. more probably than not) veridical unless there is reason to doubt them, whether or not we have independent evidence for the truth of the beliefs in terms of which they were 'interpreted'.

It is not enough to show that religious experiences, though

"interpretations", may yet form part of a cumulative argument for religious claims: we must go deeper and strike at the roots of the vicious circle challenge, presuppositions (i) and (ii). Those who treat religious experiences as being 'interpreted' in a way that less controversial perceptual experiences are not must be shown the extent to which all perceptual experiences, even the most straight-forward perception of a table, involve interpretation, and the extent to which beliefs, concepts, and experiences all interact in the development of our cognitive life. The discussion which follows is more psychological than philosophical, but it is relevant neverthe-less, since it will confirm the need for cumulative justification and for a principle of credulity, show that some of the alleged epistemological differences between religious and other perceptual experiences are not so great, and provide the understanding of perceptual experience on which Chapters VII and VIII are based.

2. THE INTERACTIVE NATURE OF CONCEPT FORMATION

One assumption which seems to underlie the vicious circle challenge is the 'association' theory of concept formation.[2] Accord-ing to this theory, the formation of concrete concepts requires little input from the subjects; they need to do no more than remember their past experiences, note the resemblances in the stimuli, and associate a label with the common features (e.g. if every time one notices a small furry creature with big ears one is told, "That's a rabbit," then eventually one forms the concept of a rabbit). The formation of abstract concepts and logical relations will follow. Concepts which cannot be acquired by ostension are applied to an experience rather than derived from it in any way, and so (argues the sceptic) their application in specific cases requires justification. It would thus be viciously circular to use an experience on which such a concept had been imposed as evidence that that concept was instantiated in the real world. In the religious case, it is claimed that since one cannot "point to God", the concept of God is not derived from experience; we must therefore have proof that God exists

---

[2] For discussions of this and other theories of concept formation, see Neil Bolton, *Concept Formation* (Oxford: Pergamon Press, 1977), chs. 1, 2, and 7; Lyle E. Bourne, Jr., *Human Conceptual Behaviour* (Boston: Allyn & Bacon, 1966), chs. III and IV; and Bruner, *Beyond the Information Given*, chs. 8, 9, and 20.

before we are warranted in applying the concept of God to an experience.

As will soon become clear, this view of concept formation fails to take into account the extent to which our understanding of concepts and our ability to perceive the world in terms of them develop together. Concepts, beliefs, past experiences, and present stimuli all interact in important ways. But the association theory has other faults, the most glaring of which is the fact that it cannot explain the formation of many types of concept. Observation of sensory resemblances alone will not lead to the acquisition of concepts based on 'family resemblances', concepts in which the common feature is something non-visible such as 'function', or concepts which depend on some special relation between the features. Even the acquisition of ordinary concrete concepts poses problems, since, as has often been noted by philosophers, pure ostension cannot unambiguously direct the attention to a particular aspect of a sensation (e.g. shape rather than colour), and many fortuitous sensory regularities do not generate concepts. It is also difficult to see how abstract concepts and logical rules could ever be 'abstracted' from pure sensory experiences, since sensations have no intrinsic significance or order. As Bruner points out, "associations do not just happen".[3]

This does not imply that the rival 'hypothesis-testing' theory of concept formation is correct. According to this theory, people approach their environment already armed with hypotheses, which they test through experience, modify, and eventually order into a conceptual system. But hypotheses, even unconscious ones, cannot be formed prior to experiences except at a very high level indeed, when a wide range of past experiences can be taken into account.

The most plausible theory of concept formation appears to be one which combines elements from both the association and hypothesis-testing theories. Although very young children and older persons faced with extremely unfamiliar stimuli tend to use a procedure close to association, and very advanced concept formation by intelligent subjects against a background of extensive experience approaches pure hypothesis testing, the theory of *general* concept formation which best accounts for the evidence is the "reciprocal interaction of cognitive structures and environmental

[3] Bruner, ch. 20.

events".[4] A person's noetic structure is not a linear hierarchy of inferred beliefs based on basic beliefs based on "direct sense experience", with a corresponding conceptual hierarchy of complex concepts abstracted from concrete concepts passively learned by ostension; nor are concepts formed in a cognitive vacuum and then imposed on experiences. There is, rather, a continual interplay between concepts, beliefs, events, reflection, the creative imagination, and other cognitive and perceptual factors. Far from being mere enumerations of properties observed to be associated by similarity or contiguity in space or time, concepts require the active participation of the subject; they represent ways of organizing experience, and usually involve the interpretation of past experiences and expectations about future experiences. As the psychologist Neil Bolton puts it,

the subject elaborates his repertoire of concepts at the same time that he organizes his environment and, consequently, we should speak of the construction of reality occurring in parallel with the development of cognitive structures such as hypotheses, concepts and plans.[5]

The ability to have detailed and accurate perceptual experiences thus develops *along with* increased understanding of the things we are perceiving.

Johnson-Laird's notion of *mental models* is extremely useful to an understanding of the way we use and develop concepts.[6] Though we do employ propositions and images in our mental representation of the world, Johnson-Laird argues, we also create very important "structural analogues" of the world which he calls "mental models". These depend on prior knowledge and experience and are continually "recursively revised" in the light of the current context and new knowledge, experiences, and events. The mental model theory shows what an active role our mind plays in our apprehension of the world, for these models are crucial to the way we represent the world to ourselves in thought and perception, to our capacity for expressing that representation, and to the way we respond to it. The theory also explains how we can use so many concepts in daily life whose 'rules' we are unable to articulate, for mental models tend to be based on an unformalized,

[4] Bolton, p. 5.
[5] Ibid., p. 3.
[6] See Johnson-Laird, *Mental Models*, especially chs. 7 and 15.

though rational assessment of background knowledge and the experiences of real life rather than on formal rules. Proponents of the vicious circle challenge tend to think of concepts as rule-governed and articulable (and, indeed, some are, though not (generally) the ones in which we are interested here); but an argument that we cannot have an experience "of God" unless we already know how to define God in terms of perceptible predicates simply does not do justice to the real nature of our concepts and to the way they interact with experience.

Like schemata, stereotypes, and the other elements of 'incorporated interpretations',[7] mental models can contribute to misapprehensions if they are inappropriate in a particular context. It is our model of surgeons as male, for instance, which makes the riddle of the surgeon's son so difficult (the surgeon says, "I can't operate on this boy; he's my son;" but the surgeon is not the boy's father).[8] But, as the next section will show, mental models also generally enable very rapid understanding, perception, and problem-solving, and they are flexible enough to adapt to most non-paradigmatic situations (such as the three-legged dog which causes traditional accounts of concepts so much trouble). The fact that an experience has been 'interpreted' in terms of a specific conceptual framework or mental model (religious or otherwise) cannot in itself make that experience evidentially suspect; the sceptic must show that the model or concept was inappropriate in some way. These points will be given further support in the next section, which explains in more detail how various factors interact in the 'incorporated interpretation' of an experience.

3. INCORPORATED INTERPRETATION[9]

Proponents of the vicious circle challenge maintain that experiences are only seen as religious because a religious interpretation has been imposed on the 'given' element in an experience, and that 'interpretations' are only warranted if we have prior, independent evidence that the beliefs they involve are true and the concepts instantiated. Psychological studies paint a very different picture of

---

[7] See Ch. I.4 above, and, for a fuller account, the next section.
[8] See Sanford, *Cognition and Cognitive Psychology*, ch. 11.
[9] Most of this section should be taken to apply to reflexive interpretation as well.

perception, however. If the vicious circle challenge took into account the extent to which all experiences are 'interpreted', it would lead us into scepticism, for it would require us to perform such impossible feats as proving that material objects exist quite apart from any putative experiences of them. Interpretation, far from being an extraneous element imposed from without, is absolutely essential to there occurring a perceptual experience at all.

Perception of any type is never a purely physical activity; it involves the whole person. We are not passive recipients of ready-made representations of our environment; rather, stimuli from that environment must be processed by various interpretive mechanisms before they can have any significance for us, and constitute a perceptual experience (as opposed to mere sensation). Such an experience is thus the product of complex intellectual activity in which we have, in the psychologist Jerome Bruner's well-known phrase, 'gone beyond the information given'.[10] This claim can be supported by many illustrations from the field of cognitive psychology, of which a few are given below.

Incorporated interpretation may be carried out before we are even aware that there is something there to perceive, as has been shown by studies in which biologically or emotionally important signals were found to have a much lower recognition threshold than neutral signals. Somewhere in his subconscious, for instance, a sleeping person is able to carry out the classification which distinguishes words such as his own name, which elicit a response, from irrelevant words, which do not.[11] Incorporated interpretation is thus clearly not a matter of carrying out inferences in the rapid but conscious manner of a Sherlock Holmes, making highly ramified deductions from less ramified sensory clues. It is, rather, an unconscious process *analogous* to conscious inference and interpretation. The way things seem to us to be 'goes beyond' the information given in the stimuli alone, and it does so in a systematic manner best explained by the model of unconscious rules of inference, interpretation, and selection procedures. Because the process is unconscious, what seems to a person to be 'given' in an experience has already been interpreted. The empiricist's 'given', sense-data, are not 'given' at all from the subject's point of

[10] Bruner, ch. 13.
[11] Neville Moray, *Attention: Selective Processes in Vision and Hearing* (London: Hutchinson Educational, 1969), ch. 3.

view; in fact, it is very difficult and usually requires training to see the world in terms of them, as any textbook on the 'phenomena of constancy' (see below) will show.

The innate and learned 'rules' which guide the selection, processing, storage of, and response to perceptual 'cues' are part of what is called a 'set'. A perceptual or cognitive set, in its widest sense, is the background which subjects bring to their experiences, and which interacts with the stimuli to make the experiences what they are for those subjects. Many different factors can be at work together in a perceptual set: innate 'rules of inference' (e.g.— probably—binocular disparity and the recognition of basic emotional states in oneself and others); linguistic and cultural background (e.g. the tribal African concept of causality as 'personal' rather than 'physical', and concepts such as 'Wanderlust' and 'Gemütlichkeit', for which a word is available in some languages and not others[12]); upbringing (e.g. being taught that persons in a certain category are 'dirty'); beliefs and expectations (e.g. that red-haired people have quick tempers, that objects fall when unsupported, that trembling is associated with fear); training (e.g. to recognize animal tracks); needs, desires, and emotional state (e.g. the need to believe a certain person approves of you, a woman's fear that a man wants only 'one thing' from her); personality (e.g. the 'anxiety neurotic' who is 'set' to perceive emotionally negative material); and physiological states and drives (e.g. dizziness, hunger).

Psychologists have attempted to discover some of the unconscious rules which shape perceptual experience by deliberately making the 'cues' misleading or ambiguous. Some of the perceptual illusions which result are well known. When a photograph of shadowed craters on the moon is turned upside-down, for instance, it looks like a picture of hillocks, despite our knowledge that the objects are craters. This is due to our learned expectation that light always comes from above; shadows inside concave objects are expected to be in the upper portion, shadows on convex objects on the lower portion.[13] Another classic example, the Ames Room, plays on our expectations that rooms are rectangular and that any apparent incongruities lie in moving objects rather than in the

---

[12] See section 4 below.

[13] See R. H. Day, *Human Perception* (Sydney: John Wiley & Sons, 1969), chs. 6 and 8, for a fuller discussion of this illusion.

environment. When observers look through a peephole in one wall, they seem to see a normal room containing objects which mysteriously change size as they move about. What they are actually seeing is a tilted room with a trapezoidal floorplan. Objects in the corner of the room farthest from the observers appear to be their correct size, while objects in the corner closest to the observers appear to be grossly enlarged, because the observers have unconsciously projected them on to an imaginary far corner of the presumed rectangular room and then, still unconsciously, performed the appropriate size calculations.[14]

Even such 'non-cognitive' experiences as emotions employ unconscious rules of inference. The studies in 'attribution theory' which deal with the labelling of one's own emotions and bodily states and the ascription of certain states to certain causes have shown that subjects label their states of arousal according to the meaning they perceive in their situation, unconsciously attributing certain sensations to the factors most likely to have caused them in that situation. In a classic experiment by Schachter and Singer,[15] students who were injected with adrenalin and then placed in a context suggestive of anger or euphoria (e.g. for anger, an insulting questionnaire and a 'fellow subject'—an actor—saying "it's unfair") experienced the corresponding emotions when they had no other explanation for their state of arousal; those who were told what sensations to expect from the adrenalin did not experience the emotions, as they had no need to attribute their sensations to anger or euphoria. Mark Cook describes another interesting experiment in which men looking at pin-ups were fed what they were told was their own heart-beat through headphones: they ended up claiming to prefer the pin-ups associated with a faster false heart rate, since they unconsciously correlated a faster heart rate with heightened emotion or sexual desire.[16] And in a very intriguing experiment by Festinger and Carlsmith,[17] subjects who were given a twenty dollar

[14] For a good description of the Ames Room, see N. R. Hanson, *Perception and Discovery* (San Francisco: Freeman, Cooper & Co., 1969), ch. 9.

[15] Stanley Schachter and Jerome E. Singer, "Cognitive, Social and Physiological Determinants of Emotional State", *Psychological Review*, 69 (1962), 379–99. The example of Stephen Bradley's conversion experience in Ch.VIII.3 shows how attribution theory might be applied to certain religious experiences in which a state of arousal is given a religious label.

[16] Mark Cook, *Perceiving Others* (London: Methuen, 1979), ch. 5.

[17] L. Festinger and J. M. Carlsmith, "Cognitive Consequences of Forced Compliance", *Journal of Abnormal and Social Psychology*, 58 (1959), 203–11.

bribe to lie that a boring task was interesting still believed the task to be boring afterwards, whereas subjects who were given only one dollar to tell the same lie began to believe the task really was more interesting than they had thought at first. Even unconsciously, we need to feel we have good reasons for our actions, and if a one dollar bribe is not a good enough reason for lying that a task was interesting, then the task must actually have been interesting.

In the above cases, the relevant factors in the subject's set led to unveridical perceptual experiences and mistaken attributions; it is essential to recognize, however, that these are highly artificial cases, designed to be illusory in order to isolate certain rules of inference. Both innate and acquired sets generally *aid* perception— otherwise the human race would have died out long ago. The rules incorporated into our perceptual sets enable the rapid and accurate perception of important or likely percepts, and the associated screening mechanisms prevent our perceptual processes from being bogged down by irrelevant information. The rule that light always comes from above, for instance, enables us to classify shadow-casting objects much faster than if we had to look about for the light source every time; and the size and distance inferences involved in the Ames room illusion are part of the 'phenomena of constancy', which ensure that our perceptual experiences present us with a stable world of objects which 'look' the same under varying conditions, so that they can be quickly recognized. A Rolls-Royce in the distance looks larger than a Mini in the foreground, though the retinal image is smaller (this 'size constancy' shows up in infants of a few months); tilted plates look round, though the retinal image is elliptical. It is only when the context is obscured, or the percipient is a trained artist (or philosopher!) that these unconscious rules do not always mould the way things look (epistemically).[18]

Without such perceptual sets, the cognitive strain involved in making sense of our environment would be intolerable. It has been shown that one of the thought disorders suffered by schizophrenics is an inability to screen out irrelevant stimuli; for instance, they find it more difficult than normal to state the colour of green letters which happen to form the word "red".[19] Unconscious selection of

[18] For more information on the perceptual constancies, see R. H. Forgus and L. E. Melamed, *Perception: A Cognitive Stage Approach* (New York: McGraw-Hill, 1976), chs. 7 and 8; and D. W. Hamlyn, *The Psychology of Perception* (London: Routledge & Kegan Paul, 1957), ch. II.

[19] For an illustration of the disastrous effect of this inability to screen out

relevant stimuli is essential if we are to perceive the world in manageable, meaningful structures. The rare cases of individuals who must perform consciously what most of us perform unconsciously show just how much we rely on incorporated interpretation, and how far we take it for granted. N. R. Hanson cites the example of some adults, congenitally blind due to cataracts and then cured by an operation, who required intensive training before they could see normally; by day thirteen, for instance, they could still only distinguish a triangle from a square by counting the angles.[20] Rarer still are those unfortunate individuals who—usually because of brain damage—must carry out all perceptual interpretation by laborious conscious deductions; they "see" but do not "perceive". These people appear frequently to reach the wrong conclusions: shown a photograph of an indoor scene with a Christmas tree, for instance, one subject reasoned that it must be a picture of the exterior of a house because of the "shrub with decorative stones underneath".[21] Fortunately, most of us find it very easy to transform the barrage of stimuli with which we are constantly bombarded into meaningful perceptions—and we usually get it right. If we had to "infer the tiger from its stripes" (as Wolters puts it),[22] we would lead a precarious existence indeed; but the fact that the 'sets' involved in these inferences are unconscious means that instead of wasting our mental energy deducing books, tabletops and tigers from the sense-data, we can direct them to higher pursuits—such as philosophy.

Incorporated interpretations make it possible for us to experience a world of objects and persons, causes and consequences—a world in which rational action is possible. Interpretations and the influence of perceptual sets should not be treated as corrupting influences, unwarranted unless supported by independent evidence; rather, they should be considered innocent until proven guilty, for they are essential to all types of perceptual experience. One could never begin to perceive the world if one always had to justify incorporated interpretations before trusting them. In fact, we go

irrelevant stimuli, see the case history of Norma McDonald in M. B. Bowers and D. X. Freedman, "'Psychedelic' Experiences in Acute Psychoses", ch. 31 of Tart (ed.), pp. 463–76.

[20] *Perception and Discovery*, p. 151.

[21] The case of John Strange, in G. W. Humphreys and M. J. Riddoch, *To See But Not To See* (London: Erlbaum, 1987); see also Bolton, ch. 3.

[22] A. W. P. Wolters, *The Evidence of our Senses* (London: Methuen, 1933), ch. 11.

through life trusting our incorporated interpretations unless there is reason not to, and are normally unaware of them *as* interpretations. This is, in effect, the principle of credulity from another angle: the interpretations incorporated into perceptual experiences must be taken as probably correct unless there is reason to believe otherwise.

We have seen that all perceptual experiences and many non-perceptual experiences involve incorporated interpretation. It is not that perceptions of value, beauty, causality, and religious signifi-cance are 'interpretations' in a way that perceptions of material objects are not. However, it is true that some experiences are more shaped by an interpretive set than others. The visual perception of an apple is not open to the same degree of influence by culture, personality, and so on as is the perception of an immoral act or of a generous person, just as the perception of an apple under optimum viewing conditions is not as open to the influence of a set as is the perception of an apple when the stimuli are ambiguous. One way of discovering whether the stimuli were ambiguous or whether the set played a large role when such information is not directly accessible (unlike controlled experiments) is to collect many accounts of what is allegedly the same percept and see whether and how the accounts differ. This is the basis of the conflicting claims challenge to religious experiences, which aims to show that the religious aspects of such experiences are nothing *but* interpretation. We will deal with one version of that challenge in the next section, and its strongest version in the next chapter; the purpose here is merely to show that one cannot drive a wedge between 'experience' and 'interpretation' in the way proponents of the vicious circle challenge would like.

'Unconscious interpretation' would only be good grounds for a challenge if it could be shown (i) that the set which influenced the experience incorporated incorrect rules of inference or (ii) that the set was of a type which generally leads to misperceptions.

(i) People do sometimes use faulty 'mental models'. Psychol-ogists have discovered, for instance, that we often operate with incorrect 'implicit personality theories' (such as the unfortunately very prevalent one which correlates good character with good looks and bad with bad), which can lead to misperceptions of character and motives.[23] But the onus is on the sceptic to show that

---

[23] Cook, chs. 5 and 6.

a particular unconscious rule of interpretation or inference is incorrect (and that it is in fact being used). For this challenge to work in the religious case, the sceptic would have to show that religious beliefs incorporated in a set, such as the belief that God created the world, are very probably false; and the vast majority of religious beliefs have not been shown to be so.

(ii) Sets may also be likely to lead to misperceptions because they involve psychological or physiological states and traits which tend to affect perception adversely, often by leading to the incorrect application of otherwise correct rules of inference—states of intoxication, for example, and schizophrenia. Whether religious experiences generally arise out of such 'pathological' sets is a question for Chapter VIII, but I will deal with one aspect of it here. It is sometimes suggested that needs and desires come into this category—for instance, the fact (if it is one) that people have unconscious needs and desires for a protective and punishing parent-figure, 'meaning' to life, and a 'face' to the universe is often stated as if it were proof that religious experiences are nothing but wishful thinking. But needs and desires usually aid perception, helping us to identify and respond to those things which will satisfy us and to avoid things which are dangerous or unpleasant. A hungry person is more likely to notice a source of food, a person afraid of wild animals more likely to notice a rustling in the underbrush. Of course, like any other set, needs and desires can distort perception in certain circumstances; but again, the onus is on the sceptic to show that in the religious case the influence is a distorting one. (Other aspects of the 'Freudian' challenge will be discussed in Chapter VIII.)

4. IS RELIGIOUS EXPERIENCE "NOTHING BUT" INTERPRETATION?

To back up their claim that experiences are religious only when a religious interpretation is 'imposed' on them, proponents of the vicious circle challenge maintain that religious experiences tend to conform to cultural paradigms and that mystical experiences usually occur only after a rigorous course of training and indoctrination. The previous section should have made it clear that all experiences involve some interpretation in accordance with the subject's set; religious experiences are not unusual in that respect, as some sceptics may have thought. There may, however, be a significant difference in the *degree* to which concepts, beliefs, and training influence religious experiences. This section will not be able conclusively to overcome the challenge that religious experiences are "nothing but" interpretation—all the resources of the next three chapters are required for that task—but it will provide a response to the 'vicious circle' component of that challenge, the claim about conformity to training and tradition.

That quintessential proponent of the vicious circle challenge, Antony Flew, argues that the character of religious experiences

seems to depend on the interests, background, and expectations of those who have them rather than upon anything separate and autonomous. . . . the expert natural historian of religious experience would be altogether astounded to hear of the vision of Bernadette Soubirois occurring not to a Roman Catholic at Lourdes but to an Hindu in Benares, or of Apollo manifest not in classical Delphi but in Kyoto under the Shoguns.[24]

This challenge would have little impact on an argument from religious experience in its present form, since it is restricted to visions. Flew seems to believe that if visions are to have any evidential value, their alleged objects must exist as quasi-physical autonomous entities, and that if such entities did exist, they would appear in the same quasi-physical form to everyone. The latter claim has some force in the case of historical figures, though it is conceivable that even these could choose to appear in a form familiar to the subject rather than in the form they took in life. When one takes the view of visions put forward in Chapter II, however, their conformity to cultural paradigms becomes largely irrelevant. Whether visions are seen as the objectified "idea-patterns" of a community[25] or as religious insights conveyed in 'picture' form, their quasi-sensory aspects should be expected to conform to individual or cultural models and should not normally be regarded naïvely as features of some quasi-physical entity.

Interpretive religious experiences might support the sceptic's argument, since they do seem to owe their religious character largely to a religious world-view which deeply permeates the subject's life. As was pointed out earlier, however, it is for this very

---

[24] Flew, pp. 126–7.
[25] For a fuller account of Tyrrell's theory of "idea-patterns", see Chapter VIII.2.

reason that interpretive religious experiences have little evidential force outside a cumulative argument.[26]

What of mystical experiences, which often appear to depend on years of intensive training within a particular tradition? Spontaneous mystical experiences do occur, particularly in the realm of nature mysticism, but it is true that the introvertive experiences so highly prized by mystics are usually correlated with training. But mystical training is not necessarily a course of brainwashing. It serves three very respectable functions: (i) it enables subjects to fulfil certain basic requirements which make mystical experiences more likely; (ii) it directs subjects' attention to certain percepts and sharpens their skill at perceiving them; and (iii) it provides them with the concepts needed to understand their experiences and the language with which to express them. *All* perceptual experiences are made possible by such training; the fact that training is required before certain sorts of perceptual experiences occur in no way implies that those experiences are determined entirely by that training and not by any independent reality. Let us look more closely at the three types of training mentioned above.

(i) In the first place, it should be no more worrying that we must undergo exercises of purification and quieting of the mind and body before we are likely to have a mystical experience than that we must have our eyes open and in good working order and not be distracted by other percepts and thoughts if we are to have a visual perceptual experience of a small object in front of us. Granted, such requirements are not nearly as rigorous in the religious case as in the secular, since 'spontaneous' mystical experiences are possible; but this only helps to undermine the sceptic's argument.

(ii) It is well known that if people are given prior instructions to look out for a certain percept, they will perceive that percept more quickly and accurately than if they had not been given that 'instructional set'—in which case, they might have overlooked the percept completely. Training can 'tune' subjects to an aspect of reality they are not normally 'set' to perceive and enable them both to perceive new features and to discriminate finer degrees of one feature, as when a music student learns to distinguish between notes a quarter-tone apart, which she previously *heard* as the same. In science, too, discoveries—even those which come as a 'flash of

---

[26] Culturally determined differences among visions and interpretive experiences will be discussed further in Chapter VII.2.

insight'—are made by those who have an appropriate set. Scientific training and reflection, combined with a capacity for creative insight, lead to the perception of patterns and anomalies and the invention of fruitful models and analogies. Bruner talks of discovery favouring the well-prepared mind,[27] Koestler of "ripeness":[28] Kekulé, for instance, was "ripe" for discovery when he had his 'benzene ring' dream (described above, Chapter V.2), for he had been dwelling on the problem for some time.[29]

Since we learn over the years to occupy our attention almost wholly with worldly matters, it should not be surprising that it takes training to divert it to a more spiritual realm and to focus it on features there in a knowledgeable way. Moreover, as Moray points out, the attention we focus (unconsciously as well as consciously) on certain 'cues' is often a function of cue *value* rather than cue strength.[30] (He adds, typically, that at present we have no idea how this 'value' is represented in the nervous system.) Religious training heightens the value of religious 'cues' by presenting a religious goal as the *summum bonum*; to a person embroiled in secular society, they would have no value.

(iii) That mystical experiences are usually described using the terminology of the subject's own tradition is to be expected, given their 'ineffable' nature. Soskice points out, for instance, that

the mystic . . . often feels a crisis of descriptive language because there do not seem to be words and concepts in the common stock adequate to his or her experience. This straining of linguistic resources leads to the catachretical employment of metaphor, of phrases like 'the dark night', 'the spiritual marriage', and 'mystic union'. . . . Often, indeed almost always, the mystical writer is influenced by a particular tradition of descriptive imagery and philosophical presupposition. John of the Cross, for example, uses scholastic terminology (although not always with the sense the scholastic writers intended) and the theme of 'mystic night' and 'cloud of unknowing' is itself a biblical theme, harking back to the Cloud of Exodus and to the Night of the Song of Songs.[31]

As Chapter VII will show, understanding such metaphors within the context of the mystic's own tradition is vital, as one can easily

---

[27] "The Act of Discovery", ch. 22 of his *Beyond the Information Given*.
[28] Koestler, *The Act of Creation*, pp. 113 and 119.
[29] For further discussion of prior preparation, creativity, and discovery, see N. R. Hanson, *Patterns of Discovery* (Cambridge: CUP, 1958), and Yee, sections 3.3 and 4.1.2.
[30] Moray, ch. 9.   [31] Soskice, p. 151.

be led astray by the language used. Most mystical terminology is deeply embedded within a network of associations produced by the experiential and linguistic history of a community.[32] Only rarely do subjects undergo mystical and other intense religious experiences with such frequency, and have such fertile imaginations, that they are able to develop their own system of classification, as St Teresa did.[33] In describing experiences so often claimed to be 'ineffable', then, it is hardly surprising that the most detailed and articulate auto-descriptions tend to come from those people who have acquired a rich store of religious concepts from their community—and that their descriptions are in terms of those concepts.

The important question here, however, is whether the terminology which subjects learn through their traditions influences not just the expression of the experiences, but the experiences themselves, and to what degree.

The influence of language on thought and experience has long been debated.[34] However, of the three versions of the Whorfian (or "Sapir–Whorf") hypothesis—the 'strong' one, that language is crucially formative of thought and experience; the 'weak' one, that language influences perceptual experience; and the 'weakest' one, that language mainly affects the memory and expression of experiences—only the weakest version has survived psychological investigation. Linguistic factors appear to have little effect on perceptual experiences themselves, but they do affect one's ability to codify percepts and thus to remember experiences, to communicate experiences to others, and to relate experiences to each other. For instance, the fact that Germans have the word "Gemütlichkeit" while the English have no exact translation does not mean that Germans experience comfortable, genial, cosy, friendly, snug 'atmospheres' while the English do not. Though English speakers can and do experience 'Gemütlichkeit', however, they have to grope around to express their awareness of the phenomenon,

---

[32] Cf. the discussion of 'critical realism' in Chapter I.2.

[33] See the *Interior Castle* and *Life*.

[34] For discussions of the influence of language and sources of the conclusions cited in this paragraph, see Bruner, ch. 21; J. A. Fishman, "A Systematization of the Whorfian Hypothesis" and H. Maclay, "An Experimental Study of Language and Nonlinguistic Behaviour", both in J. W. Berry and P. R. Dasen (eds.), *Culture and Cognition* (London: Methuen, 1974); and B. B. Lloyd, *Perception and Cognition: A Cross-Cultural Perspective* (Harmondsworth: Penguin Books, 1972), ch. 2.

whereas German speakers can express it easily and are thus more likely to call attention to it where it exists and to use the term in auto-descriptions. The many studies done on the relation between the codifiability and the perception of colour in different cultures— colour being a good subject for such studies, since it is a real continuum whose divisions depend on cultural tradition—have shown that colours for which the percipient had a word were more easily recognized when they appeared again in a larger array than were colours which the percipient could not easily codify.[35] The importance of encoding to memory and expression will be discussed further below.

Though purely linguistic factors may have little influence on our perception of the world, the conceptual frameworks underlying language certainly do exert some influence. The previous two sections discussed the role of concepts, mental models, and other elements of a subject's set which are involved in incorporated interpretation, but some further comments are in order here. The perception of causality, 'person' perception, and perceptions which involve evaluative judgements are clearly affected by cultural conceptual frameworks at a highly ramified level, though it is important to note that studies have shown these types of perception to be fairly free from cultural influence at more 'primitive' levels (e.g. the perception of one billiard ball causing another to move[36] and, to a great extent, the perception of other persons' emotional states[37]). S. H. Irvine shows, for instance, how the Shona (of Zimbabwe) perception of causality is affected by the traditional world-view, according to which everything contains 'force' which can be activated by man and the ancestor spirits, and relations with the kin group (living and dead) are of prime importance.[38] Events are thus always perceived within a model of personal, social, and spiritual causality. Culturally-influenced "affect-laden" concepts can also influence perception,[39] often through stereotypes. Different aspects of an insect will be apprehended, for instance, depending on whether one recoils from it in disgust or views it as a

[35] See Lloyd, ch. 2; Fishman in Berry and Dasen (eds.); and Bruner, ch. 21.

[36] See e.g. A. Michotte, *The Perception of Causality* (London: Methuen, 1963).

[37] See Cook, ch. 4; Lloyd, ch. 4; and Forgus and Melamed, ch. 15.

[38] "Contributions of Ability and Attainment Testing in Africa to a General Theory of Intellect", in Berry and Dasen (eds.).

[39] See Bourne, ch. VI; Cook, ch. 5; and Ninian Smart, *Beyond Ideology* (London: Collins, 1981), ch. 2.

welcome source of food; and one's perception of individuals is likely to be distorted if one believes members of their ethnic group are "dirty animals". As Lippman pointed out back in 1922, "we pick out what our culture has already defined for us, and we tend to perceive that which we have picked out in the form stereotyped for us by our culture."[40] However, like all elements of incorporated interpretations, culturally conditioned stereotypes and conceptual frameworks *aid* perception in an appropriate context. In one experiment which showed how a world-view could enable rapid comprehension if appropriate and hinder it if inappropriate, subjects were allowed brief glimpses, and then better views, of pictures with various themes; subjects with a religious world-view quickly perceived one picture as that of a man with his head bowed in prayer, while subjects who saw the world in terms of business thought it was a picture of a man at work and required many more viewings before clues such as the Gothic window led them to the correct interpretation.[41]

In all the above examples of the influence of conceptual factors on perception, the experiences were by no means entirely determined by those factors. Indeed, conceptual training sometimes only affects the degree of ramification of one's perceptual experience— whether one sees a light bulb or merely a glass object, a goal being scored or merely a series of movements. It has been claimed that while people lacking an appropriate understanding of concepts such as 'light bulb' and 'the scoring of a goal' can nevertheless perceive instantiations of those concepts in the 'transparent' sense, not knowing what (or the full significance of what) they are perceiving, people lacking the concept of 'God' never have an experience of his 'presence', even transparently. Of course, proponents of this argument recognize that there are interpretive religious experiences—two people might describe exactly the same medical symptoms and only one perceive the disease as an example of 'punishment from God'. But experiences of "the presence of the divine" are a much more serious issue: if people only have experiences which could be given such a hetero-description *after* they have acquired religious concepts, then surely such concepts are ideas only and have no basis in experience? The account of concept formation given in section 2 should have exposed some of this

[40] Quoted in Cook, p. 49.
[41] See Bruner's description of this experiment, Bruner, p. 99.

challenge's faults, but at this point I wish to show that it does not even have the facts right.

Chapters III and VII both contain examples of religious experiences at odds with the received tradition, and examples of spontaneous 'senses of a presence' unrelated to the subject's prior religious concepts (if any) abound. Many cases are documented in which the subjects had overwhelming, puzzling experiences which they only realized were religious after they had read a religious text or talked with someone more experienced. One of Hardy's respondents writes, for instance, "I was not able to interpret this experience satisfactorily until I read—some months later—Rudolf Otto's 'Das Heilige'. Here I found it—the 'Numinous'."[42] Others realized their experiences were religious, but found that these experiences challenged their prior conceptions. St Teresa found this situation very distressing:

> I did not know that God was in all things, and, when He seemed to me to be so very present, I thought it impossible. I could not cease believing that He was there, for it seemed almost certain that I had been conscious of His very presence. Unlearned persons would tell me that He was there only by grace; but I could not believe that . . . and so I continued to be greatly distressed. From this doubt I was freed by a very learned man of the Order of the glorious Saint Dominic: he told me that He was indeed present . . .[43]

For others, the conflicting experiences were more welcome: in Hardy's collection, an elderly woman doctor, "brought up to fear and obey God" in a household where little was heard of love and much of sin and hell, writes of the way her childhood conception of God was transformed into a loving one and her dread into joy.[44] Another example is that of the nineteenth-century nature mystic Richard Jeffries, who, Happold maintains, discovered mystical concepts in his experiences akin to Eckhart's (e.g. the "eternal now", the divinity of the soul, "the unutterable existence infinitely higher than deity"), but who had to fumble to express his insights, since he had not read the mystics and such concepts were alien to the religious thought of his society.[45]

Childhood experiences unrelated to religious teaching are especially revealing. Some of Hardy's respondents wrote that as young children they had experiences of an "It" or a "Presence"

---

[42] In Hardy, p. 85.   [44] Hardy, pp. 87–8.
[43] *Life*, pp. 110–11.   [45] Happold, pp. 384–7.

which they only later called "God" or recognized as "divine".[46] In Edward Robinson's study of childhood religious experiences,[47] it was found that many people had vivid memories of profound religious experiences as very young children, experiences which they could not possibly have expressed in religious terms at the time. Some had had no religious training before the experience; many were familiar with some religious concepts but not with the ones they later said the experience had revealed; and many did not connect their 'Sunday School' religious concepts with their experiences, because those concepts were far too inadequate and naïve. Some even had two 'Gods', one for church, the other the object of their numinous and mystical experiences. If such reports can be trusted (and Robinson gives many reasons for trusting them), then it certainly seems that mystical and numinous experiences are not confined to those who have been through 'training and indoctrination'.

Though the above experiences are very useful as evidence that religious experiences do not depend entirely on the subject's conceptual set, they are not always the most informative type of experience. As section 2 showed, our ability to perceive and understand the world develops along with our repertoire of concepts; and, as was mentioned above, the ability to 'encode' a percept can aid memory and communication. It is far easier to remember a formula than an unstructured mass of data, and so we tend to store a 'mental model' of discourse, events, and experiences rather than uninterpreted, meaningless details.[48] This encoding may be performed consciously if the concepts are unfamiliar or the stimuli puzzling, but more often it takes the form of an incorporated interpretation. The information stored in this way, in the 'symbolic' mode, is easier to articulate and tends to last better than information stored in the 'iconic' (or 'sensory') mode, which must be frequently rehearsed if it is to be retained.[49] Encoding a religious experience in terms of culturally learned schemata can thus greatly enhance later recall and articulation of the experience.

This is not to say that relatively unencoded religious experiences are soon forgotten. Religious experiences tend to be more difficult

---

[46] See, for instance, Hardy, pp. 75 and 82.
[47] *The Original Vision.*
[48] See Sanford, chs. 5 and 6.
[49] See Bruner, ch. 18, for an account of the different types of memory.

to codify than the experiences of sensory perception, partly because they are 'private' experiences, partly because they are relatively unusual and infrequent. But they are also well suited to memory in a non-symbolic mode. Encoding is most helpful where the percept is complex; it eases the strain on the memory by organizing the details into manageable schemata.[50] Non-symbolic memory modes can cope with experiences which do not involve many discrete bits of information, and religious experiences are typically of this sort. Moreover, a highly unusual or anomalous thing is often more conspicuous than one which easily fits our mental models, so that our attention is drawn to it and we may remember it better than everyday experiences.[51] The religious experiences in question are unencoded precisely because they are so anomalous; they do not fit neatly into any of the subject's existing mental models. Such experiences tend to fascinate the subject so much that they are vividly retained while an attempt is made to understand and describe them. The childhood experiences discussed above show how the significance of religious experiences can unfold over time, as the subject acquires a more sophisticated conceptual framework (a phenomenon which the interactive account of concept formation given above helps to explain).

Encoding is not universally helpful. The theory that we store 'mental models' rather than unstructured details explains why our memories sometimes contain systematic distortions. For instance, because we tend to remember the meaning of a person's discourse rather than the actual words in their correct order, we may sometimes introduce plausible details, omit information deemed irrelevant, and 'screen out' or 'normalize' incongruent, unexpected, or undesired features. This also occurs with visual percepts: Manet apparently painted some Romanesque arches of Notre Dame as Gothic arches, because he knew that it was a Gothic cathedral.[52] It is for this reason that very highly ramified auto-descriptions of religious experiences (e.g. ones which involve highly sophisticated concepts of the Trinity) are sometimes of less value to an argument from religious experience than the less doctrine-laden descriptions.

It should be remembered, however, that encoding normally does not distort information, that it usually provides a fuller understand-

---

[50] Bruner, ch. 21.
[51] See Sanford, ch. 8.
[52] So Katz reports in his own contribution to Katz (ed.).

ing of the thing remembered, and that it generally enables better recall and articulation. It may well be that religious experiences which yield relatively uninformative and poorly articulated insights—for instance, many of those contemporary ones which refer vaguely to 'reality', 'understanding life', or 'just *knowing*'[53]—are the very experiences whose subjects were not equipped with a rich network of mental models from a religious tradition. "The fullest and most informative experiences might be those for which the subject was prepared beforehand", writes Peter Moore;[54] and the evidence certainly favours such prior preparation.

It should be clear from the foregoing that concept formation, the justification of beliefs, the acquisition of knowledge, and the ability to perceive the environment accurately are all interrelated, cumulative activities. Since perception is a matter neither of a hierarchy of beliefs based on categorized sensations nor of hypotheses imposed as arbitrary structures on the stimuli, there is no absolute dichotomy between concepts derived from experience and concepts brought to experience, or between 'experience' and 'interpretation'. It should hardly be surprising that the best way of justifying our experiential claims itself turns out to be cumulative. It is not, as the proponent of the vicious circle challenge suggests, a case of first finding evidence for religious beliefs and then being allowed to interpret experiences in terms of them. Nor is it a case, as some theists have suggested, of taking religious experiences to be self-authenticating, unanalysable experiences which never stand in need of justification. Religious incorporated interpretations, like all incorporated interpretations, must be regarded *prima facie* as probably trustworthy, but challenges are always possible. The 'conflicting claims' and 'reductionist' challenges which follow aim to show that religious interpretations are unjustified, and it is to those that we must now turn.

<hr>

53 See e.g. Hardy, p. 110.
54 Moore in Katz (ed.), p. 112.

7

THE CONFLICTING
CLAIMS CHALLENGE

The great diversity of religious experiential claims gives rise to two powerful challenges to religious experience: the challenge that since subjects cannot agree on a description of the alleged percept, their experiences must be at worst, illusory, at best, serious misperceptions, and in any case, generally unreliable; and the challenge that since the different descriptions tend to be correlated with the subjects' different traditions, a reductionist explanation involving prior beliefs is more plausible than any explanation involving an autonomous holy power. The second challenge was considered in the previous chapter and will be dealt with further in Chapter VIII; in this chapter some responses to the first will be explored.

The conflicting claims challenge is often found expressed in a form which does not do it justice. Flew's version, for instance, charges that

religious experiences are enormously varied, ostensibly authenticating innumerable beliefs many of which are in contradiction with one another . . . the varieties of religious experience include, not only those which their subjects are inclined to interpret as visions of the Blessed Virgin or senses of the guiding presence of Jesus Christ, but also others more outlandish presenting themselves as manifestations of Quetzalcoatl or Osiris, of Dionysus or Shiva.[1]

Swinburne rightly points out,[2] firstly, that such differences do not necessarily entail conflict, since "God may be known under different names to different cultures"; secondly, that accepting Flew's type of example as veridical does not usually commit one to the conflicting doctrinal systems associated with such beings; and thirdly, that in cases where an auto-description does commit the

---

[1] Flew, pp. 126–7.   [2] Swinburne, pp. 265–7.

subject to a doctrine which adherents of other religions can give good reasons for regarding as false, the subject can normally retreat to a less ramified auto-description (e.g. "some supernatural being" rather than "Dionysus") without casting doubt on religious experiences in general. If there were "vastly many experiences apparently of an omnipotent Devil", whose existence would be incompatible with God's existence, then the theist's position would be threatened; but, says Swinburne, "there are not [vastly many] such experiences".[3]

This response is correct as far as it goes, but it fails to take account of the quite substantial amount of *prima facie* conflict encountered when one goes beyond the quasi-sensory, anthropomorphic visions of Flew's examples. Flew could have made his challenge much stronger if he had appealed to numinous and mystical experiences and included atheistic as well as theistic traditions. Subjects of such experiences usually claim to have apprehended the nature of *ultimate* reality; and what might be acceptable diversity at lower levels often becomes conflict at this level. Consider the following very representative types of experience, for instance: (i) a numinous experience of 'creature-consciousness' when one feels oneself to be in the presence of an awe-inspiring and supremely holy power; (ii) a rapturous theistic mystical experience apparently of loving intimacy with a personal 'Other'; (iii) a monistic experience of seeming to transcend "all barriers, all sense of duality, differences, separateness", including the idea of a God with personal attributes, and arriving at the realization of "profound Silence or Supreme Peace, wherein all thoughts cease and you become identical with the Supreme Self";[4] (iv) a 'natural mystical' experience of a fundamental unity behind but going no further than the things of this world, with 'perceptions' such as R. M. Bucke's,[5] "that all men are immortal; that the cosmic order is such that . . . all things work together for the good of each and all; that the foundation principle of the world . . . is what we call love . . ."; (v) a Buddhist experience going "beyond Yogin identity with the universe, beyond Christian union

---

[3] Ibid. p. 267. Although the natural reading of Swinburne's sentence is that there are *no* experiences apparently of an omnipotent Devil, he explained to me that the correct reading is the one I have given.

[4] Swami Sivananda, pp. 379 and 372 respectively.

[5] See the quotation above, Ch. II.4.

with God, to limitless expansion, to the unthinkable"[6]—in its most extreme form, an experience in which the meditator sees that all, even Brahman, suffers from 'impermanence, imperfection, and non-self', and in which he "truly knows that he is no self, either bodily or spiritually, but only a series of processes and thoughts; that all other 'realities' are also thus empty and transient."[7] Taken at face value, these five experiences could not all be veridical together. Since they represent some of the major mystical traditions of the world, this poses a serious threat to any argument from religious experience. The main task of this chapter is thus to attempt a reconciliation of such experiences (though not necessarily of the doctrines with which they are typically associated) while preserving a substantial amount of their evidential force.

That last qualification is important, for there are several ways of dissolving the conflict between religious claims which leave religious experiences with no evidential force. Apparent conflict is of no consequence to those who hold the non-cognitive views of religious experience described in Chapter I, for instance; and the narrow one-true-religion approach, according to which the doctrines and experiences of all but the "true faith" are false and illusory, consigns religious experience to an extremely low evidential rung indeed, since the criteria by which they are judged veridical presuppose the truth of one religion's doctrines. Similarly, any approach which requires radical revision of most religious auto-descriptions before they can be seen as compatible makes religious experience in general epistemologically suspect (though some revision is acceptable).

Before moving on to more promising attempts to resolve the *prima facie* conflict among numinous and mystical auto-descriptions, we should say a few words about alleged conflict among the other types of religious experience.

2. CONFLICT AMONG THE LESS 'INTRINSICALLY RELIGIOUS' TYPES OF EXPERIENCE

(i) Conflict among interpretive religious experiences generally presents little difficulty, since they have so little evidential force of

---

[6] Mettānando Bhikkhu, in conversation.
[7] King, *Buddhism and Christianity*, p. 162.

their own. It may seem as natural to a Hindu to see illness as the result of bad *karma* from a past life as it does to a Christian to see it as a God-given chance to 'suffer with Jesus', but both would probably be willing to admit that their interpretation of events arose from a prior belief in certain doctrines rather than from any intrinsic features of their experiences of illness. This is not to deny that their experiences are *different*; indeed, the course of their illness may vary considerably because of the attitude they take towards it. But such experiences can only provide evidence for religious doctrines within a cumulative argument, where the weight of evidence from many different sources may favour one interpretation over the other, or show both interpretations (or neither) to be valid in some sense.

(ii) Alleged conflict among quasi-sensory experiences apparently of lesser supernatural beings can be dealt with along the lines suggested by Swinburne, above (see also the discussion in Chapter VI.4). Traditions which accept the existence of any supernatural beings below God can generally accommodate a wide variety of such beings, and where a being is described in a way which conflicts with another tradition's doctrines—experiences of "the risen Christ" conflict with the Jewish and Muslim stance against incarnation, for instance, and Hindu experiences of Krishna as the incarnation of God conflict with the Christian doctrine of unique incarnation—the issue becomes one of conflict with 'background beliefs' rather than with experiences. Where those background beliefs are very well supported, they may constitute a defeater to an experiential claim. As Chapter V showed, however, most beliefs which are a source of *widespread* conflict with religious experiences are highly controversial, and so do not provide an effective challenge.

The one type of experience with which all visions of supernatural beings conflict is the purported mystical revelation of the 'unreality' of *all* entities—but then, most types of religious experience conflict with that one; it will be dealt with below.

As was pointed out in Chapter II.3, a great many quasi-sensory religious experiences are not taken by their subjects to represent an actual external state of affairs, but they are nevertheless believed to be 'pictures' sent by a divine source and thus to be a reliable source of religious insight, when correctly interpreted. Julian of Norwich's vision of the 'allegory' of the Lord and his servant was one such,[8] but even experiences apparently of supernatural beings can be of this type: a vision of Shiva might be taken only as a reminder that God has fearful and awe-inspiring aspects as well as loving ones, while a vision of the Virgin Mary might be taken as a reminder of the reverse. These quasi-sensory experiences would not then conflict in themselves, though they could give rise to conflicting retrospective interpretations.

There are, however, other types of quasi-sensory experience—usually 'voices'—which present themselves as direct revelations from the divine and for which little, if any, retrospective interpretation is required. Many of these 'revelations' are about personal matters and so generally do not conflict: instructions to become a missionary, found a convent, or 'take up and read' are only a source of conflict if they are taken to imply that the subject's tradition is therefore the one true faith or if the course of action conflicts with someone else's allegedly divinely ordained course of action, an occurrence one does not often come across. More troublesome are those alleged revelations regarding religious truths, such as the nature of the afterlife, and rules of behaviour supposedly binding on all men, such as food laws. How can one reconcile Peter's vision of a sheet full of animals and a voice saying, "Rise, Peter; kill and eat. . . . What God has cleansed, you must not call common",[9] with the Lord telling Moses and Aaron that those same animals are "unclean",[10] if both are supposed to be pronouncements of one unchanging God?

One very plausible solution is provided by David Brown's model of revelation as a 'dialogue' in which "God progressively unveils the truth about himself and his purposes" according to the recipients' intellectual capabilities and culture.[11] Since God values human free will highly and since too fundamental a challenge to the subject's presuppostions or too confusing a communication might lead the subject to reject his experience altogether, God does not impose fully-fledged, word-perfect revelations of knowledge and morality on people. Conflict among quasi-sensory revelatory

---

[8] See Ch. II.3.

[9] Acts 10: 13, 15.

[10] Leviticus 11.

[11] Brown, ch. 2; see also the suggestion in Swinburne, p. 273 n., though this is highly anthropomorphic. For a more traditional explanation of the fact that some of God's laws are not binding for all time or for all men, but were designed for specific situations, see Irenaeus, *Adversus Haereses*, Book 4, chs. xv and xvi.

experiences does not tend therefore to show that those experiences are generally illusory or even misperceptions of God's message, though it does prevent us from taking purported revelations as absolute, unrevisable truth. The principles behind this solution are widely accepted by non-fundamentalists, but the somewhat anthropomorphic and interventionist characteristics which it pre-supposes of God can make it look suspiciously *ad hoc*. Further evidence is required to show that God does interact with humans in this way, and a non-naïve account of that interaction must be spelled out. Since the need for "non-crude interventionism" is discussed in Chapter VIII, I will not discuss the issue further at this point.

(iii) 'Flashes of insight' which are not part of a quasi-sensory revelation or of a mystical experience very often deal with personal matters; like voices which offer personal guidance, these 'revela-tions' should not generally conflict. Insights of more universal import are, as we saw earlier, largely treated as unreliable sources of knowledge, guilty until proven innocent, as are 'intuitions' in the secular realm. Conflict is therefore of little consequence to their general evidential force, since they only have such force within a cumulative argument. The more serious conflict among mystical pronouncements on ultimate reality is discussed below.

(iv) Auto-descriptions of regenerative experiences are very diverse, but they do not usually conflict unless they involve conversion to a particular creed, describe the regenerative effect in a highly ramified way, or attribute the effect to a source characterized in a highly ramified way. In such cases, the beliefs involved in the maximal auto-description may be defended, or else a 'moderated' auto-description may be given which leaves out the more highly ramified aspects of the experience while preserving its evidential force under the moderated description. Regenerative experiences which involve the sense of a nonhuman 'presence' are intrinsically religious and as such are included in the discussion of numinous and mystical experiences below.

3. CONFLICT AMONG NUMINOUS AND MYSTICAL EXPERIENCES

How can 'ultimate reality' be both a personal being and an impersonal principle, identical to our inmost self and forever 'other', loving and utterly indifferent, good and amoral, knowable and unknowable, a plenitude and 'emptiness'? Is our *summum bonum* a dynamic, passionate communion with a holy power or a static, tranquil state of undifferentiated unity? Is the world around us a temporary prison of suffering, ignorance, and imperfection or a basically good participant in God's glorious reality?

Scholars and mystics have attempted many different resolutions of these 'mystical paradoxes'. One rather brazen approach, that of W. T. Stace, simply accepts the conflict as irreducible: "the paradoxes . . . are in fact incapable of rational solution"; mysticism "is simply nonlogical".[12] But inherently contradictory experiences are poor evidence for the existence of their alleged object; one would need to be convinced of its existence on other grounds before accepting such unorthodox experiences as veridical in the first place. In the secular realm, for instance, light is a familiar and common public object of experience, and so when scientists tell us they have perceived it behaving as a wave in one experiment and as a particle in another, and that those are mutually exclusive categories, we accept the paradox, and hope that one day our understanding will advance so that it is resolved. But conflict among mystical experiences cannot be so readily accepted: 'God' is not similarly universally perceived by all normal human beings and recognized as one and the same phenomenon, and there is no general faith that if a mystical paradox seems intractable now, a solution will be found in the future.[13]

The claim that mystical experiences are irreducibly paradoxical can be made to look more respectable by bringing in the argument that such experiences conform to a *different* logic which transcends our everyday 'common or garden variety' (though Stace rejects such a move as a "bogus solution"; mystical experiences conform to *no* logic for him). Otto writes at one point of

the peculiar logic of mysticism which discounts the two fundamental laws of natural logic, the laws of contradiction and excluded middle. As non-Euclidean geometry sets aside the axiom of parallels, so mystical logic disregards these two axioms; and thence the "coincidentia oppositorum," the "identity of opposites," and the "dialectic conception" arise.[14]

[12] Stace, pp. 264 and 268.

[13] I owe the 'light' example to R. W. Hepburn, *Christianity and Paradox* (London: Watts, 1966), ch. II.

[14] Rudolf Otto, *Mysticism East and West*, tr. B. L. Bracey and R. C. Payne (London: Macmillan, 1932), p. 45.

Could it be that the normal laws of logic are based on our narrow experience of a world divided up into discrete packages of spatio-temporal properties and personal identities, according to which a thing cannot be both *a* and non-*a*, in the same respects and sense of *a*, and that a mystical experience which saw a fundamental unity in all that diversity would transcend that limited logical system? Perhaps: but, unlike non-Euclidean geometry, this higher, mystical logic has yet to be developed and to be shown to work (though some (non-mystical) systems have now been developed which reject the law of excluded middle). Since we can as yet make no sense of logical contradictions, and since, as we shall see below, alternative solutions are proposed by mystics themselves, we should seek an understanding of mystical utterances which does not treat them as straightforwardly self-contradictory or contradictory in conjunction.

In many Eastern religious traditions, there has evolved a theory of two levels of truth which neatly disposes of religious conflict. According to the strictest interpretation (Shankara's Advaita Vedanta), experiences of a God with personal attributes (*saguna-Brahman*) belong to the lower level of truth, which is perfectly adequate for everyday life. From the transcendent point of view, however, there is only one undifferentiated reality (*nirguna-Brahman*), and the personal Brahman is seen to belong to the realm of illusion. But this theory cannot help an argument from religious experience, for it is really only another version of the narrow one-true-religion approach: it treats all experiences other than the realization of identity with the undifferentiated Brahman as ultimately illusory. (More liberal interpretations of the saguna–nirguna-Brahman theory will be discussed below.)

One widely accepted approach to mystical conflict is based on the assumption that 'experiences' never conflict; only doctrines and interpretations do. Usually a 'common core' of the experiences is given, a sort of 'perennial philosophy' left behind when the conflicting 'interpretations' are strained out.

This position is plausible, but in the form in which it is often presented it suffers several defects. Firstly, it assumes that highly ramified auto-descriptions are always the result of retrospective interpretation. Chapter VI showed, however, how the subject's 'set' can interact with the stimuli to produce an interpretation incorporated into the experience itself, so that even highly ramified auto-descriptions may reflect the way things appeared to the subject to be at the time. 'Experiences' can and do conflict.

Secondly, it is a disguised version of the one-true-religion approach, since it regards any deviations from the perennial philosophy as misinterpretations of the core experience. Stace even goes so far as to suggest that many of these misinterpretations are due to ecclesiastical pressure[15]—Eckhart and al-Ghazali *would* have been pantheistic (the true religion) if they had been allowed to be— but his theory lacks empirical support. Much evidence would be needed to show that the minimally ramified doctrines of a true 'common core' were the only true doctrines, for if they are, then a great many experiences must be considered misperceptions under their maximal auto-descriptions. Moreover, as was pointed out in Chapter VI, the true significance of an experience can be missed as much by under-interpretation as by over-interpretation.

Thirdly, most purported 'perennial philosophies' are not true common cores, since they tend to be distilled from mystical experiences only (disregarding numinous experiences), and they often appear to have been biased by the proponent's own beliefs (e.g. Stace's pantheism).

This approach should not be totally rejected, however, since it can be reworked into a much more subtle, complex, and empirically grounded attempt to resolve experiential conflict. Though the argument for this approach will inevitably be somewhat programmatic—we cannot go into the empirical evidence in anywhere near enough detail here—it should suffice to show that the following conclusions are plausible:

(i) There are four basic types of numinous and mystical experience which cannot be reduced to 'the same type of experience with differing interpretations'.

(ii) Most alleged conflict among introvertive mystical experiences is superficial.

(iii) All four types of experience can be found in each major religious tradition, though with differing frequency and interpretations; the major religions have thus developed theories to reconcile the apparently incompatible experiences and integrate them in one system, though not all these theories preserve the veridicality of all four types of experience.

---

[15] See Stace, p. 114.

(iv) Taking into account different sets, different theories of integrating numinous and mystical experiences, the role of models and metaphors in the expression of religious experiences, and the importance of evaluating auto-descriptions within the context of the subject's life and understanding, we will see that (a) it is possible to reconcile many numinous and mystical experiences at a high level of ramification, but only by theories which themselves require support beyond the experiences, so that cumulative arguments are needed; and (b) at a very low degree of ramification, it is possible to distill a 'common core', for which most numinous and mystical experiences are direct evidence.

It should be noted that I am not attempting here to argue for a 'universal religion' or to claim that there are no fundamental conflicts among the doctrines of different traditions. One must know something of a tradition's doctrines in order to understand its experiences, but doctrines involve much more than experiential reports. Though a comparison of doctrinal systems would be illuminating, it is far beyond the scope of this book.[16] The object here is to see if the alleged conflict among *experiences* is such that no coherent account of a unitary divine percept is possible. The fact that we will uncover a "common core" of experiential claims (not to be equated with a 'universal religion') shows that the challenge of experiential conflict can be overcome.

4. IRREDUCIBLE TYPES OF NUMINOUS AND MYSTICAL EXPERIENCE

It is true that even where an interpretation has been incorporated into an experience, it is often possible to distinguish it from other features of the experience. One may be able to show that it was due to the subject's set rather than to any intrinsic feature of the stimuli, or identify the influence of highly ramified beliefs on an experience which might have been given a more moderated description by a less knowledgeable subject. A secular example[17] would be the case of two men who give identical moderated auto-descriptions of their experiences, viz. "I see a hat of such-and-such a description",

[16] Some very useful comparisons of religious traditions are W. L. King, *Buddhism and Christianity*; Rudolf Otto, *Mysticism East and West*; and the books by Ninian Smart cited in the bibliography.
[17] From Wainwright, *Mysticism*, pp. 108–10.

but who give conflicting maximal auto-descriptions, viz. "I see Jack's hat" and "I see Tom's hat": the conflict is easily seen to be a conflict in background beliefs only, and the experiences are still evidence for there being a hat there. A similar case in the mystical realm would be an experience which both a Christian and a Buddhist describe in a relatively unramified way as a sense of blissful, total freedom and a transcendence of all the cares and limitations of ordinary existence: the conflict arising out of the Buddhist's more highly ramified description of his experience as a liberation from the cycle of rebirth can be put down to 'background beliefs'. Highly ramified incorporated interpretations may also be recognized to be due to a *model* of the divine, often one embedded in the subject's culture. Experiences of God as lover, mother, or king, for instance, do not conflict, for the subjects realize these are all supposed to be models of the same divine reality. Where interpretations which can thus be ascribed to background beliefs (etc.) clearly conflict, and moderated auto-descriptions are available, the experiences are still evidence for any religious claims entailed by the moderated auto-description. Which, if any, are veridical under their maximal auto-description, must be decided by other types of evidence. An outline of the way these other types of evidence can work together with religious experience to support highly ramified interpretations is provided in the final chapter.

Not all numinous and mystical experiences can be 'reduced' to the same type of experience, however, or even to experiences which are clearly consistent. As Katz says, "There is no intelligible way that anyone can legitimately argue that a 'no-self' experience of 'empty' calm is the same experience as the experience of intense, loving, intimate relationship between two substantial selves."[18] Many mystics distinguish between different types of experience which they have had themselves—St Teresa describes both dualistic loving intimacy with God and a union with God in which all sense of duality is lost, for instance.[19] There are, moreover, a substantial number of cases of auto-descriptions at odds with the received tradition. The theistic auto-descriptions of Ramanuja in the Hindu Vedantist tradition, the monistic auto-descriptions of Meister Eckhart and al-Hallaj from theistic traditions, and even

[18] S. T. Katz, "Language, Epistemology, and Mysticism" in Katz (ed.), pp. 39–40.

[19] Though the former predominates. See p. 180 for an example of the latter.

St Teresa's report of a sense of the real presence of God in all things when all those around her said he was "there only by grace"[20] are unlikely to be products of background beliefs as opposed to reflections of intrinsic features of the experiences. A preliminary study[21] of the mysticism of Advaita Vedanta (monistic Hinduism), Ramanuja's theistic 'qualified non-dualist' Hinduism, Zen and Theravada Buddhism, 'cosmic consciousness' and 'nature mysticism', Sufism, Spanish, German, English medieval, and Eastern Orthodox Christianity, and some contemporary experiences suggests four basic types of numinous and mystical experience which cannot be reduced to 'the same experience under different interpretations' without rendering some of them almost completely illusory: (i) experiences of an awesome 'numen'; (ii) experiences of a loving (etc.) relationship with a personal 'other'; (iii) extrovertive mystical experiences of unity in multiplicity; and (iv) introvertive mystical experiences of unity devoid of all multiplicity. There are many subtle variations within each category, many ways of expressing the experiences, and, as always, many borderline cases.

In section 6 we will discuss ways of showing these irreducible types of experience to be compatible, for it is not immediately obvious that they are. It is largely because there are such different ways of experiencing what is alleged to be one reality that we must contend with those highly paradoxical descriptions of "ultimate reality" given at the beginning of section 3. Moreover, many versions of Hinduism and Buddhism see only the last type of experience as veridical, and relegate the others to the realm of illusion (as seen from the position of enlightenment). Before we attempt to reconcile all four types of experience, however, we must take a closer look at the experiences of category (iv), for even "unity" can be described in apparently conflicting ways.

5. CONFLICT AMONG INTROVERTIVE MYSTICAL EXPERIENCES

The introduction to mystical experience in Chapter II described three types of introvertive mystical experience: the attainment of

---

[20] *Life*, pp. 110–11; and see also Ch. VI.4, above.

[21] This would be an enormous programme of research, done thoroughly. Some idea of the soundness and scope of my 'preliminary study' can be gained from the bibliography, though sources such as conversations and lectures are not listed.

internal unity (including Buddhist 'emptiness'), the realization of identity with the Absolute, and union with God, not amounting to identity. A closer look at the reports in question would show that mystics generally admit that little interpretation is possible *during* such an experience, and so most auto-descriptions are reflexive interpretations. Now, reflexive interpretations are covered by the principle of credulity, and there seems to be no reason to think that mystical experiences described merely as a profound stilling, emptying, or unifying of the mind, with no further metaphysical entailments, are not just that. Real difficulties arise, however, with experiences of apparent union with an eternally distinct 'Other', literal identity with God, and transcendence of the "illusory" notion of God, which look as if they cannot all be veridical under their maximal auto-descriptions.

This section will attempt to show that a less superficial reading of those auto-descriptions, drawing on the teachings of mystics and theologians themselves, yields experiences which are not in such conflict after all. We will see that mystics very probably have the same sort of experience, viz. freedom from all sense of time, space, personal identity, and multiplicity, which leaves them with a blissful, 'naked awareness' of perfect unity and a sense that 'this is it', the ultimate level of reality. During the experience, the lack of duality is so complete that there is no sense of a distinct 'other' with whom they are united or of a separate 'self' which is isolated from other things. On emerging from the experience, however, they reflexively interpret it, usually in accordance with their doctrinal set, as 'union with God', 'isolation of the eternal self', 'liberation from *samsara*', and so on. Previous experiences can also play a role: if the mystic previously experienced senses of a numinous presence before which he almost felt annihilated, or slipped into this blissful 'oneness' from an experience of loving intimacy, then it would be natural for him to interpret his mystical experience as some kind of union with an 'other', whereas a mystic without these experiences and from a monistic tradition would rarely reflexively interpret his experiences in dualist terms. Further differences emerge in the struggle to verbalize the experiences—'via negativa' models versus 'via positiva' models, subtle doctrinal ramifications, and much more. The experiences themselves can also vary in many ways. All traditions allow for different stages along "the mystic way" and would accept a wide variation in quality and depth, from a beginner's brief experience of 'pure consciousness' to the supreme experiences of the great mystics. The experiences are also coloured by the subjects' beliefs, personality, culture, and training, making the bliss passionate love or deep tranquillity, the unity more 'dazzling' or more 'dark', and so on. The experience a Theravada Buddhist calls 'nirvana' would be very different on that score from the experience a Christian calls 'spiritual marriage'. But the crucial similarities among mystical auto-descriptions make it probable that conflict can be ascribed to sources other than the experiences themselves.

It is not possible in the space available here to present adequate empirical evidence for the above claims; readers are invited to read the mystics for themselves. It is hoped that the illustrations and arguments which follow, in addition to the examples presented in Chapter II.7, will show that the claims are at least very plausible.

Chapter V listed several reasons for believing that auto-descriptions which include the claim to literal identity with God or Brahman ought to be revised. I shall say no more here about the facts that the subjects do not exhibit the divine attributes one would expect if they were literally God and that there are severe difficulties with the doctrine that there is one God with whom we are all literally identical (difficulties which are often pointed out by members of monistic traditions themselves), but shall give grounds for believing that those who utter such auto-descriptions do not always themselves wish them to be taken literally.

Subjects from theistic traditions may express their experiences in terms of literal identity because, as was mentioned above, there is no sense of a distinct 'other' during the experience, the subject–object distinction disappears, and they are aware of what seems to be undifferentiated unity. In their more sober moments they may revise their impulsive, reflexive interpretation and give an auto-description in terms of union rather than identity. Consider, for instance, this passage from the Sufi mystic al-Ghazali:

The mystics, after their ascent to the heavens of Reality, agree that they saw nothing in existence except God the One. Some of them attained this state through discursive reasoning, others reached it by savouring it and experiencing it. From these all plurality entirely fell away. They were drowned in pure solitude: their reason was lost in it, and they became as if dazed in it. They no longer had the capacity to recollect aught but God, nor could they in any wise remember themselves. Nothing was left to them but God. They became drunk with a drunkenness in which their reason collapsed. One of them [Hallaj] said, "I am God (the Truth)." Another [Abu Yazid] said, "Glory be to me! How great is my glory" . . . But the words of lovers when in a state of drunkenness must be hidden away and not broadcast. However, when their drunkenness abates and the sovereignty of their reason is restored . . . they know that this was not actual identity, but that it resembled identity as when lovers say at the height of their passion:

> "I am he whom I desire and he whom I desire is I;
> We are two souls inhabiting one body."

. . . This condition is metaphorically called identity with reference to the man who is immersed in it, but in the language of truth (it is called) union.[22]

It is not only these passionate, unorthodox Sufis who report theistic experiences which are phenomenologically monistic; many Christians report similar experiences without thereby claiming to be identical with God. Meister Eckhart, for instance, is well known for such 'shocking' statements as:

There was never union so close; for the soul is far more closely united with God than are the body and soul that form one man. This union is far closer than if one were to pour a drop of water into a cask of wine; there, we still have water and wine, but here we have such a changing into one that there is no creature who can find the distinction.[23]

Even St Teresa of Avila, of unimpeachable orthodoxy and generally much more inclined to use dualistic models of marriage than monistic models of absorption, writes of the highest state of union with God:

But here it is like rain falling from the heavens into a river or a spring; there is nothing but water there and it is impossible to divide or separate the water belonging to the river from that which fell from the heavens.[24]

This is strikingly similar to the passage from the *Katha Upanishad* which states that

---

[22] From *Mishkāt al-Anwār*, quoted (and tr.) by Zaehner, pp. 157–8. A similar translation can be found in *Al-Ghazzālī's Mishkāt al-Anwār* ("The Niche for Lights"), tr. W. H. T. Gairdner (London: Royal Asiatic Soc., 1924), pp. 60–1 (Arabic text pp. 19–20).

[23] *Counsels on Discernment* 20, tr. Colledge, p. 272.

[24] *Interior Castle*, p. 214. This passage was also quoted above, Chapter II.7.

as pure water raining on pure water becomes one and the same, so becomes . . . the soul of the sage who knows.[25]

Several models and distinctions are available which allow Christian mystics to reconcile their experiences of undifferentiated unity with the alleged eternal gulf between creature and creator. The sense of union can be expressed as a oneness of 'spirit' (supported by St Paul's "he who is united to the Lord becomes one spirit with him"[26]), which is then contrasted with illicit forms of union such as oneness of nature or substance. Bernard of Clairvaux writes, for instance:

God is present in a man in such a way . . . that he infuses or rather is infused and partaken of; this occurs in such a way that someone need not fear to say that God is one spirit with our spirit, even if he is not one person or one substance with us.[27]

Others may use the complex mystical doctrine of 'deification',[28] which can be spelled out in many ways: with the model of a 'divine spark' already in the deepest part of the soul and rediscovered by the mystic, the models of 'the birth of Christ in the soul' and of 'the indwelling of the Holy Spirit', and the model of the progressive transformation of the soul in imitation of Christ, ending with a perfect union of wills.

Hindu mystics can appeal to very similar doctrines to explain the experiences they so often express as literal identity with Brahman. Eric Lott's careful study of Vedantin systems shows that even in Shankara's strictly monistic system, the person who discovers his 'identity' with Brahman does not claim that his everyday, empirical self has become a creator-god but that his true, inner self, "the transcendent consciousness underlying individuality",[29] partakes of that eternal, divine nature, the 'ground of being'—a picture very similar to that of the 'divine spark', above. Rudolf Otto also reports that Shankara's equation of Brahman with Atman (the self) does not mean strict identity, but rather something more like "I am

---

[25] *Katha Upanishad* 4.15, tr. Mascaró.

[26] 1 Cor. 6: 17.

[27] *De consideratione* V. v. 12, from John D. Anderson and Elizabeth T. Kennan, trs., *Five Books on Consideration* (Cistercian Fathers Series No. 37, Kalamazoo: Cistercian Publications, 1976), pp. 153–4.

[28] For a comprehensive account of deification, see W. R. Inge, *Christian Mysticism* (London: Methuen, 1912), Appendix C.

[29] Eric Lott, *Vedantic Approaches to God* (London: Macmillan, 1980), p. 39.

'essenced' by Brahman" or "Brahman exists me".[30] There are, moreover, theistic interpretations of apparent statements of identity in Hindu scriptures. Ramanuja interprets the refrain, "He is the Self; That Thou art", for instance, in accordance with the many references to Brahman as the 'inner controller'.[31] For him it epitomizes the following analogical relationship: as the finite self is to the body, so Brahman is to the universe; and Brahman is the Self of each finite being (like the 'divine spark' of deification) as well as the controlling Self of the universe.[32]

A sensitive reading of those troublesome Buddhist experiences of the 'emptiness' of everything, including God, shows that this apparent source of conflict, too, can largely be eliminated. (i) The concept of 'God' which Buddhists say they have transcended is very probably the highly anthropomorphic 'Lord' of their meditation exercises. Even Christian mystics would say such a concept is imperfect and should not be considered 'ultimate reality'.

(ii) Buddhists do not say the world is illusory, just transient and imperfect. The only 'illusion' is that what we take to be permanent entities (and to which we therefore grow attached) are really only a continuous series of processes—a view very much in line with contemporary physics. Even theists often talk of the world as 'unreal' in comparison with the 'true reality' of their numinous and mystical experiences. The only tradition which describes the world as literally illusory, as in a dream, is Shankara's Advaita Vedanta—and that appears to be an intellectual doctrine rather than a datum of experience.

(iii) Despite their 'no-self' doctrine, most Buddhists claim to attain some sort of 'true self' in nirvana; the loss of personal identity is not literal 'emptiness', in spite of the use of the word. The Zen Buddhist Suzuki wrote that

The denial of *Atman* as maintained by earlier Buddhists refers to *Atman* as the relative ego and not to the absolute ego, the ego after enlightenment-experience.[33]

and a Theravada monk of the 'Dhammakaya' school explained that nirvana is not dispassionate emptiness or extinction (for who would want such a state? "Why be a stone?") but everything the

---

[30] Otto, *Mysticism East and West*, p. 85.
[31] See the *Brihadaranyaka Upanishad*.
[32] See Lott, ch. 4.
[33] D. T. Suzuki, *Mysticism Christian and Buddhist* (London: Unwin, 1979), p. 33.

world of "impermanence, suffering and not-self" is not—a permanent, blissful true self.[34] Though this self cannot be described, ("it is beyond all words"), and though metaphysical questions about the state of this self in nirvana are to be avoided (they are distractions on the path to enlightenment), it is very real indeed.

One must be wary of importing Western, non-mystical conceptions into Buddhist doctrines. Nirvana, for instance, is often compared by Buddhists to the extinction of a flame. But it is not extinction in the Western sense:

the ancient Indians did not believe that a flame was ever either absolutely lit or absolutely extinguished. They thought that quiescent fire, a kind of essential fire, was present practically everywhere, but especially in inflammable substances. A flame when lit was simply fire become visible, and when extinguished, become invisible again. It is therefore plausible to suppose that an extinguished self was not, in the Buddhists' imagination, absolutely destroyed, but remained in some inexpressibly quiescent state.[35]

We should also remember here the extent to which all other mystical traditions speak of a 'loss of self'. Mystics agree that in the mystical experience (and in many numinous experiences as well), it is not only self-centred thoughts and desires which disappear, but one's whole sense of ordinary personal identity. Whether this is described as 'dying to oneself', 'total surrender to God', 'losing oneself in the Absolute', or 'successful detachment from all transient ideas of self', the salient feature of the experience seems to be the same: the loss of ordinary ego-consciousness and of all sense of oneself as a separate personality with clearly defined boundaries. But the similarities run even deeper than this: many theistic comments on 'denying oneself' are almost identical to the Buddhist teaching that one must sever all attachment to and utterly transcend the notion of 'I' to achieve nirvana. The author of *The Cloud of Unknowing* writes, for instance, that

you will find that when all other things and activities have been forgotten . . . there still remains between you and God the stark awareness of your own existence. And this awareness, too, must go, before you experience contemplation in its perfection.[36]

---

[34] Mettānando Bhikkhu, in conversation.
[35] Ben-Ami Scharfstein, *Mystical Experience* (Baltimore: Penguin Books, 1973), pp. 14–15; see also Happold, p. 79.
[36] Ch. 43, tr. Wolters, p. 111.

The injunction to "wipe off the dust of selfhood from thy soul"[37] is echoed by Attar in the rich and lyrical style so typical of the Sufi mystics:

If thou dost desire to reach this abode of immortality, and to attain this exalted station, divest thyself first of self, and then summon unto thyself a winged steed out of nothingness, to bear thee aloft. Clothe thyself with the garment of nothingness and drink the cup of annihilation. Cover thy breast with a nothingness, and draw over thy head the robe of non-existence. . . .[38]

Several other examples of "no-self" experiences are cited in Chapter II.7.

(iv) As in other mystical traditions, the Buddhist language of negation is employed towards a positive end:

Beneath the negations of Buddhism, especially its negation of the self . . . there is a nonnegated Something in whose positive interests the not-self is negated.[39]

Buddhists strenuously maintain that their experiential reports and teachings are *not* nihilistic (as is commonly assumed), but rather the highest affirmation, beyond all petty affirmations which can be expressed in words. It is here that we must recall the discussion of 'critical realism' of Chapter I, and the conclusion that it is possible by means of models and metaphors to refer to spiritual realities even if they are ultimately indescribable in literal terms. Many mystics, such as Ramanuja and St Teresa, developed positive models of the divine, while stressing the superiority of ultimate reality to even our most exalted notions of majesty or goodness. These 'via positiva' mystics usually experienced a 'mysticism of love', an indescribably intimate relationship with a holy, loving "other". Other mystics, perhaps more austere and intellectual, preferred the path of negation, the "desert" and the "darkness"; they regarded all positive models as grossly inadequate and likely to mislead. Their negations and contradictions are nevertheless models of a sort, always striving to refer to something beyond the reach of human language. In the Upanishads we read, for instance, that the Atman is "soundless, touchless, formless, imperishable . . . without

[37] From a Sufi poet, quoted by Happold, p. 98.
[38] In Happold p. 258.
[39] King, p. 193.

beginning, without end . . .",[40] and ultimately "not this, not that (*neti, neti*)";[41] but the negations should be taken to imply not just *other* than but *more* than, for it is also written:

That which is the finest essence—this whole world has that as its soul. That is Reality. That is Atman [soul, self]. That art thou. (*tat tvam asi*)[42]

Dionysius the pseudo-Areopagite, a major proponent of the Christian 'via negativa' tradition, has a similar 'not this, not that' passage (also quoted in Chapter I):

[The ultimate Reality] is not soul, or mind . . . nor can It be described by the reason or perceived by the understanding, since It is not number, or order, or greatness, or littleness . . . It is not immoveable nor in motion, or at rest . . . nor does It belong to the category of non-existence or to that of existence . . . nor can any affirmation or negation apply to IT. . . inasmuch as It transcends all affirmation by being the perfect and unique Cause of all things, and transcends all negation by the pre-eminence of Its simple and absolute nature—free from every limitation and beyond them all.[43]

The *Cloud* author, too, writes:

Let go this 'everywhere' and this 'everything' in exchange for this 'nowhere' and this 'nothing'. Never mind if you cannot fathom this nothing, for I love it surely so much the better. It is so worthwhile in itself that no thinking about it will do it justice. . . . Who is it then who is calling it 'nothing'? Our outer self, to be sure, not our inner. Our inner self calls it 'All' . . .[44]

And from Meister Eckhart (as always, abundantly cited in cross-cultural mystical studies):

You should love [God] as he is One not-God, One not-spirit, One not-person, One not-image, but as he is a pure, unmixed, bright "One," separated from all duality; and in that One we should eternally sink down, out of "something" into "nothing".[45]

Negative the language may be, but it conceals a supremely positive purpose.

---

[40] *Katha Upanishad* 3.15, tr. R. E. Hume, p. 353.
[41] Throughout the *Brihadaranyaka Upanishad*.
[42] *Chandogya Upanishad* 6.10.3 and many other places in that Upanishad; tr. Hume. See also the discussion by Lott, ch. 3.
[43] *The Mystical Theology*, ch. v, tr. Rolt.
[44] Tr. Wolters, pp. 142–3.
[45] Sermon 83, tr. Colledge, p. 208.

It may be objected that the foregoing arguments are based on superficial linguistic similarities. Just as the cry "Fire!" can mean something completely different, depending on whether one is standing in front of a burning house or a firing squad, so, it is argued, 'nothingness' can mean the Yogin undifferentiated, empty, calm consciousness, the inexpressibly rich "dazzling darkness" of the Christian, or other 'ultimate realities', depending on the context. But though context is extremely important to the understanding of auto-descriptions, in this sort of case it seems more likely that mystics chose a word such as 'nothingness' because in its primary, everyday meaning it was the most apt description of their experience, and the doctrinal ramifications came afterwards.

There is, moreover, non-linguistic evidence that introvertive mystical experiences from different traditions probably share important features. The meditation techniques which lead to such introvertive experiences all tend to focus the mind inward and to empty it of mundane thoughts and ordinary self-consciousness. In some cases the actual techniques are almost identical: the 'Jesus Prayer' of Eastern Orthodox mysticism, for instance, functions like a Hindu 'mantra', a sacred word or sound repeated silently during meditation. One would expect such similar techniques to give rise to similar experiences.

6. THE RECONCILIATION OF THE NUMINOUS AND THE MYSTICAL

Most traditions have developed some kind of synthesis of the very different experiences of internal undifferentiated unity, extrovertive mystical experiences, and experiences of numinous and loving (etc.) presences. Strictly atheistic and some monistic systems relegate the last type of experience to the realm of illusion, however; and so our first task must be to show that there is no good reason to reject such experiences (ignoring reductionist arguments, for the moment).

Fortunately for theists, there are good grounds for accepting the 'theistic' experiences of numinous and other presences. (i) It is certainly *possible* to account for both numinous and mystical experiences within a single, coherent system, as this section will show. (ii) Though mystics from non-theistic traditions do not tend to have theistic experiences, this does not in itself entail that such experiences are illusory; usually they are rejected by such mystics on doctrinal grounds alone, and since those doctrines are too controversial to count as 'background knowledge' (I have yet to see a demonstration of their overwhelming probability, at any rate), the challenge is not effective. (iii) Mystics who have had both experiences of undifferentiated unity and theistic types of experience do not generally regard their theistic experiences as illusory. (iv) Even Buddhists[46] claim to have found something eternal, perfect, and real during their experiences. They would not want to call this 'God', but the possibility is there. (v) The Hindu scriptures become progressively more theistic. In fact, the strict monist Shankara had great difficulty fitting the *Bhagavad Gita*, a relatively late work, into his system, and his interpretations are often very strained.[47] (vi) As Parrinder notes throughout his book, monism at the popular level usually has theistic elements; and even Shankara's followers tend to be theists in practice.

The synthesis favoured by most Hindus involves a distinction between saguna-Brahman, Brahman the personal creator-God, worshipped and loved, and nirguna-Brahman, the transcendent, unknowable, formless goal of mystical experience. For Shankara only the nirguna-Brahman was truly real, but the more liberal version of this theory sees the two as complementary aspects of the one Brahman, or the former as a sort of emanation from the latter. Thus the *Mundaka Upanishad* can say of Brahman, "Far, far away is he, and yet he is very near, resting in the inmost chamber of the heart."[48] Worshippers can have a personal relationship with the saguna-Brahman, mystics can discover the fundamentally unitary nirguna-Brahman behind the multiplicity of the world and in their deepest, purest self: it is all one.

There are many striking similarities between this and the Christian syntheses of Meister Eckhart and the Greek Fathers. Eckhart distinguished the formless Godhead (*deitas*) from God the Father (*deus*): though the Trinity is a real product of the Godhead, and love of and devotion to the Father and Son are essential, the divine 'spark' in the soul (like the *Atman*, our divine true self,

---

[46] Except possibly some Theravada Buddhists from Sri Lanka; but they are a minority within Buddhism, and there is no way I could deal with every variation of the major traditions in this work.

[47] See Parrinder, p. 38.

[48] *Mundaka Upanishad* 3.1.7, tr. Mascaró, p. 80.

waiting to be discovered) seeks union with "the hidden God, in the ground of the soul, where God's ground and the soul's ground are one ground";[49] "it wants to go . . . into the quiet desert, into which distinction never gazed, not the Father, nor the Son, nor the Holy Spirit"[50] (like the formless *Brahman*). The Greek fathers reconciled experiences of God as immanent and transcendent, indwelling and object of worship, through doctrines of deification (Dionysius' theory of the gradual divinization (*theosis*) of man[51] has parallels in Brahman–Atman identity) and the distinction between the energies (*dunameis*) of God, through which God is present throughout creation, and in which we can participate, and the essence (*ousia*) of God, God in himself, transcendent, unknowable, the 'dazzling darkness' of the mystic quest. This could also be expressed as the distinction between God in his love and humanity, especially as revealed in the incarnation, and the unknowable God in his greatness and glory.

R. C. Zaehner proposed a Christian synthesis which allowed monistic and nature mysticism spiritual worth, but only as preliminary stages of a spiritual journey culminating in love of God.[52] His first stage, 'personal integration', is a re-entry into undifferentiated consciousness and the integration of the conscious and the unconscious in the wholeness of a unified personality: successful nature mystics can advance this far. The second stage is the isolation of the immortal soul and complete detachment from worldly things: this is the monist's resting place. To stop here is dangerous, however, Zaehner claims, since it leaves the soul empty and purified, ready for an invasion by the proverbial seven devils, incursions from the unconscious. One must proceed with God's grace to the third stage, theistic union, and fill the purified soul with love for and of God.

Zaehner's solution is similar to one from a very different theistic tradition, Ramanuja's 'qualified non-dualist' Hinduism. For Ramanuja, experiences of unity are a real release from karma and the attainment of a kind of deification, but true salvation comes with the recognition of the Lord's majesty and love, for "the isolated self does not share in the joy of basking in the glory of the

---

[49] Sermon 15, tr. Colledge, p. 42.
[50] Sermon 48, tr. Colledge, p. 198.
[51] See Parrinder pp. 10 and 147.
[52] In *Mysticism Sacred and Profane.*

Lord".[53] The key to the scriptures for Ramanuja is the *Bhagavad Gita* passage, "And now again give ear to this my highest Word, of all the most mysterious: 'I love you well'";[54] as with Zaehner, theistic love is placed above monistic liberation.

Unlike the previous authors, Evelyn Underhill and Ninian Smart both provide syntheses which do not exalt one type of experience above the rest.[55] Underhill draws a contrast between the person of artistic or poetic temperament who in awe and rapture discovers the immanent God (e.g. St Teresa), and the austere metaphysician who turns from the created order to find the formless, transcendent ground of being (e.g. Eckhart); in Christianity, she says, we have an excellent home for both, since the doctrine of the Trinity shows that the indwelling spirit, the personal mediator, and the transcendent Absolute are complementary parts of a whole. It is clear that personality can make a great difference to religious style and expression, even at less 'mystical' levels. One individual may prefer a highly emotional religious service with music, rituals, and passionate oratory, while another prefers a rather calm service with an emphasis on information and exhortation; a religion which does not embrace both styles will not appeal to all people, whatever its doctrines. It should not be surprising, then, that if there is one God who manifests himself or relates to us in different ways, mystics of different temperaments should have perceived different aspects of his activity and nature.

Smart agrees that a religion must incorporate both the numinous and mystical 'strands' if it is to have universal appeal, and illustrates the difficulty of keeping any one-strand religion pure with the examples of Sufism in Islam (an explosion of unitive experience within a religion stressing the gulf between man and God) and Pure Land Buddhism (in which one attains salvation by worshipping Amida Buddha). Like Underhill, Smart believes Christianity provides an excellent synthesis, but he also provides non-doctrinal

[53] Ninian Smart, *Doctrine and Argument in Indian Philosophy* (London: Allen & Unwin, 1964), p. 113; see also the expositions of Ramanuja's theology in Lott, *Vedantic Approaches to God*, and in Parrinder, pp. 97–8.

[54] *Bhagavad Gita* 18: 64, tr. R. C. Zaehner (London: OUP, 1969), p. 108.

[55] Underhill, *Mysticism*, ch. 5; and Ninian Smart, *Reasons and Faiths* (London: Routledge & Kegan Paul, 1958), chs. III and V. Further arguments for regarding Christianity as the best synthesis of the two apprehensions of the divine, as immanent 'true self' and utterly transcendent 'other', can be found in Happold, chs. 22–4.

grounds for identifying the One of mysticism with the numen who is worshipped and loved: having supreme value as an object of worship is closely linked to having supreme salvation (or libera-tion) value; both are experienced as eternal, uncompounded, indescribable in literal terms, and 'truly real', far above this derivative and transient world; and experiences of both generate self-naughting attitudes. Which type of experience one has, which aspect of the divine one perceives, may be linked both to personality and to cultural and doctrinal background, since different religions emphasize different 'strands'. But the latter is not a strictly determining influence (one only needs to look at some of the mystical examples above to see how uncorrelated with the received tradition experiences can be), and Smart believes the strands reflect truly different types of experience:

It is easier to explain a dualism between God and the soul by reference to the experience of prophets and worshippers than to explain the latter by reference to a current doctrine of dualism. It is easier to see that the Lord who is worshipped is also the God of metaphysics than to see why the God of metaphysics should be worshipped at all.[56]

7. A 'COMMON CORE'

The experiences themselves do not favour any one of the above syntheses over the others. Numinous and mystical experiences do not unambiguously support such highly ramified doctrines as the identity of the true self with Brahman or the activities of the three persons of the Trinity in the world and the soul; for these, cumulative arguments incorporating other types of evidence are required (see Chapter IX). The experiences do support several relatively unramified but very important doctrines, however, and the fact that they can be woven into a consistent synthesis, whatever its further doctrinal ramifications, turns these relatively unramified propositions into the sort of 'common core' the perennial philosophers were seeking above.

A survey of many different numinous and mystical experiences shows that they can provide good evidence on their own for the following claims:

[56] *Doctrine and Argument*, p. 144.

(i) The mundane world of physical bodies, physical processes, and narrow centres of consciousness is not the whole or ultimate reality.

(ii) In particular, the phenomenal ego of everyday consciousness, which most people tend to regard as their 'self', is by no means the deepest level of the self; there is a far deeper 'true self' which in some way depends on and participates in the ultimate reality.

(iii) Whatever *is* the ultimate reality is holy, eternal, and of supreme value; it can appear to be more truly real than all else, since everything else depends on it.

(iv) This holy power can be experienced as an awesome, loving, pardoning, guiding (etc.) presence with whom individuals can have a personal relationship, to whom they are profoundly attracted, and on whom they feel utterly dependent; it may be described positively in terms of goodness, wisdom, and so forth, but all such descriptions are ultimately inadequate.

(v) Though introvertive mystical experiences cannot in themselves show that union with something else has been attained, since only the unity is experienced, the evidence of numinous experiences and the fact that experiences of awe before the numen and love of the numen can easily slip into mystical experiences when all sense of self has been annihilated make it probable that at least some mystical experiences are experiences of a very intimate union with the holy power, however that is spelled out. (Other mystical experiences may nevertheless be no more than the integration or purification of the meditator's mind.)

(vi) Some kind of union or harmonious relation with the ultimate reality is the human being's *summum bonum*, his final liberation or salvation, and the means by which he discovers his 'true self' or 'true home'.

The above claims constitute what might be called 'broad theism'. In practice, few people are such 'broad theists'; they adhere to systems of a much higher degree of ramification. We have shown that the conflicting claims challenge cannot defeat the experiential evidence for fundamental theistic claims of a low degree of ramification, but for the finer points of most actual religions, further evidence will be required where there is conflict. Some maximal auto-descriptions will then have to be rejected; others will be accepted; many will be forever controversial. We would do well to remember the ancient analogy of the six blind men describing an elephant; we are like blind men groping after an elusive and many-faceted reality, and perhaps we should be more surprised at the amount of agreement there is in religious matters than at any disagreements we find.

8

THE REDUCTIONIST CHALLENGE

Perhaps the most popular current challenge to religious experience is the 'reductionist' challenge: "Nowadays we know that science can explain all that." But can the secular disciplines actually explain all religious experiences, and does that constitute 'explaining them away'?

It is true that no putatively reductionist accounts of religious experience can *disprove* theism. No matter what subject-related challenges sceptics produce and how plausible their rival explanations are, since 'God moves in mysterious ways', it is always *possible* that he brought the experience about and was a real percept to the subject. One can only show conclusively that a religious experience was not veridical by showing that God does not exist.

An argument from religious experience requires more than the mere possibility that God is the ultimate cause of such experiences, however, since the reductionist challenge can be presented in two powerful forms which allow the possibility that religious experiences might be veridical but rob them of any evidential force. (i) The first is a correction of subject-related challenges which appeal to such 'pathological' explanations of religious experience as hyper-suggestibility and abnormal physiological states. The operation of such factors has been shown in non-religious cases to increase the likelihood of unveridical perceptual experiences; and in conjunction with certain sets, these factors can make it highly probable that the subject will have certain perceptual experiences, whether or not the apparent percept is actually present. Even theists are often reluctant to give support to religious experiences in which pathological factors have played a part. Experiences produced by such factors cannot provide good evidence on their own for the alleged percept, and neither the possibility that God reveals himself more to the psychologically unstable and to those who have been 'opened up' by drugs, nor the fact that God, if he exists, is indirectly the cause of *all* occurrences can turn these experiences into good evidence on their own.

(ii) The second version of the reductionist challenge is a cumulative challenge: those religious experiences which cannot be explained by reference to pathological factors can nevertheless be explained by reference to nonpathological processes such as the labelling of states of arousal in accordance with a belief set, and further evidence, it is claimed, shows such nonpathological naturalistic explanations to be better than any explanations involving religious factors. Though religious experiences are not abnormal or unhealthy, then, they allegedly provide no more evidence for theism than non-religious experiences do. The strength of such nonpathological reductionist accounts will be debated in section 3, and the "further evidence" discussed briefly in section 4.

It can be seen that the causes of religious experience are much more relevant to an argument from religious experience than the origins of religious beliefs are to the question of the probability of those beliefs. One may arrive at a belief through non-truth-related processes such as peer pressure or wish-fulfilment, but later discover good truth-related grounds for the belief.[1] A reductionist account of belief can only show at the most that one should not infer the truth of a belief from the fact that people hold it; such an account is irrelevant to the question of the belief's probability. The corresponding 'fruits, not roots' approach to religious experience is not so successful, however, since the way an experience is caused and its veridicality are inextricably linked. An argument from religious experience cannot be built on experiences which have therapeutic value but no evidential force; and to say that "all experiences are ultimately caused by God" only preserves the evidential force of religious experiences if they play a very minor role in a cumulative case, as will be shown in section 3. Naturalistic accounts of religious experience must therefore be taken very seriously.

---

[1] L. Scott Frazier describes such a process in his D.Phil. thesis, "The Psychodynamics of Religion" (Oxford, 1978).

2. PATHOLOGICAL EXPLANATIONS OF RELIGIOUS EXPERIENCE

If religious experiences can be shown to be the product of factors which are normally associated with misperceptions and nonperceptions, then whatever other factors may be involved, they cannot be regarded as generally reliable sources of knowledge. Their role as evidence will then be very small indeed, reduced to an inferior element in a cumulative case whose other elements provide copious evidence for the existence of God and for his propensity to reveal himself through normally untrustworthy processes. As we shall see in this section, however, the empirical evidence for the widespread operation of such pathological factors in religious experience is far from conclusive, and the psychological research dealing with such factors is plagued by empirical and conceptual problems. There are four main groups of explanation which must be considered 'pathological': (i) hypersuggestibility, (ii) deprivation and maladjustment, (iii) mental illness, and (iv) abnormal physiological states.

Before we look at the empirical evidence for these pathological reductionist challenges, a general caution about that evidence must be stated. Most psychological studies have been concerned with the correlates of 'religiosity',[2] seeking to establish a psychological profile of 'the religious person'. But to what extent are "religious people" and "subjects of religious experiences" co-extensive?

In the first place, religiosity itself is not a simple, easily measured characteristic. A great deal hinges on the way experimenters pick out the class of 'religious' people. For instance, if a questionnaire implicitly distinguishes between 'religious' and 'non-religious' people on the basis of belief in the literal truth of the Bible, then the correlations obtained may be valid for Christian fundamentalists, but not for religious people in general. It has been found that fundamentalism correlates highly with authoritarianism, and so if one's criteria of religiosity pick out only fundamentalists, one may proclaim that "religious people are highly authoritarian", and mislead all those who have not read the experimental report. Similarly, if one picks out the religious according to church membership or church attendance, one will include the large

---

[2] It should be remembered that I am using the term "religiosity" in its neutral, psychological sense.

number of people who attend church or claim affiliation for non-religious reasons such as social status and conformity. Since studies have consistently shown that the majority of churchgoers are of this 'extrinsically oriented' type (as opposed to the 'intrinsically oriented' 'genuinely devout'; the distinction was originally made by Gordon Allport, and has since been refined[3]), studies using this measure of religiosity are biased against the 'genuinely devout'. This has been taken to explain, for instance, the surprising correlation which was found between 'religiosity' and racial prejudice before more refined measures were introduced; people concerned with social status and conformity tend to be the most prejudiced. Even the measurement of religiosity according to beliefs is risky, since some people who consider themselves 'highly religious' do not hold orthodox beliefs. Subjects with what Batson and Ventis call a 'quest' orientation to religion,[4] who are open-minded and critical but for whom the 'spiritual side of life' is very important, usually get lost somewhere in the 'non-religious' category of psychological studies. It is being suggested with increasing vehemence that this 'quest' orientation is the missing factor that would destroy all the 'traditional' correlations between religiosity and authoritarianism, prejudice, suggestibility, and so on.

Another factor which ought to be taken into account (but rarely is) in any study on the correlations of 'religiosity' is the fact that 'being religious' has different connotations in different cultures. The difference between Great Britain and the United States alone is striking: Argyle and Beit-Hallahmi report that the many reliable surveys carried out between 1962 and 1970 showed that Americans were more 'religious' than the British on every measure of religiosity and that religiosity correlated positively with socio-economic status in Britain but negatively in the USA.[5] They

---

[3] See the selections from Gordon Allport and from R. O. Allen and B. Spilka in L. B. Brown (ed.), *Psychology and Religion* (Harmondsworth: Penguin Education, 1973). It should be noted that an 'extrinsic' orientation is not necessarily hypocritical; it includes people who go to church because they feel it is their moral and patriotic duty, and those who go for the social fellowship it provides.

[4] Their very useful discussion of "ways of being religious" is found in C. Daniel Batson and W. Larry Ventis, *The Religious Experience: A Social-Psychological Perspective* (New York: OUP, 1982), ch. 5.

[5] Michael Argyle and Benjamin Beit-Hallahmi, *The Social Psychology of Religion* (London: Routledge & Kegan Paul, 1975), chs. 2 and 11. The higher religiosity of Americans was also found by Hay and Morisy (see n. 11, below).

explain these differences not by appealing to any truly greater religiosity on the part of Americans (particularly working-class ones), but primarily by social factors: in the United States, the working class is composed largely of immigrants from very religious ethnic backgrounds; and at all levels, the American church has become 'internally secularized', so that membership is often a matter of social conformity and respectability, giving the member social status, security, ethnic identity, and political clout. In Britain, on the other hand, there is a strong socialist movement in the working class which is against religion, and the church itself has retained its religious character while society has become more secularized. Moreover, within the United States, differences between black and white religiosity have been observed: one study showed that religiosity correlated much more positively with well-being for blacks than for whites, *with socio-economic factors controlled.*[6] This may be due to the fact that religious meetings were the only regular community gatherings the black slaves were allowed, so that the church came to serve much more important social functions for the black community than for the white.[7] The differences discussed so far have all obtained within a relatively homogeneous Western culture, and so one must wonder which psychological and sociological correlates would be found in vastly different cultures such as India and China. How many of the psychologists' conclusions would still hold true, for instance, in a society which truly believed in a cycle of rebirth, which regarded the life of a wandering holy man as the highest ideal, in which most religious rituals were carried out in the home, or in which visions were encouraged and taken seriously? Since nearly all studies in the psychology of religion have been carried out in the West on Christian (or Judaeo-Christian) populations, their validity is very limited. Until more cross-cultural data are available, it is surely premature for psychologists to talk of the characteristics of the 'religious' person.[8]

Even if we confine ourselves to the 'Western' scope of the

[6] Arthur St George and Patrick McNamara, "Religion, Race and Psychological Well-Being", *J. Sc. Stud. Rel.*, 23 (1984), 351–63.

[7] See the discussion in Batson and Ventis, ch. 2.

[8] One noted Western psychologist/sociologist of religion, B. Beit-Hallahmi, is properly pessimistic about the ability of scholars to provide "a psychological profile of the religious person". See his article, "Psychology of Religion—What Do We Know?" *Archiv für Religionspsychologie*, 14 (1980), 228–36.

available studies, is there any reason to think that the correlations found with 'religiosity' also apply to subjects of religious experience as a class? I have found only two sources which shed light on this question. Ralph Hood has carried out many studies which show that the intrinsically religious[9] are significantly more likely to have undergone religious experiences than the extrinsically religious.[10] This is good news for subjects of religious experiences, for in those studies which make the distinction, intrinsically oriented persons generally come out much more favourably than the extrinsically oriented. However, a great many subjects of religious experiences are not 'religious' at all according to the criteria used in psychological studies. In a study comparing trends in reports of religious experiences in Great Britain and the United States, David Hay and Ann Morisy[11] found that in Britain, 45 per cent of those reporting religious experiences never attended church apart from 'rites of passage' such as marriage, and almost 25 per cent of those calling themselves "agnostic", "atheist", or "don't know" reported the "awareness of a presence or power"; and while the Americans were three times as likely to say they were 'religious' (see the discussion above), the positive response rate for experiences was very similar. It is true that 56 per cent of the British who attended church regularly reported religious experiences, and that 75 per cent of those who said the 'spiritual side of life' was very important to them reported religious experiences, but it is clear nevertheless that studies into the correlates of 'religiosity' tend to miss out a substantial proportion of subjects of religious experience, and to include many who have not had such experiences.

The philosopher investigating religious experience is thus faced with a dilemma: either ignore the vast majority of research in the psychology of religion, and dismiss pathological challenges to religious experience on grounds of insufficient data (which probably would not satisfy proponents of the reductionist challenge), or enter the fray more or less on the psychologist's terms, regarding the research into 'religiosity' as indirectly applicable to the majority

---

[9] See above for a brief explanation of 'intrinsic' and 'extrinsic' religious orientations.

[10] A list of these can be found in his article, "The Construction and Preliminary Validation of a Measure of Reported Mystical Experience", *J. Sc. Stud. Rel.*, 14 (1975), 29–41.

[11] "Reports of Ecstatic, Paranormal, or Religious Experience in Great Britain and the United States—A Comparison of Trends", *J. Sc. Stud. Rel.*, 17 (1978), 255–68.

of subjects of religious experience, though with certain limitations (e.g. the 'extrinsically' religious are probably much less representative of subjects of religious experience than are the 'intrinsically' religious), and paying special attention to any research which does deal directly with religious experience. I have opted for the latter course, since it is more likely to prove effective in quelling reductionist challenges. Bearing in mind the limitations of this evidence, then (both for and against the case for religion), let us see how far it supports pathological explanations of religious experience.

2.1 Hypersuggestibility

It has been claimed that religious experiences are the product of something akin to hypnotic suggestion, either self-induced or brought on by external factors. As such, they would simply conform to the hypnotic suggestion, whatever the real nature of the world might be, and so would provide little evidence for theism. There is some support for this view, as the following points make clear; but further considerations will show that the evidence falls far short of linking most religious experiences to hypersuggestibility.

(i) Gibbons and De Jarnette conclude their study with the claim that

The present data support the conclusion that the existential phenomena which comprise the experience of conversion and salvation—and, by extension, perhaps other types of transcendental experiences—are in reality "hypnotic" phenomena, which occur without a formal induction in response to implicit or explicit suggestions conveyed by the speaker, the setting, or the attendant ceremony.[12]

Their study found that of 49 students at a college in the American "Bible Belt", chosen for very high or very low hypnotic susceptibility, those with very high susceptibility were significantly more likely than those with very low susceptibility to say they had been 'saved'; and while the 'saved' members of the former group had without exception undergone profound experiences with "perceptual, affective, and ideomotor responses" (e.g. "warm tingling glow"), the unsusceptible 'saved' students all emphasized

---

[12] Don E. Gibbons and James De Jarnette, "Hypnotic Susceptibility and Religious Experience", *J. Sc. Stud. Rel.*, 11 (1972), 152–6.

the cognitive, moral, or social aspects of their rather unemotional conversions.

(ii) It is well known that brainwashing techniques are used at many revival and sect meetings. Hypersuggestibility can be induced through emotional and physical arousal and exhaustion, which can be brought on by prolonged singing and dancing, those fire-and-brimstone sermons laced with emotional propaganda and oratorical devices which arouse anxiety and guilt, and stressful activities such as the handling of poisonous snakes.[13] In such a state, subjects are particularly likely to respond to suggestions which offer relief from their extreme tension (such as suggestions to accept Jesus Christ and to be filled with the Holy Spirit) and to follow others in activities such as public commitment displays and the speaking in tongues.

(iii) Research into the correlation between religiosity and suggestibility has yielded the following tentative results: religious people may be higher in 'primary' (psychomotor) suggestibility (e.g. they respond better to placebos, exhibit hysterical symptoms at revival meetings) and in 'prestige' or 'social' suggestibility (e.g. they change their opinion more readily in accordance with social influence), though they have not been found to be higher in 'secondary' suggestibility (they do not tend to 'perceive' or 'recall' things suggested by another in a complex or ambiguous situation).[14] Sceptics would argue that it is 'primary' suggestibility which lies at the back of most religious experiences (and that it is 'prestige' suggestibility which lies at the back of most religious beliefs).

(iv) Some meditation techniques, such as prolonged staring at a coloured disc, bear marked similarities to techniques used to induce hypnotic states.

The sceptic has, therefore, a *prima facie* case, but there are further points to consider.

(a) The Gibbons and De Jarnette study was confined to the experience of being 'saved' during meetings at which 'salvation sermons' were preached. What kind of 'hypnotic phenomenon' is

---

[13] See William Sargant, *Battle for the Mind* (London: Heinemann, 1957); and R. H. Thouless, *An Introduction to the Psychology of Religion*, 3rd edn. (Cambridge: CUP, 1971), ch. 4.

[14] See the discussions in Argyle and Beit-Hallahmi, ch. 6, and Geoffrey Scobie, *Psychology of Religion* (London: Batsford, 1975), ch. 7.

occurring when no such agent of suggestion is apparent? One would be making an unwarranted extrapolation if one argued that because some highly suggestible individuals have religious experiences under conditions which clearly suggest those experiences, the experiences of individuals who are not particularly suggestible under conditions which do not appear to suggest a religious response (or that particular religious response) must also be due to hypnotic suggestion. Until further 'hard evidence' is found to connect religious experiences of all types with hypnotic suggestion, the majority of religious experiences must be considered innocent; for an explanation involving hidden, postulated factors can only defeat a perceptual claim if there are very good reasons to believe in those factors generally and to believe they are operating in a specific case. (This is an important point, and it is developed further in sections 3 and 4.)

(b) The tentative correlation between religiosity and primary suggestibility also fails to constitute a strong defeater: most of the studies were carried out before the notion of 'religiosity' had become more differentiated; the links found between religiosity and suggestibility were not very strong; and where religious *experiences* were studied, they were limited to conversion experiences. Even if one assumed that all the 'religious' people who had had religious experiences were highly suggestible (meaning that the rest of the 'religious' people would have to be relatively unsuggestible), one would also have to assume that 'non-religious' subjects of religious experience were highly suggestible and that religious experiences occurred in situations which in some way suggested the experience. So many assumptions do not make a viable defeater.

(c) A study by Basil Douglas-Smith, though generally poorly designed, did find that of 249 subjects of mystical experiences, only 38 could clearly be suspected of hypersuggestibility.[15] Of these, nine were subjects who responded affirmatively to the question whether they were able to undergo a mystical experience at will. The other 29 failed the 'glow-card' suggestibility test: all subjects were sent a card with a small spot of printer's ink on it, and were asked to report the time elapsed before they saw the spot glow in pitch darkness. Though the spot could not actually glow in the

[15] *The Mystics Come to Harley Street* (London: Regency Press, 1983).

dark, the subjects did not know this; they must have thought it was a test of night vision. Only 29 managed to "see" the spot glow, and they were then eliminated from Douglas-Smith's study on grounds of suspected hypersuggestibility.

(d) Suggestibility can be heightened in practically anyone by the techniques used at revival meetings, and there is good reason to think many experiences occurring under such conditions are due to a form of hypnotic suggestion, particularly since such experiences tend not to have long-term effects. These experiences can therefore play only a minor role in an argument from religious experience. However, most religious experiences do not occur under such suspicious circumstances.

(e) The experiences discussed in Chapter VI.4—childhood experiences of a divine presence not connected with the 'Sunday School God', and certain adult experiences—provide counter-examples to the charge that religious experiences are a form of auto-suggestion, with the subjects experiencing just what their strong beliefs lead them to expect. It is also relevant that certain categories of paranormal experience—particularly 'near-death' experiences, which are often religious—have been shown not to depend on the subject's prior beliefs. Tyrrell reports that expectancy often seems to have an inhibiting rather than an encouraging effect on the seeing of apparitions;[16] and in Michael Sabom's study of near-death experiences, it was found that people who had heard of such experiences before their crisis event or who were regular churchgoers were no more likely to have them than people who had not heard of these experiences, did not attend church, or were agnostics.[17]

(f) Any vigorously preached ideology is bound to have a large proportion of suggestible adherents. Political movements are similar to religious ones in this respect. The correlation may therefore not be with religiosity in so far as it is religious, but with religiosity in so far as it is a product of normal social dynamics. One must always be wary of taking statistical correlations to indicate causal relationships, in any direction.

(g) Hypnosis is still a very poorly understood phenomenon. It is sometimes even treated as a reliable means of uncovering infor-

---

[16] Tyrrell, ch. v.
[17] Michael Sabom, *Recollections of Death: A Medical Investigation* (Corgi Books, 1982); see pp. 84, 180–1, 216–17, 228–30, and 264.

mation—for instance, when it is used to dredge up repressed memories. A correlation between hypnotic susceptibility and religious experience may not show that religious experiences are the product of suggestion but may rather, as Hood suggests, "be indicative of an ability to become aware of 'wider' or 'deeper' aspects of reality of which hypnosis is only another indicator".[18]

The challenge of hypersuggestibility overcomes the *prima facie* evidential force of some religious experiences, then, but certainly not of all. We will soon see that this conclusion is true of most pathological reductionist challenges.

2.2 Deprivation and Maladjustment

If it can be shown that religious experiences occur only to those who are severely deprived, frustrated, anxious, or under stress, then it might seem that such experiences are operating as a self-generated palliative or defence mechanism. Like hypnotically suggested experiences, then, religious experiences might be veridical, but could provide little evidence for their apparent percepts, since they would be brought about by epistemically unreliable mechanisms and would have occurred in just the same way, whether or not their apparent percepts were there. The following discussion will show, however, that this challenge has insufficient empirical suppport.

(i) *Deprivation.* Many studies in America have shown that people who could be classed as 'deprived' in some way—the elderly, women, the uneducated, the poor, the rural, and blacks—are more religious than more privileged people. The evidence is not clear-cut, however, and it would certainly be hasty to conclude either that religion functions as "the opium of the people" or that religious experiences are psychological defence mechanisms, for the following reasons:

(a) In Britain, while correlations for the elderly and women are similar to the American findings, socio-economic status correlates positively with religiosity. This was explained above, and shows that factors other than the need for 'compensatory' religious beliefs may lie behind the American correlations. Moreover, when religious *experience* was studied, it was found to be positively

---

[18] Ralph Hood, "Hypnotic Susceptibility and Reported Religious Experience", *Psychological Reports*, 33 (1973), 549–50.

correlated with social class and education in both Britain and the United States.[19]

(b) Women are more religious than men for a variety of reasons, many of which have nothing to do with their 'deprived' status (e.g. they are more conforming; church may be more important to them socially). But, again, the correlation seems to decrease when one focuses on religious experience. Many studies have found that in spite of women's greater religiosity, men report almost as many (and in some studies more) religious experiences as women.[20]

(c) It is true that American blacks tend to report more religious experiences than American whites, but the different functions of the black church (see above) and its generally more emotional style of worship could help account for this.[21] One must also remember that in the study which showed that religiosity was much more highly correlated with personal wellbeing for blacks than for whites, socio-economic status was controlled; it was not that blacks turned to religion because they were deprived of worldly goods or status.[22]

(ii) *Sexual frustration*. This has been a common theme in reductionist accounts of religious experience, particularly of adolescent conversion and mystical experiences. Three theories must be considered here:

(a) Adolescent conversion is often regarded as a means of resolving the guilt feelings and stress which result from the emerging sexual urges. In support of this, sudden conversion experiences in adolescence have been found to be associated with guilt feelings, neuroticism, and anxiety.[23] But many factors are at work here. Adolescent conversion experiences are frequently associated with fundamentalist training, and many occur during revival-type meetings. The problems associated with adolescence—insecurity, the desire to be 'in' in some group, emotional instability—make the subjects even more susceptible to peer pressure, suggestion, and anxiety arousal. Many adolescent conversion experiences therefore have little evidential force. Others do

[19] Hay and Morisy.
[20] See Hay and Morisy, pp. 262–3; Douglas-Smith; and Michael Carroll, "Visions of the Virgin Mary: The Effect of Family Structures on Marian Apparitions", *J. Sc. Stud. Rel.*, 22 (1983), 205–21.
[21] See Batson and Ventis, ch. 2.
[22] St. George and McNamara.
[23] See Argyle and Beit-Hallahmi, chs. 4 and 8.

not succumb to these challenges, however; and the mere fact that they occur during the turbulent years of adolescence should not disqualify them or brand them as a sexual phenomenon. 'Conversions' of many types occur during this period, since it is a time of heightened interest in values, beliefs, and identity, and of decisions for or against such things as religion and parental values.

(b) The super-ego projection theory, which is derived from Freud, maintains that conflict between the super-ego (the conscience) and the id (instincts) is relieved by a projection mechanism which transforms the super-ego into God and the id into the devil.[24] Thouless hypothesizes, for instance, that the 'diabolical visitations' of the great mystics were the mystics' suppressed natural instincts, particularly the sexual instinct, breaking through and being reified as evil impulses attempting to distract the mystic from his or her single-minded quest for God.[25] Argyle and Beit-Hallahmi report not inconsiderable support for the super-ego projection theory in the general field of religion: sexual activity (i.e. a forbidden instinctual activity) is lower among the devout; a study of eighty primitive societies yielded a high correlation between degree of sexual restriction and development of religion (though there is no indication of the criteria used to measure 'development of religion'); regular churchgoers are less delinquent (though irregular attenders who are church members or orthodox believers are not); for Protestant females there is a correlation between religiosity and guilt feelings; and religion does have "an irrational super-ego quality about it"[26]—the believer tends to have doubts but feels he ought to be more pious; religion makes strong moral demands; authoritarian believers see God as a forbidding, chastising figure; and the conflict between instincts and the super-ego can be found in much religious literature.

That one of religion's functions should be to restrain our instinctual impulses is hardly surprising. Such impulses get in the way of all sorts of 'higher' pursuits and spiritual ideals. Moreover, this is clearly not the only function of religion; and religious experiences are often characterized by such things as love, comfort, and a sense of freedom. But most importantly, no amount of

[24] Ibid. ch. 11.
[25] R. H. Thouless, *The Lady Julian: A Psychological Study* (London: SPCK, 1924), ch. iv.
[26] Argyle and Beit-Hallahmi, p. 189.

empirical testing can decide whether the God-concept operates in some respects as a super-ego because it is merely a projection or because there is something in reality which does relate to us somewhat as a super-ego.[27] If super-ego explanations of religious experience are to be successfully reductionist, they must have the support of the sort of cumulative argument which will be examined in section 4.

(c) Religious experiences are considered by some (particularly by Freudians) to be sublimations of blocked sexual or aggressive impulses which cannot be expressed directly and which reactivate the repressed impulses of the Oedipal period.[28] Indirect empirical evidence for the sexual sublimation theory abounds: in Michael Carroll's study of visions of the Virgin Mary, the vast majority of his fifty cases were sexually mature subjects who apparently lacked regular sexual partners; the elderly, unmarried, and widowed are more religious than younger or married people; the classical saints and mystics had no overt sexual satisfaction; and religious literature contains many erotic images and expressions of tenderness, intimacy, and love.

The theist can reply that alternative explanations are available for the greater religiosity of the elderly, the unmarried, and the widowed; that the imagery of love is only one of many forms of imagery in devotional literature which are considered theologically appropriate and sanctioned by centuries of use; that many subjects of religious experience lead perfectly satisfactory sex lives—saints and mystics are usually special cases, chaste because they refuse to let their attention to higher ideals be diverted by wordly pleasures and cares—and finally, that some mystical traditions (e.g. some forms of Tantrism) actually use sexual intercourse as a mystical technique.

Such counter-evidence is unlikely to impress those Freudians who see attempts to disprove their theories merely as further proof of the theist's repressed impulses. Freudian theories thus often appear impossible to test empirically, for they can be stretched to explain any state of affairs (a charge more often levelled against religious beliefs). Carroll's study, however, does not appear so *ad*

---

[27] John Bowker makes this point in *The Sense of God* (Oxford: Clarendon Press, 1973), p. 131.
[28] See especially Carroll, "Visions of the Virgin Mary".

hoc. Unlike many Freudians, he not only gives an explanation of Marian visions in terms of sexual sublimation, but attempts to back up the explanation with empirical data. There are data showing a widespread lack of sexual partners among subjects of visions (mentioned above); facts about Italian family structure which would make visions of the Virgin particularly common among Italian men and women (which they are) if the sexual sublimation theory were true; information about the Spanish Inquisition's attitude to rural miracles which would make Marian visions less likely to be reported there, although the family structure is like the Italian; and statistically significant, though far from perfect, correlations between being male and having a vision devoid of father-figures and being female and having a vision with a father-figure (e.g. the adult Christ, a male saint), as predicted by the Oedipal theory.

Does this mean we must look upon most religious experiences as nothing but the disguised sexual impulses of the sexually frustrated? Far from it. Carroll's study deals with a limited number of one type of quasi-sensory religious experience, all of whose subjects were pre–1896 and were studied at third-hand (from a study by Walsh); his supporting data were far from conclusive; and his explanation rests primarily on a very convoluted theory of male and female Oedipal complexes which is by no means uncontroversial. Some form of sexual sublimation may underlie a large proportion of visions (indeed, some seem to invite this interpretation—St Teresa's vision of the angel who pierced her with a long golden spear and left her moaning and "afire with a great love for God" is an obvious candidate, for instance,[29] though it must be said that she seldom had this type of experience), but it has yet to be shown to be a highly probable explanation of the majority of religious experiences of all types.

(iii) *Defence mechanisms.* Is there any evidence that religious experiences are a defence mechanism conjured up to help people cope with extreme fear of that most intransigent of human problems, death? Many studies have shown that religious people are more likely to have a positive attitude towards death, and that the correlation is especially strong among the intrinsically oriented, the group in which religious subjects of religious experience are

[29] *Life*, pp. 192–3.

concentrated.[30] Sabom found that near-death experiences (many of which were religious) clearly reduced death anxiety.[31] It is not that certain people were excessively afraid of death and then manifested normal attitudes after a religious experience, nor that (except possibly among the extrinsically oriented) religious people denied or masked their real fear of death in order to give their religious beliefs credibility. Religious people had a more positive attitude towards death than non-religious people; and the subjects in Sabom's study showed from their behaviour in the face of death that the reduction in fear was real, which one would not expect if the experiences were merely a palliative or defence mechanism.

(iv) *Regression.* One popular theory about mystical experiences explains them as regressions to a prenatal or infantile state in order to resolve unconscious conflicts—"regression in the service of the ego".[32] The mystic withdraws from life and its attendant stresses, and regresses to a state which gives a sense of unity and loss of self, leads to a sense of 'rebirth', and is psychologically adaptive. This theory implies that people who undergo mystical experiences should have relatively weak ego strength, whereas Hood's 1974 study[33] and a study of Zen Buddhism by Douglas MacPhillamy[34] both show the opposite; in fact, MacPhillamy found that training in a co-educational Zen monastery improved ego strength measures, especially among those who had undergone an enlightenment experience. Moreover, the meditation experiences which one proponent of this theory likens to drug-induced regressions to perinatal states are very different from most mystical experiences, being disruptive and painful.[35] The 'regression' theory is in any

---

[30] See Argyle and Beit-Hallahmi, ch. 11; Thouless, *Introduction*, ch. 8; and John Patrick, "Personal Faith and the Fear of Death Among Divergent Religious Populations", *J. Sc. Stud. Rel.*, 18 (1979), 298–305.

[31] Sabom, pp. 88–9, 172–4, and 285.

[32] See Raymond Prince and C. Savage, "Mystical States and the Concept of Regression"(1965), in John White (ed.), *The Highest State of Consciousness* (Garden City, NY: Doubleday Anchor Books, 1972), pp. 114–34; and Christopher Bache, "On the Emergence of Perinatal Symptoms in Buddhist Meditation", *J. Sc. Stud. Rel.*, 20 (1981), 339–50.

[33] Ralph W. Hood, Jr., "Psychological Strength and the Report of Intense Religious Experience", *J. Sc. Stud. Rel.*, 13 (1974), 65–71.

[34] Douglas J. MacPhillamy, "Some personality effects of long-term Zen monasticism and religious understanding", *J. Sc. Stud. Rel.*, 25 (1986), 304–19. This is one of the few longitudinal studies available on religious experience—i.e. a true 'before-and-after' study.

[35] Bache (see n. 32, above).

case still too much in the speculative stages to constitute an effective pathological challenge. It may well be that, nonpathologically, some of the tranquillity, harmony, and loss of self experienced in mysticism is due to revived memories of life in the womb, but, besides being difficult to prove, this would not show such experiences to be unveridical.

(v) *Maladjustment.* It has been suggested that religious experiences occur to maladjusted, insecure, or anxious subjects with a religious set, as a culturally approved method of escaping from reality and finding solace. Such factors can affect non-religious perception— for instance, anxiety neurotics are better at perceiving 'emotionally negative' material while others tend to 'repress' it;[36] in intense need, we may perceive things according to that need; and insecure people are generally more suggestible. Beardsworth suggests that senses of a presence may be projections of the subject's own feelings and needs, so that the 'other' appears to be comforting, chastising, and so on, as required.[37] But most of the evidence links religious experience with psychological *health*. An exception is the wide support for the correlation of subjects of sudden adolescent conversion and religious college students with emotional insta-bility, inadequacy, guilt feelings, and anxiety.[38] For subjects of religious experience who are not in those narrow classes, however, the following evidence is relevant (in assessing this evidence, it should be remembered that subjects of religious experiences are more likely to be 'intrinsically' religious than 'extrinsically' religious): it is widely reported that the elderly are better adjusted if they are religious; Argyle and Beit-Hallahmi report that regular churchgoers are less likely to commit suicide; Batson and Ventis found that the intrinsic and quest orientations to religion were associated with good mental health while the extrinsic orientation was associated with mental maladjustment; Baker and Gorsuch found that trait anxiety correlated negatively with the intrinsic orientation but positively with the extrinsic;[39] the extensive study by Hay and Morisy showed that people reporting religious

---

[36] Bruner, ch. 1.

[37] Beardsworth, *A Sense of Presence*, chs. 5 and 6.

[38] Batson and Ventis, and many other sources.

[39] Mark Baker and Richard Gorsuch, "Trait Anxiety and Intrinsic-Extrinsic Religiousness", *J. Sc. Stud. Rel.*, 21 (1982), 119–22. The other sources in this paragraph have already been cited.

experiences were significantly more likely to report a high level of psychological wellbeing; and Ralph Hood (1974) found that 'intense religious experiences' (which often involve the loss of the sense of personal identity) are associated with ego strength rather than with the ego weakness predicted by proponents of the theory of regression to infantile ego–states. On the whole, then, it appears that subjects of religious experiences are not psychologically unhealthy.

Hood and others[40] have also discovered that one widely used measure of psychological factors, the "Minnesota Multiphasic Personality Inventory", is strongly biased against religion, since it assumes on a very questionable theoretical basis that religiosity is indicative of ego weakness and maladjustment. A response affirming 'trust in God', for instance, would count against a subject's psychological health. Though MacPhillamy used the MMPI, he was only interested in change in psychological health over time and was happy to use an objective scale which went against his own bias. He noted that any attempt to interpret the absolute MMPI scores of members of religious communities in the standard ways would "result in inaccurate conclusions and in substantial overstatements of pathology". Any study which uses the MMPI to measure the correlation between religiosity and psychological strength is therefore biased against religion from the outset, and must be considered useless. (The dangers of such inadequately controlled psychological research are well known in many other fields, such as education.)

2.3 Mental Illness

Some sceptics have approached the question of psychological explanations of religious experience from the other side, not by pointing out the defects of their subjects, but by pointing out their similarities to experiences known to be 'pathological'. Mackie writes that

Hysteria, delusions, cycles of mania and depression are known and reasonably well understood psychopathic phenomena in innumerable cases where there is no religious component; but experiences which have such

---

[40] Hood (1974); MacPhillamy. MacPhillamy also cites works by J. Dittes and J. McConahay which support this finding.

components, which count as religious *par excellence*, share many features with these pathological ones.[41]

He lists other 'natural' experiences to which religious experiences are similar and then concludes that, as there is no *intrinsic* difference between experiences ascribed to God and those pathological experiences which even theists would want to explain in psychological terms, religious experiences have no force as evidence for religious claims.

If religious experiences are to be explained by the same mechanisms which produce the delusive experiences of the mentally ill, one would expect subjects of religious experiences to share the psychological characteristics of the mentally ill which make those mechanisms operative. But the evidence overwhelmingly supports the view that most subjects of religious experiences, even subjects of those relatively rare, intense mystical states which come closest to psychotic experiences, have no underlying pathology. The previous section showed that subjects of religious experiences cannot generally be accused of psychological maladjustment; here we will deal with more serious accusations. Argyle and Beit-Hallahmi point out that successful religious leaders are more in touch with other people and are more skilful organizers than most psychotics. Great mystics and religious leaders, who because of their "odd" practices and experiences are prime targets for psychopathological accusations, are, as Underhill puts it, "almost always persons of robust intelligence and marked practical or intellectual ability".[42] One would not expect a person suffering from psychotic delusions to have St Augustine's philosophical acumen or his ability to govern the troubled diocese of Hippo, or to have the practical skills of St Teresa in reforming her order and founding convents, of St Catherine of Genoa in administering her hospitals, or of St Catherine of Siena in advising rulers. Of the nine Buddhist monks studied by Carrithers who were living a life of renunciation in the forest, only one was mentally imbalanced, and he failed to complete his training; several were clearly "mentally robust, highly intelligent, and hardy individuals who would not only have been successful but very influential in any field they chose."[43] B. Groeschel writes of St Catherine of Genoa:

[41] J. L. Mackie, *The Miracle of Theism*, p. 180.
[42] Evelyn Underhill, *Mysticism*, p. 59.
[43] Carrithers, ch. 1; quote from p. 16.

Her own doubts about the supernatural origin of her fasts and illnesses, her willingness to listen to others, to be skeptical about the spiritual value of something as dramatic as a forty-day fast, attest to a degree of reality testing inconsistent with any psychotic process. Her ability to relate to antagonistic personalities, including initially her husband's, counterbalances her withdrawal into unusually recollected states. Her ability to rouse herself on a moment's notice for the good of some other person is totally inconsistent with any pathological withdrawal symptoms.[44]

The young visionaries of Medjugorje, Yugoslavia, who have recently come to the world's attention, have been extensively tested by psychologists and pronounced to be "perfectly normal and balanced".[45] The list of psychologically sound and socially active subjects of religious experience is endless.

Despite claims such as Scharfstein's, that "if the writing of admitted mystics and admitted psychotics is compared line by line . . . they will often not be distinguishable",[46] a comparison of psychotic and mystical utterances and experiences exposes crucial differences between the two. These differences are not 'doctrine-bound'; it is not that "genuine" religious experiences are those which agree with Scripture while those which conflict are labelled "pathological", as is sometimes alleged. It may be that some of the differences are due to the supportive, structured environment in which mystical experiences generally occur, but this cannot be the whole explanation: there are spontaneous mystical experiences, and a psychotic experience in a monastery is still psychotic. Marghanita Laski's comparison of "genuine" and drug-induced ecstasies,[47] a study by Bowers and Freedman of those psychotic experiences which are very similar to "healthy" religious experiences in their early stages,[48] Kenneth Wapnick's comparison of the mystic St Teresa of Avila and the schizophrenic Lara Jefferson,[49] and even Scharfstein's study of mysticism[50] all reveal non-theological ways

---

[44] *Catherine of Genoa*, tr. and notes by Serge Hughes, intro. by Benedict J. Groeschel (London: SPCK, 1979; Classics of Western Spirituality), p. 9.

[45] *The Facts About Medjugorje*, pamphlet by Richard Foley.

[46] Scharfstein, *Mystical Experience*, p. 164.

[47] *Ecstasy* (London: Cresset Press, 1961), pp. 263–73.

[48] "'Psychedelic' Experiences in Acute Psychoses" in Tart (ed.).

[49] "Mysticism and Schizophrenia", in R. Woods (ed.), *Understanding Mysticism* (Garden City, NY: Doubleday/Image Books, 1980), pp. 321–37. See also the study of three schizophrenics with 'religious' delusions in Milton Rokeach, *The Three Christs of Ypsilanti: A Psychological Study* (London: Arthur Barker, 1964).

in which psychotic experiences differ markedly from their accepted religious counterparts:

(i) The insights obtained during religious experiences are seen as valuable afterwards, while psychotic revelations are generally regarded by their subjects as nonsense after they have recovered.

(ii) The specifically religious components of pathological and non-pathological convictions often differ. Argyle and Beit-Hallahmi point out that religious leaders tend to develop ideas with a universal appeal which meet the needs of many people besides themselves, unlike the severely limited ideas of psychotics with a religious bent.[51] The 'three Christs of Ypsilanti' often introduced bizarre sexual and science-fiction notions into their religious delusions, for instance,[52] and the psychotic judge, Daniel Paul Schreber, believed he could see rays, or nerve-filaments, which "led from God to his own brain and from there to all other souls, transmitting both voices and poisons".[53] Such ideas are clearly of a different order from mystical insights about such matters as seeking inward peace, to which many people can relate.

(iii) Subjects of religious experiences may feel fear in the sense of awe, but not the panic or feeling of torture which overcomes many subjects of drug-induced and psychotic experiences. Though many psychotic experiences begin with a refreshing, almost ecstatic sense of awakening or heightened awareness which is described in terms identical to those used by many mystics, there is "usually a vague disquieting, progressive sense of dread which may eventually dominate the entire experience".[54]

(iv) The thought disorders characteristic of schizophrenic patients—e.g. the inability to screen out irrelevant stimuli, mentioned in Chapter VI.3—are not associated with religious experiences, even those most similar to psychotic experiences.

(v) Psychotic experiences which bear many similarities to religious experiences very often occur in the context of other psychotic experiences which are far from religious—e.g. secular delusions of grandeur, hallucinations of fantastic objects, fears of extra-terrestrial forces. One of the 'three Christs', for instance,

---

[50] See Scharfstein, chs. 8–10.
[51] Argyle and Beit-Hallahmi, ch. 8.
[52] See Rokeach, chs. IV and XIII.
[53] See Scharfstein, pp. 134–5.   [54] Bowers and Freedman.

believed that the President of the United States was his father,[55] and Schreber believed

that he would be transformed into a woman, and that this would be a preparation for the renewal of mankind, that the weather was 'to a certain extent' dependent on his actions and thoughts, and that he was the human being around which literally everything in the universe turned.[56]

(vi) In psychotic and drug-induced experiences, overwhelming significance is often seen in trivial external details (e.g. Huxley's trouser leg, a stranger's glance) in a way which is very different from the unifying transformation of external things in extrovertive mystical experiences.

(vii) Subjects of psychotic experiences are unable to control their delusions and they are terrified by the sense of loss of control. Mystical experiences are usually sought after, and where there is a sense of loss of control, it is welcomed.

(viii) Scharfstein refers to mystical phenomena such as "the loss of oneself in fusion with other people and things" as "psychotic traits".[57] But though mystical and psychotic experiences of 'depersonalization' sound similar when described in such general terms, an examination of actual auto-descriptions reveals important differences. For instance, where mystics talk of the dissolution of "the ego" or "individuality" (see the examples in Chapters II.7 and VII.5), psychotics talk of the fragmentation or merging of the *body*.[58] A mystic who loses all sense of 'I' in ecstatic union with God does not thereby lose the ability to distinguish his body from his neighbour's; subjects of psychotic and drug-induced experiences are often not so sure. A psychiatrist writes of an experience with LSD, for instance:

At certain times I could not tell where I ended and my physical surroundings began. Nor could I tell whether I was I or whether I was the two other people who were attending me. To find out, I had to explore the contours of my own face, arms, and shoulders, and then theirs.[59]

The mystical and psychotic senses of 'unreality' must also be different; for while psychotics withdraw from a 'dead' world which they may see populated with 'automata',[60] mystics act in the world,

---

[55] Rokeach, ch. XVI.			[58] See the examples, in Scharfstein, p. 137.
[56] Scharfstein, p. 135.			[59] Rokeach, p. 289.
[57] Ibid. pp. 133–4.			[60] See Scharfstein, pp. 137–8.

guiding novices or caring for the sick. The nature mystics' sense of heightened awareness and of profound significance in the world also has a different quality from apparently similar psychotic experiences, for the emotional intensity of the psychotics' experiences and their inability to screen out insignificant details prevent them from relating properly to other people and to their environment.[61] It is as if the mystic remains conscious of the "lower truth" of the material, non-unitary world, can integrate the mystical vision with it, and does not see that vision in physical or bizarre terms, while the psychotic's superficially similar experiences are pathological delusions.

(ix) Most importantly—and related to the previous point— religious experiences are generally "life-enhancing"; psychotic experiences generally are not. Mystics' experiences enable them to free themselves from dependence on or attachment to the material and social world, while psychotic experiences are an escape from a world in which the patient is unable to function.[62] Subjects of religious experiences are able to integrate those experiences into their lives, benefit from them in many ways, and continue to explore the spiritual realms they open up. Psychotic experiences are chaotic, destroy the subject's ability to function as a normal social being, and seldom lead after recovery to a desire to continue exploring the 'inner world' into which the victim was so rudely thrown. As Wapnick notes, "The mystic provides the example of the method whereby the inner and outer may be joined; the schizophrenic, the tragic result when they are separated."[63]

It should also be remembered that religious communities themselves usually distinguish between 'healthy' and 'neurotic' religious experiences.[64] Eastern mysticism abounds with cautionary tales of disciples who "strained too hard" and so were subject to all manner of mental and physical ailment until they pursued a less fanatical course;[65] St Teresa, as was mentioned above

---

[61] The case studies in Bowers and Freedman are good examples of these features of psychotic experiences.

[62] Wapnick, p. 336.

[63] Ibid. p. 337.

[64] See religious criterion (iv) in the comparison of religious experience and sense perception above, Chapter III.3.

[65] See, for instance, Carrithers, ch. 11, for the story of a Buddhist monk who recovered from such "over-exertion" and is now a trusted teacher; and see Scharfstein, pp. 17–19, for the tale of a Zen master.

(Chapter III.3), discounted 'voices' heard by subjects who were "melancholy" or had "feeble imaginations"; the author of *The Cloud of Unknowing* warns in typically exuberant tones of the dangers into which overenthusiastic, vain, or misguided novices may run, when their soul "festers in feigned and fiendish fantasies";[66] and the fanatically religious mother of one of the 'three Christs of Ypsilanti', who was reported to hear voices and was probably psychotic, was admonished by her priest for having "too much religion, not healthy religion. Catholics like strong, healthy religion."[67]

Religious experiences are in any case too common[68] for highly pathological explanations to be plausible as general accounts of the experiences; a society composed largely of hysterics, schizophrenics, and manic depressives would be unlikely to last long. Cultural differences are relevant here, too, as some cultures (e.g. Zulus) and sub-cultures (e.g. sects) encourage and accept experiences which would be regarded as pathological elsewhere, while the subjects of those experiences are well adjusted by all other criteria. These passages from an introductory psychology textbook are illuminating:

Lee (1961), investigating a syndrome of screaming among the Zulu in which the victim might yelp for hours, days or even weeks, found from two large random samples (416 and 200 women respectively), that in each case almost 50 per cent of the sample reported a history of such screaming. Now here we have behaviour that is, by Western standards, grossly abnormal. But among the Zulu women it was as usual to be a screamer as not to exhibit this behaviour. . . . Similarly, in the same investigation it emerged that some 30 per cent of Zulu women suffered visual and auditory hallucinations of 'angels', 'babies', 'little short hairy men', etc. In the West this would be regarded as grossly abnormal. Yet few of these women showed any other signs of mental disorder and, within the limits of their culture, their hallucinations were reasonably legitimate.

. . . in cultures where angels, familiars or other non-material objects are expected to be seen by many people, and this expectation has been fostered in each individual from birth onwards, these are indeed legitimate . . .[69]

[66] See the *Cloud*, chs. 45, 46, and 52.

[67] Rokeach, p. 49. The priest was an immigrant from Europe (as was the mother); hence the somewhat broken English.

[68] In Hay and Morisy's study, over a third of the random national sample reported what could be called religious experiences.

[69] D. S. Wright *et al.*, *Introducing Psychology* (Harmondsworth: Penguin Books, 1970), pp. 543, 560; the reference is to S. G. M. Lee, *Stress and Adaptation* (Leicester: Univ. Press, 1961).

Exactly what the authors mean by "legitimate", it is difficult to be sure, but they almost certainly mean something more like "not maladaptive" or "not pathological" than "veridical". As we saw in Chapter II.3, however, strict veridicality is not usually important to religious visions; they are more often regarded as divinely inspired 'pictures' or as quasi-sensory accompaniments to a religious insight than as perceptions of a quasi-physical being. Unfortunately the authors do not explain how such visions could ever come to be produced in a non-pathological way. Perhaps we should take seriously Tyrrell's suggestion that experiences such as these Zulu hallucinations and visions of saints and angels can be explained in terms of "collective idea-patterns".[70] When a community believes a certain entity to exist, Tyrrell argues, and has a clear picture of its characteristics, the collective idea-pattern thus created can appear in the same way as other apparitions, by an interaction of the subject's own beliefs and perceptual faculties and the "telepathic agency" of others. If the notion of telepathic agency is unpalatable, another suggestion with some support from cognitive psychology might be more acceptable. In societies such as the Zulu, social skills are extremely important—one's whole life is geared towards relationships with one's kin, living and dead, and even causality is seen in personal terms. It has been shown that a "field-dependent" cognitive style (as opposed to the more ana-lytical "field-independent" style extolled in the West) is associated with good interpersonal perception, and so is more adaptive in societies which stress personal relations.[71] Field-dependence may also be associated with suggestibility, and so it could be that well-adapted members of Zulu communities and other close-knit communities such as sects are also the sort of people who would be more prone to hallucinations suggested by deeply ingrained cultural ideas and widely encouraged by the community.[72] This speculative suggestion does not of course show such visions to be veridical, but nothing in my argument rests on their veridicality; I

---

[70] See Tyrrell, especially chs. III, v, and vi.

[71] I owe this information to John Berry, in conversation. See also H. A. Witkin, "Cognitive styles across cultures", in Berry and Dasen (eds.), pp. 99–117; Bolton, ch. 9; Bruner, chs. 1, 9, and 21; Cook, ch. 6; Forgus and Melamed, chs. 15 and 16; and Lloyd, ch. 6.

[72] However, a study by G. Jahoda showed that Ghanaian university students were not more likely to believe traditional superstitions if they were field-dependent; indeed, the older ones were more likely to hold such beliefs if they were field-*independent*. See his "Supernatural Beliefs and Changing Cognitive Structures Among Ghanaian University Students" in Berry and Dasen (eds.), pp. 142–57.

wished merely to show that experiences which appear pathological may not always be so when cultural context is taken into account.

Perhaps there is no *intrinsic* difference between the experiences theists reject as pathological and many they accept, if by 'intrinsic difference' it is meant that subjects must appeal to 'external' defeaters such as lack of fit with background knowledge and with other experiences before they can be sure that the way things seem is not the way things are. But vivid sensory hallucinations in the secular realm are also normally 'intrinsically' indistinguishable from veridical perceptions in this way. No one has suggested that because of this, sense experiences ought to be explained by reducing them all to hallucinations. To insist that the experiences themselves must carry some mark of their veridicality would be to impose far harsher conditions on religious experience than on non-religious perceptual experiences.

2.4 Abnormal Physiological States

The issue of drug-induced religious experiences is highly controversial. It has been argued that experiences induced by such artificial means could not be genuine perceptions of God, that other religious experiences are so similar to drug-induced ones that they must all be products of some (albeit well-concealed) abnormal physiological state, that drugs awaken the dormant 'mystical consciousness' and 'open us up' to realms to which we are normally blind. The evidence, as we shall see, supports all of these claims to some extent, but none of them overwhelmingly.

It should be noted first of all that drug-induced experiences ought not to be considered suspect simply because the subject's mental state has been affected by physical factors. As H. D. Lewis points out, we do not worry when physical factors such as fresh air and a good night's sleep induce mental alertness: "There seems to be nothing in principle against there being specific physical conditions of elevated mental states."[73] The problem, however, is that the physical factors in question usually impair cognitive and perceptual functioning. If drug-induced religious experiences are to retain any evidential force, it must be shown that drugs do not have that effect in the religious case.

---

[73] H. D. Lewis, *Our Experience of God*, p. 168.

There is a great deal of evidence that drugs cannot produce religious experiences on their own, in the way that, say, a blow to the head produces an experience of 'stars'. At the most, it appears they can act as a catalyst, and so it is open to the theist to argue that it was other, nonpathological factors which were crucial to the religious content of the experience. John Bowker informs us, for instance, that drugs do not introduce anything new into the mind or behaviour or affect stored information in a discriminatory and meaningful manner, but can only initiate or inhibit brain activity;[74] and Alister Hardy writes:

> It should not worry us if it is shown that altered states of consciousness may be produced by chemical means; the chemicals themselves do *not* produce the divine ecstasy, but affect the brain in such a way that a rarely accessible region of the sub-conscious mind becomes available to those who already have, perhaps unknown to them, a mystical streak within them.[75]

Hallucinogenic drugs appear to produce a general state of arousal which has no meaning in itself, but is labelled by the subject according to set and perceived setting. Under conditions of sensory deprivation, with no setting and no particular set, it is known that subjects receiving such drugs report none of the usual hallucinatory effects.[76] It thus seems likely that drugs do not produce religious effects on their own, but that they make a subject more prone to religious experiences where set and setting are appropriate. They might divert one's attention from ordinary matters, challenge one's normal patterns of thought and perception, make one feel 'something special' is happening, and intensify experiences so that anything which could have religious significance is elevated to a vivid 'religious experience'.

It is *possible*, then, that in the religious case, drug-induced states do not impair perceptual powers. This possibility also exists in the case of experiences which appear to be intense religious experiences but are associated with psychosis, extreme sensory deprivation (see below), or other abnormal states. Perhaps psychotics sometimes apprehend profound mystical truths—for instance, that there is a deeper level at which we are 'all one'—but because of their

---

[74] Bowker, ch. VII.
[75] Hardy, p. 97.
[76] See Bowker, p. 150.

psychosis and their inability to relate to the world at an ordinary level, this apprehension remains unintegrated, is overladen with delusory elements, and contributes to inappropriate behaviour. Perhaps techniques which impair normal functioning and generate hallucinations also allow brief glimpses of a state which our minds are usually too regimented, too 'outer-directed', to perceive.[77] Such suggestions are merely possibilities at this stage, however, and so they do not carry enough weight to overcome the pathological challenges.

Drug-induced religious experiences might find more support within a cumulative argument, but there are some features of these experiences which could persuade even theists to reject them. The discussion in the previous section showed that, in some respects, typical drug-induced experiences are like psychotic experiences in the way they differ from typical mystical experiences. It is, moreover, clear from the literature that drug-induced mystical experiences are almost always extrovertive rather than the intro- vertive type extolled by most mystical traditions,[78] and there is rarely a sense of personal presence or of union with another being. The use of drugs to induce religious experiences cannot be recommended, partly because of the dangers of drug use, and partly because experiences produced in such a way tend to be regarded as something separate from normal life and so may not become properly integrated into the subject's religious, psycho- logical, and cognitive development.[79] Most importantly, one must wonder how experiences which can be so easily manipulated can be reliable sources of knowledge about an uncontrollable, autono- mous reality. In Pahnke's "Good Friday Experiment", for instance, nine out of the ten seminary students who were given psilocybin and then attended a long religious service reported mystical experiences (a significantly higher rate than the placebo subjects), and the one drugged subject who did not report a mystical experience was highly sceptical of drug-induced experiences and was determined not to have any such experiences while drugged.[80]

---

[77] See Ronald E. Shor, "Hypnosis and the Concept of the Generalized Reality-Orientation", in Tart (ed.), pp. 233–50.

[78] See Wainwright, *Mysticism*, ch. 2.

[79] See the discussion of this point in H. D. Lewis, p. 171.

[80] See Walter Pahnke and Wm. Richards, "Implications of LSD and Experimental Mysticism" in Tart (ed.), pp. 399–428.

It may be that drug-induced experiences of nature mysticism, at least, are veridical, but there is insufficient evidence to overcome this pathological challenge directly; drug-induced religious experiences will have to play their evidential role, if any, in a cumulative argument. Fortunately for this argument, relatively few religious experiences are induced by hallucinogenic drugs.

It might be argued that experiences apparently not induced by drugs are actually drug-induced in a more subtle way, through the release of natural drug-analogues produced by the brain. However, the only natural drug-analogue which might serve this purpose, B-endorphin (which mimics morphine), is primarily a long-term pain-killer which tends to bring on drowsiness rather than anything approaching religious experience.[81]

Religious—especially mystical—experiences do sometimes occur while their subjects are in somewhat abnormal physiological states, produced not by drugs, but by some more 'natural' method such as fasting or breathing exercises. If this fact is to constitute an effective challenge, it must be shown that such states generally cloud judgement and distort perception.

People have been found to hallucinate and to experience feelings of 'oneness' under conditions of sensory deprivation.[82] Most religious experiences cannot be ascribed to sensory deprivation, however; and many which occur under analogous conditions—e.g. during a meditation exercise in which the attention is focused on a word or object to the exclusion of all else—do not involve the hallucinations and unpleasant experiences so common to victims of sensory deprivation. Moreover, sensory deprivation must usually continue for much longer than the average meditation session before such abnormal experiences are reported. Perhaps this helps to account for the fact that those mystical traditions which use techniques closest to sensory deprivation (e.g. some Hindu and Buddhist regimes which require the subject to sit still in isolation for days on end with eyes closed or staring fixedly at some object) are also the traditions in which one finds experiential reports of a more bizarre nature than those typical of Western mystics. As was pointed out in Chapter II.3, however, quasi-sensory hallucinations

---

[81] See Sabom, pp. 234–6. His discussion of possible reductionist accounts of near-death experiences is extremely useful.

[82] Scharfstein, pp. 117–19.

are not very highly valued even in these traditions; the real goal lies beyond them.

Breathing exercises may raise the level of carbon dioxide in the blood, and such an increase has been found to induce hallucinations and euphoria. L. J. Meduna discovered that when subjects were administered carbon dioxide (mixed with oxygen), many reported experiences which could be considered religious, such as "a sense of bodily detachment . . . ineffability, telepathic communion with a religious presence, and feelings of cosmic importance and ecstasy".[83] Other elements of the subjects' experiences, however, were not so religious: there were reports of hallucinations of coloured patterns, animated "musical notes floating by", and other bizarre effects. Again, it is primarily in those mystical traditions which take breathing exercises to extremes that one finds reference to similar non-religious quasi-sensory hallucinations, and such experiences may well be due to carbon dioxide intoxication. But these cases are not typical of most religious experiences. Most breathing exercises simply aid concentration and relaxation without producing such profound physiological changes; breathing exercises do not always bring on religious experiences; and religious experiences the world over occur without the aid of such exercises.

Less is known about the effects of such mystical techniques as fasting and self-torture. Though these techniques may alter the body chemistry, they do not impair normal perception and cognition to the degree that hallucinogenic drugs do, and so do not constitute quite as powerful a challenge. Indeed, in some cultures fasting and a certain degree of asceticism are recommended as *aids* to clear thinking and bodily health.

The less demanding meditation techniques are also beginning to gain credence in the West for their contribution to mental and physical health. Numerous experiments with Zen and Yoga meditators in the East and with practitioners of transcendental meditation and biofeedback techniques in the West have shown that such techniques tend to produce an 'alpha-wave' brain-state, which is reported to be very relaxing and pleasant.[84] Far from being

[83] Reported in Sabom, pp. 241–2; Meduna's study is "The Effect of Carbon Dioxide upon the Functions of the Brain", in *Carbon Dioxide Therapy* (Springfield, Ill.: Charles C. Thomas, 1950).

[84] See Tart (ed.), chs. 33–5.

a hallucination-inducing pathological state which impairs thinking and perception, meditation has been found to confer such benefits as better concentration, increased alertness, and a greater ability to cope with tense situations.[85] Except for drug-induced experiences and experiences related to extreme physiological techniques, then, the challenge that religious experiences are associated with states which impair perception and cognition is not very effective.

Although none of the four types of 'pathological' reductionist challenge has wide application to religious experience, it might be objected that if they were combined, most religious experiences would be defeated by at least one of them, and so the argument from religious experience would fail. The combined challenge is unlikely to have so much force, however. Pathological personality variables tend to be present in clusters (people are often anxious, insecure, *and* hypersuggestible, for instance), and many subjects of religious experience escape all of them; and it is clear that the other types of pathological factors (e.g. hallucinogens), whose presence is much easier to detect, are absent from the vast majority of cases of religious experience.

3. NONPATHOLOGICAL EXPLANATIONS OF RELIGIOUS EXPERIENCE

The nonpathological version of the reductionist challenge appeals to nonpathological naturalistic explanations of religious experience and Occam's razor. The existence of religious traditions as a whole can, it is claimed, be explained by complex 'natural histories of religion'. Through normal social processes, members of different societies acquire those societies' religious beliefs, engage in religious activities, and find themselves in religious settings. The religious 'set' thus acquired leads the subjects to attribute certain experiences and events to a divine cause, to label certain states of arousal as 'religious', and to find religious significance in certain situations—in short, to have religious experiences in accordance with their set—whether or not there is anything uniquely 'religious' there to be perceived. Since naturalistic accounts can thus explain religious experiences completely by the factors and

---

[85] See Edward W. Maupin, "On Meditation" in Tart (ed.), pp. 177–86.

processes which are known to operate in human experience, they are to be preferred to theistic explanations which appeal to unique, controversial entities and quasi-magical processes; for even if such entities and processes were not improbable, they would be redundant.

One response to this challenge is to deny that theistic explanations require the postulation of non-natural entities and processes, since God always works through natural causes. Maurice Wiles, for instance, appears to maintain a strictly 'non-interventionist' position when he rejects the notion of direct divine causation or revelation:

Talk of God's activity is . . . to be understood as a way of speaking about those events within the natural order or within human history in which God's purpose finds clear expression or special opportunity.[86]

Moreover,

when we speak of particular occasions—whether the inspiration of Scripture, a eucharistic service, the history of the church, the lives of the saints, or even special experiences of our own—as scenes of the Holy Spirit's activity, we need not (indeed I would be bold enough to say we ought not) imply thereby that they are occasions in which some special supernatural causation is to be looked for. Such a description should rather, I suggest, be understood to mean that here are places where the purpose of God has been apprehended, expressed or put into effect in a particularly profound way.[87]

This type of account is very plausible for interpretive religious experiences, general senses of 'sacredness' and 'harmony', and nature mysticism. God could so have ordained the natural world and human faculties that we are able to appreciate such things as the beauty of his creation without any intervention on his part. But for anyone proposing an argument from religious experience, strict non-interventionism gives rise to several problems:

(i) If God acts at such a fundamental, general, and remote level of the causal chain, then all specific experiences and events are caused by him in the same way and to the same degree. Religious experiences are therefore no more revelatory of the divine purpose

---

[86] Maurice Wiles, *The Remaking of Christian Doctrine* (London: SCM, 1974), p. 38.
[87] Ibid., pp. 101–2.

than are secular experiences of love, beauty, and so on—and why should we take such things as sunsets, lilies, and experiences of love and healing to be more revelatory of "the purpose of God" than famines, cancer, and the homicidal 'divine voices' of the 'Yorkshire Ripper', anyway? Strong arguments would be required to show what God's purpose is, and how human beings originally discovered that purpose, if all phenomena are equally products of his remote activity.

(ii) On such a strictly non-interventionist account, religious experiences would highlight natural features of the world such as beauty and harmony, and might even reveal something 'beyond', as in nature mysticism. Interaction with that divine "more" would, however, be impossible. Many types of religious experience would thus have to be considered unveridical on a strictly non-interventionist account. Any experiences in which it seemed to people that God or some other divine power was responding to them (e.g. forgiving or guiding), that they had a loving relationship with the divine, that they were aware of a holy, non-physical presence, or even that they were mystically united with a "living" ground of being which "sought them even as they sought it", would be impossible to explain by reference to natural features of the world and the mind alone, if veridicality is to be maintained. An argument from religious experience would suffer greatly if such fundamental and frequent types of experience had to be rejected.

(iii) In the absence of personal and interactive experiences of a living God, there would be considerable danger of God being treated as a postulated power or cause rather than as something for which we have experiential evidence. This would put the onus of proof on the theist rather than on the sceptic, and religious experiences would play little part in that proof.

Swinburne maintains that experiences apparently of God's 'presence' can be veridical even on a non-interventionist account: perceptual experiences are veridical if the alleged percept is present and was a cause of the experience; if God exists, he is omnipresent and at each moment sustains the natural laws which he created and which lead to experiences of his presence; all experiences apparently of God therefore satisfy the criteria of veridicality, if God exists.[88] (This account will not work for 'lesser' divine beings or for apparent reciprocal interactions; Swinburne, but not Wiles, would

[88] Swinburne, pp. 269-70.

allow some 'supernaturalism' for those.) I find this account unconvincing, however. For one thing, it would mean experiences such as the Yorkshire Ripper's, above, must be considered veridical perceptions of God. But it also does not seem to me to fulfil the criterion of an "appropriate" causal relationship. Consider the following analogy: Smith has hypnotized Jones, and suggests to him that there is a table of such-and-such a description—call it 'table A'—in front of him. Jones, whose eyes are closed, has the experience of its seeming to him that table A is present. Unknown to Jones, Smith has had table A brought into the room and placed in front of Jones, and is basing his description of the table on his perception of it. Table A is present where it appears to Jones to be, and it is causally related to Jones's experience. Assuming that Smith is truthful and accurate in his description, the situation is very much like that of God arranging natural laws so that humans have experiences apparently of him—yet we would not (I think) want to say that Jones was having a veridical perceptual experience of table A. Just what the right kind of causal connection *is*, I cannot say, and so have purposely left it vague; but I am not convinced that Swinburne's account yields the right one for this type of experience. Surely it is reasonable to suppose that experiences as different as nature mysticism and the sense of a loving personal presence should require different causal relationships with the divine?

This is not to say that miraculous divine intervention in the natural order is necessary, nor that God quasi-magically implants full and accurate revelations of himself in people's minds, completely bypassing all normal processes of perception and understanding. According to the 'non-crude interventionism' preferred by some theologians,[89] our apprehension of God must use the same perceptual and cognitive processes as are used in the apprehension of the natural world, other persons, and ourselves. Chapter VI showed how many different factors interact to produce perceptual experiences, and non-crude interventionism allows for the same sort of interaction in religious experiences. Our apprehensions of God will therefore be mediated by (and limited by) human

[89] I owe the term, though not all the elements of this exposition of it, to Margaret Yee. See her D.Phil. thesis, "The Validity of Theology as an Academic Discipline" (Oxford University, 1987), sections 7.3.1, 8.3, and 9.4.5. Her account of non-crude interventionism follows and expands upon Austin Farrer's theological views, especially as expressed in Farrer's *A Science of God?* (London: Geoffrey Bles, 1966) and *The Glass of Vision* (Westminster: Dacre Press, 1948).

perceptual and cognitive processes; influenced by psychological and physiological states, background beliefs, our 'mental model' of the divine, and other elements of our 'set'; and encouraged by such factors as religiously significant settings, actions, and people, great natural beauty, and moments of crisis. Particularly at the higher levels of ramification, our apprehensions will be coloured by culturally embedded models of the divine,[90] and profound religious insights may be clothed in the historical and scientific beliefs of the day. (It is for this reason that religious experiences are not generally considered a reliable source of such information.) The word 'supernatural', with its overtones of crude interventionism and magic, is therefore largely inappropriate; divine activity does not *violate* the natural order, but rather works with it and through it.

Divine responses and personal relationships are thus allowed on this account, though in a non-crude way; and it is recognized that many types of religious experience can be produced without divine intervention. In accepting that factors such as mental models play a crucial role in the way we represent the world to ourselves in thought and perception, the non-crude interventionist account rejects (as a rule) such things as word-perfect, miraculous revelations of the divine. Apprehensions of God will be partial and must be understood within the context of the subject's cultural background and personal development. Yet, just as partial and metaphorical descriptions can still be reality-depicting (see Chapter I.2), these fragmentary and context-laden experiences can still be apprehensions of the living God, the holy 'other' of numinous experiences and the unitive 'ground of being' of mystical experiences. Together, and in conjunction with other types of experiences and beliefs (the cumulative case), they can give rise to a well-grounded picture of the divine aspect of our world and life.

This is by no means an adequate account of non-crude interventionism, but it should suffice to show that strict non-interventionism and crude interventionism are not the only alternatives.

On the non-crude interventionist view, theists can accept most nonpathological explanations as true, though often incomplete, explanations of religious experience. Such explanations are only *rivals* to theistic ones when presented as complete, reductionist

---

[90] See the discussion of models and metaphors in Chapter I.2.

explanations—for instance, if they account for the traditions which give rise to religious sets and settings by appealing to psychological and social processes alone, and then explain those religious experiences which are not defeated by pathological challenges by reference to the religious set and/or setting. The reductionist has a difficult task, however. By the principle of credulity, an explanation which preserves a perceptual experience's veridicality is always *prima facie* more probable than an explanation which does not, when the rival contains no direct defeaters. Reductionist explanations must therefore be shown not just to be plausible alternatives but to be *more* probable than any explanation which preserves the veridicality of religious experiences (under moderated but still religious descriptions, if necessary).

The reductionist challenge is thus unlikely to succeed on its own. It must be worked into a cumulative challenge which shows that theism is *im*probable and hence that reductionist accounts of religious experience, which explain how people might have such experiences even if theism were false, are preferable to theistic accounts. This cumulative challenge will be discussed briefly in the next section.

Before moving on to nonpathological theories which apply to religious experience directly, I should give a very brief indication both of the sorts of 'natural histories of religion' which have been proposed to account for the traditions from which religious sets derive and of the rebuttals available.

(i) Early proponents of 'cognitive need' theories tended to focus on the sorts of cognitive factors which could make contemporary religion seem irrational, regarding religion as a pseudo-science (Tylor and Frazer) or as a 'god-of-the-gaps' explanation of such things as eclipses and good fortune. However, religion also addresses itself to 'ultimate questions' which science cannot answer, such as the purpose of one's life and the explanation of consciousness and creativity.[91] Attempts to deal with such issues by reference to religious concepts cannot be dismissed as irrational or superstitious.

(ii) The 'social learning' theory partially explains the maintenance of religious traditions in society, but it fails to show either that

[91] See the discussion of cognitive need theories in Argyle and Beit-Hallahmi, ch. 11. In chs. 3 and 11, they also present good accounts of the other 'natural histories of religion' discussed here.

religious belief is irrational or that it could have originated purely through social processes. The vast majority of our beliefs are transmitted by 'social learning' from generation to generation and are believed without particular scrutiny, without thereby being irrational; and the *origin* of religious beliefs cannot be explained by conformity to norms.

(iii) The theory that religion is only an 'opium' for the frustrated and deprived was discussed in section 2, in relation to individual experiences; most of the remarks made there also apply here, to show that religion by no means always serves such a function. Moreover, while it is true that small sects often attract the frustrated or deprived and propound 'compensatory' beliefs (e.g. 'the coming of the kingdom'), there are also militant sects and reforming movements, and many religious beliefs are far from 'compensatory'.

(iv) There is much that is right in Freud's 'father-projection' theory.[92] Accepting religion in the authoritarian and uncritical way it is traditionally taught may well keep some believers in a narrow-minded, 'infantile' state psychologically and intellectually (this may help to explain some of the correlations psychologists have found); the relationship between God and the believer can be envisaged as very like a child–parent relationship; and some studies have shown a correlation between believers' images of God and those of their preferred parent, usually the parent of the opposite sex.[93] However, a critical approach to religion *is* possible, and many religious people are well above average in psychological maturity and intellectual ability; believers' images of God often do not correspond to Freud's idea of a father-figure and may be independent of parental images in the 'spiritually mature';[94] this theory is inapplicable to highly mystical, atheistic traditions and so cannot account for all 'religion'; and the theory presupposes both a Western family structure and a Western concept of God.

(v) Durkheim saw God as the personal objectification of the

---

[92] See Sigmund Freud, *The Future of an Illusion* (London: Hogarth Press, 1962), and *Totem and Taboo* (London: Routledge & Kegan Paul, 1950).

[93] See André Godin and Monique Hallez, "Parental Images and Divine Paternity", in A. Godin (ed.), *From Religious Experience to a Religious Attitude* (Brussels: Lumen Vitae Press, 1964), pp. 79–110; see also Argyle and Beit-Hallahmi, ch. 11.

[94] Godin and Hallez; see also A. Siegman, "An Empirical Investigation of the Psychoanalytic Theory of Religious Behaviour" (1961), in Brown (ed.), pp. 225–31.

traditions and demands of society, independent realities which are external to individuals but also 'internalized' by them.[95] As with other natural histories, however, much more is needed to explain all the complex and varied aspects of religious traditions. It is difficult to see, for instance, how the Eastern mystic who has withdrawn from society and is meditating on 'emptiness' can be communing with projected social institutions.

Atheists such as J. L. Mackie admit that no natural history of religion so far developed can adequately account for the phenomenon of religion as a whole. He is confident, however, that in combination they could provide "an adequate and much more economical naturalistic alternative" to religious explanations, so that even psychologically sound religious experiences do not escape the reductionist net.[96] But Mackie offers no such account himself. Presumably the combined theory would have to be extremely complex, applying the factors discussed in this and previous sections in varying degrees and combinations to different periods, traditions, and individual believers. However, it would still be difficult to show that this was a complete account. In fact, most theists would agree with Mackie that each natural history discussed above "correctly identifies factors which have contributed to some extent to religion",[97] but that is far from admitting that together they constitute a highly probable and complete reductionist account of religion.

That all 'healthy' religious experiences can be completely explained by reference to the subject's set and/or setting—the second part of the reductionist challenge—is also dubious. Certain interpretive, drug-induced, regenerative, and revelatory experiences can be given plausible naturalistic explanations, as the examples below will show; but it will be seen that the experiences most amenable to such explanation usually involve factors which would make the experiences evidentially suspect in any case—e.g. revival meetings, anxiety, or hallucinogenic drugs. Many mystical experiences and senses of a holy presence do not lend themselves so easily to nonpathological reductionist explanations. Having survived the other challenges, their evidential force can only be

---

[95] Mackie puts Feuerbach's version of this view well in *The Miracle of Theism*, pp. 192–4.

[96] Mackie, pp. 197–8.

[97] Ibid. p. 197.

overcome by a strong cumulative challenge—and we will see how effective such a challenge is in section 4.

If an anxious man takes communion expecting to be comforted by Christ or the Holy Spirit, and he does feel more relaxed, he may report that he felt the action of Christ or the Holy Spirit within him. One could, however, give a naturalistic explanation of that relaxed state (involving, for instance, the subject's belief in the efficacy of communion and his relief after performing a mildly stressful public act), and say that his attribution of that state to a divine cause, though performed unconsciously and incorporated into the experience, was very probably entirely due to the religious set and setting. (As Chapter IX shows, however, a cumulative argument may make a theistic explanation of such experiences more plausible.)

Stephen Bradley's conversion experience, which is quoted at length by James, is cited by Wayne Proudfoot as a prime example of attribution in accordance with set, with no divine causality or real apprehension of God required.[98] One night, Bradley noticed his heart beating very fast, and because he had just been to some revival meetings, he ascribed the strange palpitations to the Holy Spirit. With this conviction, the experience began to develop, each stage arising from the beliefs about the last and confirming them. He became "exceedingly happy and humble", and the palpitations and the joy built up until he felt his heart would burst for love of God, and he could not help groaning. Then he asked himself, "What can it mean?", and immediately "saw" the New Testament verse "The Spirit helpeth our infirmities with groanings which cannot be uttered"(Rom. 8: 26). Convinced that he now truly "had religion", Bradley began the next day to talk of religion with others and to pray publicly. Proudfoot suggests that many religious experiences may similarly be due to anomalous physiological changes for which the subject's set and present situation make a religious attribution plausible, though normally the attribution is more immediately and unconsciously incorporated into the experience than it was in Bradley's case.

Set and setting are especially important to drug-induced experiences. As the discussion in section 2.4, above, showed, the states of arousal produced by hallucinogenic drugs do not have any intrinsic

---

[98] See James, pp. 194–8, and Wayne Proudfoot, *Religious Experience* (Berkeley: Univ. of California Press, 1985), ch. III.

meaning, but are labelled by the subject in accordance with his set and perceived setting. Thus Pahnke's "Good Friday" subjects, students from a religious seminary in the setting of a long, moving church service, almost all reported mystical experiences if they had (unknown to them) received the drug.[99] Proudfoot suggests that some meditative exercises may produce physiological changes which are given religious labels, and that some others, by their lack of cognitive content, might produce an "attributional tabula rasa" which can be rendered meaningful by whatever system the meditator has been learning.[100] Such considerations suggest that one could produce religious experiences in almost anybody, given the appropriate techniques and a religious set and setting. Like hypnotically suggested experiences, then, religious experiences would occur whether or not there were any religious reality to be perceived.

Not all types of religious experience can be so easily induced, however. As was pointed out in section 2, the challenges applicable to drug-induced experiences are effective in only a small fraction of cases. Moreover, drug-induced mystical experiences are almost always extrovertive rather than the introvertive type favoured by most mystical traditions,[101] and they rarely produce a sense of a personal presence or of union with another being. Pahnke's subjects did yield high scores for 'internal unity', but this may have been due to the setting being a darkened church.

Senses of a presence are particularly difficult to explain in reductionist terms. They have been explained as projections of a mind starved for love and so on, but such explanations belong to the pathological category, and as such are unsuitable as explanations of the vast majority of such experiences. One must not assume some undetected (and probably undetectable) pathology in an otherwise healthy individual when nonpathological explanations are available. One plausible nonpathological explanation of experiences in which an external power seems to be guiding, inspiring, or interacting with the subject is William James's theory of the role of 'subliminal activity':

[99] See Pahnke and Richards, "Implications of LSD and Experimental Mysticism" in Tart (ed.), and the discussion in section 2.4, above.
[100] Wayne Proudfoot and Phillip Shaver, "Attribution Theory and the Psychology of Religion", *J. Sc. Stud. Rel.*, 14 (1975), 317–30.
[101] See Wainwright, *Mysticism*, ch. 2.

Let me then propose, as an hypothesis, that whatever it may be on its *farther* side, the "more" with which in religious experience we feel ourselves connected is on its *hither* side the subconscious continuation of our conscious life. . . . it is one of the peculiarities of invasions from the subconscious region to take on objective appearances, and to suggest to the Subject an external control.[102]

As James realizes, an appeal to 'the subconscious' or 'the unconscious' does not preclude divine activity. We know very little about what goes on beyond the level of everyday consciousness, and cannot even be sure that such regions are entirely 'internal'—Jung's 'collective unconscious', for instance, goes beyond the boundaries of the individual. Because it relies on such little known, 'hidden' (postulated) factors, any appeal to such unconscious activity must be thoroughly backed up by a cumulative argument if it is to constitute an effective reductionist challenge.

It appears, then, that the 'intrinsically religious' senses of a presence, numinous experiences, and introvertive mystical experiences of healthy individuals—the very types of experience we found most valuable as evidence in Chapter VII—are the ones which reductionists have the most difficulty explaining.

Sceptics also have trouble with those religious experiences which bear no discernible relation to the subject's set or setting (see Chapter VI.4). Experiences not described by or even at variance with the received tradition, children's senses of a holy presence unlike the 'Sunday School God' about whom they have been taught, spontaneous religious experiences in secular settings, and experiences contrary to the subject's beliefs or expectations can only be ascribed to set and setting with difficulty (though the last type can often be ascribed to 'subconscious incubation' where the subject's conscious beliefs are at variance with a tradition to which he is exposed and eventually converts). The influence of set and setting in such cases is so indirect and well concealed that a reductionist explanation appealing to it must be very well supported by further evidence if it is to be an effective rival to a nonreductionist explanation.

Finally, for set and setting to have as profound an influence as the reductionist claims, subjects of religious experience would all have to be quite suggestible; and section 2 showed that the evidence

[102] James, pp. 487–8.

linking religious experience with suggestibility is far from conclusive.

This is not, of course, to deny any influence from the set and setting. As with any perceptual experience, factors such as the subjects' knowledge and cultural background will affect the way they classify the stimuli and the degree of ramification of that classification, and the activity they are engaged in will affect the types of percepts they are both set to perceive and able to perceive. There are, however, three peculiarities of religious percepts which would make one expect the influence of set and setting to be greater than in most secular perception. Once one recognizes these features, one sees that certain facts which reductionists have taken to support their case can be explained just as well by a non-crude interventionist account which preserves the veridicality of most religious experiences (at the very least under moderated auto-descriptions). Firstly, since religious percepts are generally privately experienced, elusive, and difficult to describe, it is not surprising that highly ramified auto-descriptions of them should tend to conform so closely to the subject's set. As Chapter VII showed, however, an important 'common core' can be established.

Secondly, since divine forces are non-physical, one would expect any quasi-sensory aspects of a religious experience to correspond to ideas in the subject's set.

And thirdly, if it is true that our everyday consciousness is too rigidly controlled and cluttered up with everyday concerns to apprehend spiritual realities, as has often been suggested, then it is hardly surprising that so many religious experiences occur while the subject is engaged in religious activities designed to produce more religiously oriented, undistracted, and 'receptive' frames of mind. Arthur Deikman has even proposed a theory of 'deautomatization' along these lines:[103] in the daily activities of secular life, when we are required to be alert to our surroundings, make quick perceptual judgements, and perform goal-directed actions, we employ a highly automatized selection system to screen out irrelevant stimuli and enhance useful ones (see Chapter VI), and we use a 'separate personal self' as a basic reference point. In a meditative, 'receptive' mode of consciousness, however, 'deauto-

---

[103] Arthur J. Deikman, "Deautomatization and the Mystic Experience" (1966) and "Bimodal Consciousness and the Mystic Experience" (1976), in Woods (ed.), pp. 240–60 and 261–9 respectively.

matization' may take place, so that the stimuli are no longer pre-sifted. In this state, the external world appears more vivid, real, and alive; subject–object distinctions are blurred; and the subject often has a sense of profound unity. Deikman suggests that, far from being a delusive or pathological way of experiencing the world, this may be a veridical type of experience which we tend to inhibit with the selective 'action' mode of consciousness of day-to-day life.

In nonpathological reductionist accounts of both individual experiences and whole traditions, it is the reductionist who most often appears to be postulating hidden and controversial factors and processes, whereas, beyond the factors and processes which both the theist and the sceptic accept, the theist appeals only to the alleged objects of perception. Since pathological reductionist explanations are inapplicable to the majority of religious experiences, a reductionist account of religious experience will only be preferable if the weight of evidence shows theism to be improbable. The reductionist challenge cannot therefore stand on its own; it must form part of a cumulative challenge, to which we now turn.

4. THE CUMULATIVE CHALLENGE REVISITED

As was pointed out above, the principle of credulity ensures that the sceptic has a more difficult task than the theist. If the evidence other than that of religious experience does not show theism to be improbable, then the evidence of the many religious experiences which escape pathological and other challenges will be sufficient to make some relatively unramified theistic claims probable (and the theist can then attempt to build up a case for more highly ramified beliefs). The sceptic, on the other hand, must show that theism is clearly improbable if reductionist accounts of otherwise undefeated religious experiences are to be preferred. (The sceptic does not need to show theism to be *highly* improbable; a high degree of improbability is only required when improbability is being used as a single, direct challenge to an experience. Here it is being used to back up several other challenges.) If the force of the evidence remains unclear, on the borderline of probability, then the benefit of the doubt will go to a position which maintains the veridicality of otherwise undefeated religious experiences.

By combining 'background evidence' such as the problem of evil with the facts that many apparently normal people have no experience of the divine, that many of those who do can be shown to succumb to 'pathological' challenges, that religious experiences have led to fanaticism and atrocities, and that subjects (allegedly) cannot agree on a single, consistent account of their alleged percept, reductionists claim to be able to show that theism is improbable. Since they also maintain that plausible reductionist accounts of the as yet undefeated religious experiences are available (drawing on natural histories of religion and attribution theory to explain why people would have those experiences even if no religious claims were true), they can combine the arguments and assert that there is no reason to accept somewhat improbable theistic accounts of religious experiences.

We have seen that in their non-cumulative form, pathological challenges do not succeed in a great many cases, the conflicting claims challenge does not affect the evidential force of most experiences under less highly ramified descriptions, existing natural histories of religion are inadequate, and even nonpathological naturalistic explanations are not very plausible in many cases. It is difficult to assess the weight of these challenges when combined; no numerical values of probability can be assigned, and there is considerable room for individual judgement (features of the theistic cumulative case as well; see the discussion in the next chapter). Much appears to hang on just how improbable theism can be shown to be on the background evidence. This 'background evidence' is usually made up of three types of argument: (i) those adducing direct counter-evidence to theism; (ii) those proposing rival explanations of phenomena which theists claim can best (or only) be explained theistically; and (iii) those attempting to show that theistic arguments to the existence of God do not work.

(i) The existence of so much evil and suffering in the world and the philosophical problems associated with such unusual concepts as a bodiless agent and omnipotence both threaten traditional theism. However, such plausible responses have been made both to the problem of evil and to the challenge of the incoherence of theism (see Chapter V) that, though the sceptical evidence does *count against* the probability of theism, it does not clearly show theism to be improbable.

(ii) The order and beauty of the universe, its existence in the first place, and the phenomenon of consciousness are all facts which theists have argued can best be explained on a theistic account. Some sceptics have developed materialistic explanations of them,[104] while others maintain that they are 'brute facts' for which explanations should not be sought.[105] Unlike the case of naturalistic explanations of religious experience, naturalistic explanations of the universe (etc.) do not have to be shown to be far more probable than their theistic rivals before it is reasonable to accept them. Since arguments from natural theology postulate God as an explanation rather than citing him as a datum of experience, they do not have the *prima facie* superiority granted by the principle of credulity. However, rivals to theistic explanations must be at least somewhat more probable than the most sophisticated theistic explanations if they are to be some evidence that theism is improbable, and I have yet to see naturalistic explanations which are so compelling.

(iii) Many theistic arguments *are* faulty. However, many are not; and the fact that the others do not work does not in itself show theism to be improbable. At the most, it can only show that theism may be less probable than some of its proponents have thought.

J. L. Mackie's *The Miracle of Theism* and Richard Swinburne's *The Existence of God* (supplemented by *The Coherence of Theism*) are good examples of the debate over the probability of traditional Judaeo-Christian theism. From these and other works, it would appear that theism cannot clearly be shown to be improbable on the background evidence; it is a borderline case. (See the further discussion below, Chapter IX.2.)

This is not to say that the cumulative challenge has no force at all. The challenges of the last few chapters demanded complex counter-arguments in which the theist had to make some concessions, and in combination those concessions ensure that an argument from religious experience alone will have considerably less force than many theists have hoped. Though no single challenge can defeat an argument from religious experience, together they do reduce the field of religious experiences with evidential value and lower the

---

[104] See, for instance, P. W. Atkins' rather speculative 'scientific' cosmology in *The Creation* (Oxford: Freeman, 1981).

[105] See e.g. Bertrand Russell in "The Existence of God, A Debate Between Bertrand Russell and Father F. C. Copleston" in Hick (ed.), *The Existence of God*, pp. 167–91: "I should say that the universe is just there, and that's all."

degree of ramification of the claims which such an argument can support.

It is possible, however, to respond with a *theistic* cumulative argument, in which religious experience will play a crucial part. How such an argument might be constructed, and what the theist can hope to achieve with it, are questions for the final chapter.

9
TOWARDS A CUMULATIVE CASE
FOR THEISM

The previous chapters led to the conclusions that the conflicting claims challenge does not overcome many important types of experiential claim, that reductionist explanations of religious experiences and traditions are largely inapplicable or defective, and that theism has not been shown to be improbable. When combined, these conclusions showed that religious experiences can survive the cumulative challenge. In particular, numinous and mystical experiences and senses of a "presence" provide very strong evidence for the "broadly theistic" beliefs outlined in Chapter VII. These included the claims that human beings have a 'true self' beyond their everyday 'phenomenal ego', and that this true self is intimately related to the divine nature; that there is a holy power beyond the world of the senses, which is perceptible as the ultimate, unitary ground of being, as an awesome, creature-consciousness inspiring power, as the 'something more' which shines through the world of nature, and as a personal, loving presence; and that human beings can find their most profound satisfaction in a harmonious relation with this holy power.

These claims are substantial, but they do not in themselves constitute a 'living religion'. Few people would find such basic principles immediately relevant to their lives. Because the conflicting claims and reductionist challenges do have some force, however, religious experiences on their own do not generally provide overwhelming evidence for much beyond these basic claims. It is true that one can deduce some further points from the above 'broad theism': for instance, the beliefs that we all share in divinity and that the world is guided by a loving power would have implications for morality. But most of the more highly ramified and life-guiding principles of the world's religions are not so directly related to religious experiences; they require the support of a more complex cumulative case.

Like scientific systems, religious belief systems do not follow deductively from a set of 'raw' perceptual experiences. Even Kekulé's revolutionary benzene ring theory was not based solely on his dream of the snake with its tail in its mouth.[1] Although the insight gained from that dream was crucial, it arose in the context of many years of research into the problem of the molecular structure of certain compounds, and it required further reflection and testing before it could be presented as a fully developed, well grounded theory. Similarly, religious experiences may be crucial to a highly ramified religious system, but they usually require a great deal of 'working out' before their full significance is realized.

The 'interactive' accounts of concept formation and incorporated interpretation in Chapter VI explained why experiences do not 'reveal' highly ramified truths in a conceptual vacuum. Perceptual experiences are themselves formed in a 'cumulative' way, through the interaction of many factors such as the subject's prior beliefs and experiences, and their full significance often unfolds only over time, as they are reflected upon in the light of critical debate, new knowledge, and further experiences. Where there is any reason to question an experiential claim, it should not be surprising if the defence also takes a cumulative form, drawing on evidence such as related knowledge and experiences. The more highly ramified the claim, and the more embedded it is in a network of related claims, the more cumulative the defence is likely to be.

A few philosophers and theologians have recognized the importance of religious experiences in cumulative types of argument. In Swinburne's cumulative argument for the existence of God, for instance, once the other types of evidence have shown that theism is not improbable, "the evidence of religious experience is . . . sufficient to make theism over all probable."[2] In Soskice's study of models and metaphors, religious experiences are noted as an important way of grounding reference to God,[3] and Yee's discussion of the development of early Christian belief shows the crucial role played by the disciples' resurrection experiences.[4]

---

[1] See Chapter V.2, above.
[2] Swinburne, p. 291.
[3] See *Metaphor and Religious Language*, pp. 137–40 and 150–3.
[4] See, for instance, Yee, section 8.5.2.

A theistic cumulative argument will do far more than simply provide additional support for religious experiential claims. One must remember that different pieces of evidence *interact* in cumulative arguments, so that the whole is greater than the sum of the parts. Other types of evidence help us make sense of religious experiences and increase the likelihood that they are veridical; religious experiences help us make sense of other experiences and beliefs and increase the likelihood that certain beliefs are true; and all types of evidence work together to support a network of highly ramified beliefs. In this final chapter, the additional types of evidence will be seen to supplement the evidence of religious experience in three ways:

(i) Evidence and arguments which generally support theism will make it more difficult for the sceptic to maintain the charge that theism is clearly improbable. They will thus help to defeat the direct challenge of high improbability on the background evidence and, more importantly, the reductionist cumulative challenge.

(ii) A cumulative argument provides many evidentially weak experiences with a role in the case for theism. With additional evidence for the truth of certain religious claims, some types of religious experience which succumbed to sceptical challenges might now be considered genuine sources of religious insight, and may then act as evidence in their turn. Many nonperceptual and interpretive religious experiences will also be seen to provide indirect evidence for religious claims within a cumulative argument.

(iii) By drawing on diverse sources of evidence, a good case can often be made for highly ramified theistic beliefs which do not depend on the evidence of religious experiences alone.

2. GENERAL ARGUMENTS FOR THEISM

The foregoing chapters may have given the impression that the theist is always on the defensive, always responding to the sceptic's challenges. But there are also positive arguments for theism. I am not talking here of the traditional deductive 'arguments for the existence of God', which work much better as hints towards inductive arguments or as methods of evoking religious attitudes (e.g. wonder at the fact that anything exists at all; a sense of contingency) than as attempts at logical compulsion. There are many inductive types of argument which provide positive support for theism. One quite rigorous and comprehensive presentation of these can be found in Swinburne's *The Existence of God*.

Swinburne argues that "various occurrent phenomena are such that they are more to be expected, more probable if there is a God than if there is not."[5] How, for instance, could random natural factors have created a world in which people had "great opportunities for co-operation in acquiring knowledge and moulding the universe"?[6] Many phenomena which "cry out for explanation", such as the fact that anything exists at all, cannot be given complete scientific explanations; the alternatives are theism or the acceptance of such phenomena as "brute facts".[7] And so Swinburne argues that a personal God of infinite capacities (a simple hypothesis) is a better stopping place for explanation than a complex, finite, physical universe (a version of the cosmological argument); that the beauty and order of the world (for instance, the fact that it conforms to natural laws) are more likely if there is a God than if everything were left to chance (the teleological argument); that science will never be able fully to explain mind–body correlations or the emergence of consciousness; and even that God might have had reason to create this particular type of world, as opposed to the many other types which might have come about through random or other natural processes (arguments from 'providence'). Certain events in human history and alleged miracles may also provide evidence for theism, though this evidence is more difficult to evaluate. Thus, although theism cannot be considered overwhelmingly probable on the evidence other than religious experience—it does not have high enough predictive power—its simplicity, its "remarkable ability to make sense of what otherwise is extremely puzzling",[8] and its capacity for dealing with counter-evidence show that it is certainly not *im*probable.

Some arguments which have been proposed in favour of theism—e.g. many forms of the 'ontological argument', Paley's very specific arguments from 'design', and various arguments from

---

[5] p. 277.
[6] Ibid.
[7] Attempts at 'scientific' cosmological accounts do exist—see Ch. VIII. 4 (ii)—but they are highly speculative. See also Ch. VIII, nn. 104 and 105.
[8] Swinburne, p. 289.

morality—suffer so many defects or are so controversial that they do not contribute a great deal to the theistic case. An argument from design which cites only phenomena that can now be explained by natural evolution, for instance, is unlikely to convince anyone other than a 'creationist'.[9] However, the theistic case survives without such arguments: enough evidence is available, when the positive arguments for theism are combined with counter-arguments to the sceptic's charges of improbability (such as the problem of evil), to show that theism is not improbable on the 'background evidence'.

We saw in the last chapter that the reductionist challenge could only succeed in most cases if religious claims and theistic accounts of religious experiences could clearly be shown to be improbable. Reductionist accounts of experiences which had no obvious pathological features and which succumbed to no other challenges depended either on the existence of hidden pathological factors or on the plausibility of a 'natural history of religion'; but a challenge dependent on hidden factors is extremely weak, and reductionist accounts of religious traditions and their relationship to religious experiences have so far been highly inadequate. A reductionist account of religious experiences could thus only prove more probable than an account which preserved those experiences' veridicality if there were additional evidence that those experiences were unveridical, i.e. if it were shown that the experiential claims were clearly improbable on the 'background evidence'. Since theism has not been shown to be improbable, the evidence of many religious experiences can be added to the argument; and, as was pointed out above, the cumulative case which results strongly favours a 'broad theism'. (More highly ramified beliefs require a more complex cumulative argument, as will be seen in section 4.)

Since only the barest outline could be given of the 'background evidence' for and against theism, some readers may feel the overall evidence is still inconclusive. But a cumulative argument to a complex belief system, which draws upon so many different sources of evidence, each requiring extensive specialist knowledge,

---

[9] There is a more general argument from design, however, which has more force, viz. the argument that such a delicate arrangement of scientific laws is required to produce a big bang and a 'primeval soup' capable of evolving into humans and animals that it is unlikely to have come about by chance, and a rational cause is indicated.

could never be presented completely in one book. Indeed, it would be impossible for one person to test all the evidence and formulate all the arguments for such a case. As in all fields of knowledge, much must be taken on trust.[10] No progress would be made in science, for instance, if research projects had to start from scratch; we all stand on the shoulders of our predecessors.

This inability to present all the relevant evidence in detail does, however, add to the problem of assessing the overall weight of evidence, particularly in a case such as this, where the evidence is not strictly quantifiable, nor the argument formal. In such circumstances, personal judgement inevitably plays a larger part in the weighing of the evidence than in other types of argument. But personal judgement need not, and should not, constitute subjective bias. Indeed, it is a necessary element in all areas of knowledge. A defence of the rationality of personal judgement is clearly beyond the scope of this book, but readers who are worried about the role it must play should turn to such works as Michael Polanyi's *Personal Knowledge*,[11] which argues that personal judgement is indispensable to science (and, indeed, to all knowledge), and Yee's "The Validity of Theology as an Academic Discipline",[12] which shows that though personal judgement is involved in the acquisition of all knowledge, strict attention to empirical and critical principles will yield the highest possible level of objectivity. Most of the decisions we must make, scholarly or otherwise, cannot be arrived at by a formal decision procedure, and so, as W. Abraham has observed, we use personal judgement to direct the organization and weighing of the pieces of evidence[13] (though it should be pointed out that even the application of formal decision procedures requires personal judgement). Moreover, though the evidence may not overwhelmingly support one conclusion or another, this also occurs in every discipline at times; it does not mean we cannot make a rational, well-grounded decision. Properly understood, personal judgement is an activity which requires

---

[10] W. J. Abraham makes this point well in "Cumulative Case Arguments for Christian Theism", in Wm. J. Abraham and Steven W. Holtzer (eds.), *The Rationality of Religious Belief* (Oxford: Clarendon Press, 1987), pp. 17–37.

[11] London: Routledge & Kegan Paul, 1962 (1958).

[12] See the discussions of personal judgement in Yee, 3.2, 3.4.1, 3.4.2, 4.3, 5.2.5, and 6. 2.

[13] Abraham, p. 34.

considerable skill, knowledge of the field, and rigorous adherence to the principles of rational inquiry.[14]

Since feelings about religion tend to run high, however, there is a real danger in this case that personal judgement could degenerate into personal bias. A committed atheist or committed Christian who ignored counter-evidence, put excessive weight on shaky evidence, and selected authorities to suit their purposes, would be guilty of misusing personal judgement. But a more rational sort of personal bias could manifest itself, as when a person whose son has just died of leukaemia believes that responses to the problem of evil are radically inadequate, or a person who has had an overwhelming religious experience believes reductionist accounts miss vital aspects of that experience. Where much of the evidence is drawn from life, one's experience of life will colour one's appreciation of the evidence. However, as long as one makes use of authorities in a careful and scholarly manner, subjects one's own views to empirical testing and critical argument, and weighs the evidence and arguments with all the skill and honesty demanded by the proper use of personal judgement, the result should be a conclusion that is well grounded and worthy of assent.

3. THE ROLE OF EVIDENTIALLY WEAK RELIGIOUS EXPERIENCES

Once theism has been shown to be probable on the total evidence available (including that of undefeated religious experiences), types of religious experience which were not so useful as evidence on their own can play a small evidential role, in four (not mutually exclusive) ways:

(i) The example of the drunkard and the wallaby in Chapter IV.4 showed how evidence that the alleged percept was very probable could overcome the successful challenges of intoxication and poor visibility, and even turn the experience into additional evidence for the percept. Religious experiences which are defeated by such subject-related challenges as the influence of hallucinogenic drugs, mental illness, and deprivation may similarly be backed up by the combination of evidence that theism is probable and the following arguments: the deprived (etc.) very probably turn to God more

---

[14] A good account of these principles, which stresses the need for both empirical and 'critical' testing, can be found in Yee, especially chs. 5 and 6.

often than the satisfied, and so are more likely to have experiences of him; drugs and mental illness dissociate the mind from mundane realities, leaving it open to fantasies and hallucinations, but also to the divine realities to which it is closed in more sane, sober moments; and both James and Underhill argue that unstable personalities may be more open to experiences of God.[15] There might thus be reason to take some of the religious claims made under such conditions as true.

(ii) Some evidence was cited in Chapter V which increased the probability of the truth of beliefs acquired through experiences such as dreams, 'flashes of insight', and visions—experiences which are considered in the secular realm and to a great extent in the religious realm as well to be generally unreliable sources of knowledge. If religious visions, dreams, and revelatory experiences are now placed within a cumulative argument, the probability that they are products of divine activity and that they yield valuable religious insights will be greatly increased, for there will be further evidence that there are divine agents, that they interact in this way with human beings, and that certain other religious claims (against which the alleged insights may be tested) are true. Claims accepted in this way can then become evidence in their turn, for instance, by being combined to support more complex religious doctrines, elaborated through the retrospective interpretation of the subject and others, or used as the basis for a re-interpretation of scriptures.

(iii) Although delusive experiences can sometimes have therapeutic value, lead to appropriate behaviour, or generate true beliefs, they are more likely to be 'maladaptive'—if you mistake the tiger for a pattern of shadows, you might not live long. 'Adaptive' experiences are more likely to be veridical, and so the fact that so many religious experiences have beneficial consequences is some evidence in their favour. This is the 'fruits' argument; and, despite the counter-evidence of religiously inspired fanaticism and prejudice, it has a great deal of force.

Some of the goals which religious experiences promote, such as missionary zeal, can only be seen as 'beneficial' within a certain framework. Very frequently, however, religious experiences yield benefits which would be regarded as such by any standard criteria. An apprehension of the underlying 'divinity' of the soul may help a

---

[15] James, Lecture I; and Underhill, ch. 3.

person recognize the intrinsic worth of all human beings; experiences of nature mysticism may encourage a person to cherish the environment; recognition of the love God has for us may impel a person to manifest much more love for others, perhaps caring for those whom society has abandoned. Stories of great saints and tireless 'followers of Christ' such as Mother Teresa of Calcutta continue to inspire us. For sceptics, as Basil Mitchell has pointed out, such "conspicuous sanctity must inevitably pose a problem, associated as it is, on [their] view, with manifest error".[16]

The psychological studies of Chapter VIII showed that religious experiences may well be conducive to good mental health[17] and to a healthy, positive attitude towards death.[18] They may also contribute to personal psychological development, leading to greater stability and self-knowledge. In the more dramatic cases, religious experiences appear to precipitate physical or mental healing, or conversion from a destructive lifestyle.[19] Through them one may discover new, profound meaning in life where before there had been a sense of purposelessness and despair, and be enabled, as Viktor Frankl was, to survive such traumas as a Nazi prison camp.[20] In innumerable cases, religious experiences have helped people deal with crises, anxiety, sorrow, and guilt, and have provided comfort and hope, courage, guidance, and moral strength.

Many of the above types of regenerative experience may be nonperceptual; there is no sense of a presence, no religious insight, no cognitive claim. But even these can be evidence for theism within a cumulative argument. If it is quite probable that there are divine forces at work, that they are more likely to act when people pray or otherwise prepare themselves, and that experiences such as new hope and comfort are expected results of this activity, then such nonperceptual regenerative experiences as renewed hope during prayer can reasonably be ascribed to divine activity.

(iv) All types of religious experience, even interpretive ones, can help us to make sense of religious doctrines and concepts which we did not understand so well before. Conversely, such doctrines and

---

[16] Basil Mitchell, *The Justification of Religious Belief*, p. 41.
[17] See Chapter VIII. 2.2 (v).
[18] See Chapter VIII. 2.2 (iii).
[19] For examples of these and the other types of regenerative experience mentioned in this paragraph, see Chapter II. 5.
[20] See his *Man's Search for Meaning*, especially pp. 63–4.

concepts may help us to make sense of both our religious and our secular experiences. This is the case with any conceptual system, as Chapter VI explained, for the development of concepts and beliefs is inextricably bound up with experience. Religious experiences can thus enable people to believe 'in their heart' what they had formerly only 'believed in their head', as concepts such as God's 'infinite mercy' come alive for them.[21] One may find one's commitment to a religious system strengthened as one interprets the world in terms of it, for that interpretation may increase one's self-understanding, illuminate many other experiences, give one's life added purpose and richness, enhance one's appreciation of moral values and human relationships. Even religious experiences which succumb to sceptical challenges may be indirect evidence for religious claims in this capacity, if they help the subject to understand the significance of doctrines and concepts which already have some support within a cumulative argument.

The theistic cumulative case shows how crucial ordinary, everyday religious experiences are as evidence. One must not make the mistake of thinking that only spectacular, intense revelations have evidential force, for such rare and extraordinary experiences would not have nearly the evidential force they do if they were not backed up by the countless 'minor' experiences of religious people—experiences of

the sense of the presence of God in their daily, ordinary lives, giving purpose to routine, providing courage, comfort, and hope, strengthening and deepening their moral commitment and sensitivity, leading them to worship and praise.[22]

It is these minor religious experiences—many of them interpretive —which demonstrate that religious doctrines are appropriate to the world we live in, and not merely to some esoteric 'realm of the spirit'.

4. HIGHLY RAMIFIED RELIGIOUS BELIEFS

Some quite highly ramified beliefs seem to emerge in a fairly straightforward way from religious experiences. Numinous ex-

---

[21] See the examples in Chapter II.4.

[22] Grace Jantzen, "Conspicuous Sanctity and Religious Belief", in Abraham and Holtzer (eds.), pp. 121–40; quote p. 122.

periences of awe and creature-consciousness, for instance, could reasonably lead to belief in an all-powerful God on whom everything depends utterly. Beliefs in some form of life after death, the 'divine spark', a loving God, and the efficacy of prayer could similarly be derived from religious experiences without requiring much in the way of a cumulative argument. And many models of God, from 'creator' and 'father' to 'wind' and 'void', could have received their initial impetus from religious experience. But such concepts—like all our concepts—continue to develop in the context of critical debate, community experience, and new knowledge. Most current religious doctrines are the result of so much reflection on experience, and are so embedded in a network of interlocking beliefs and models, that religious experience alone cannot fully ground them.

Some of the most crucial doctrines of the world's religions require cumulative arguments of a range and complexity that I can hardly begin to illustrate here. Issues such as the nature of the Trinity, the doctrine of atonement, whether Jesus was the unique incarnation of God, the 'three bodies' of the Buddha, the cycle of rebirth, the causes and cures of evil and suffering, the meaning of rituals, and the interpretation of scriptures all demand a wide range of evidence besides religious experience. Regarding the Christian Trinity, for instance, Austin Farrer has observed that restricting one's approach to religious experience alone would yield "a triform experience of God, not the experience of a triune deity".[23] A more comprehensive approach is required if the Trinitarian "image" (or model) of divinity is to be apprehended; one must, for instance, "ask what place [the image of the Trinity] occupies in the world of New Testament images".[24]

A good example of a cumulative method of dealing with highly ramified theological beliefs can be found in Yee's work on the grounding of theological judgements.[25] Yee stresses the necessity of carrying out "the full complement" of empirical and critical tests from all relevant disciplines in assessing theological beliefs, and shows that theological beliefs are amenable to such testing. Findings from such fields as history, archaeology, sociology, biology, and literary criticism are essential to the interpretation of

[23] Austin Farrer, *The Glass of Vision*, p. 46.
[24] Ibid. p. 47.
[25] "The Validity of Theology".

textual sources, and knowledge of the natural world, religiously significant events, and ourselves must all be taken into account if our theological judgements are to be well grounded and not merely speculative.[26] By tracing the development of the early church's beliefs about Christ, for instance,[27] Yee reveals that though the "substance" of those beliefs arose out of the disciples' crucial resurrection experiences, the final concepts were the result of the interplay of many factors as the disciples strove to come to terms with their experiences. Those experiences had severely challenged the disciples' previous thought patterns; and it was only after their initial puzzling, awe-inspiring insights had been refined against the background of Judaic tradition, Jesus' life and teachings, and the ongoing life of the church, that the full significance of the experiences emerged. Moreover, the 'working out' of matters such as these "incarnational" concepts has continued to this day, as theological models have been revised in the light of expanding knowledge in the human and physical sciences, our present-day apprehensions of God, and debate with other religious traditions.[28]

To give details of a cumulative case for any highly ramified version of theism would be impossible in a work of this scope. It is hoped that the arguments and evidence presented here have shown both the way religious experiences might be included in such an argument and their crucial role in establishing fundamental theistic doctrines. The fact that they must be embedded in a fairly simple cumulative argument to give those doctrines full support and in a more complex and ambitious cumulative argument to support the finer points of particular traditions does not mean that Antony Flew is right, that "the whole argument from religious experience must collapse into an argument from whatever *other* credentials may be offered to authenticate the revelation supposedly mediated by such experience."[29] For all the mishandling they have received, religious experiences are an essential and highly valuable source of evidence for many religious claims. Like all things with considerable force, 'evidential' or otherwise, they must be treated with caution and understanding, but can be of immense benefit.

[26] Yee, sections 7.1, 8.4, 8.5, and 8.5.1.
[27] See sections 7.3.2 and 8.5 2.
[28] See Yee, 8.6, and for an intensive examination of "incarnational-type" beliefs, ch. 9.
[29] Flew, *God and Philosophy*, p. 139, emphasis mine.

10

BIBLIOGRAPHY

Abraham, Wm. J., "Cumulative Case Arguments for Christian Theism", in Abraham and Holtzer (eds.), *The Rationality of Religious Belief*, pp. 17–37.

—— and Steven W. Holtzer (eds.), *The Rationality of Religious Belief: Essays in Honour of Basil Mitchell* (Oxford: Clarendon Press, 1987).

Achinstein, Peter (ed.), *The Concept of Evidence* (Oxford: OUP, 1983).

Almond, Philip C., *Mystical Experience and Religious Doctrine: An Investigation of the Study of Mysticism in World Religions* (Berlin: Morton Publishers, 1982).

Argyle, Michael and Benjamin Beit-Hallahmi, *The Social Psychology of Religion* (London: Routledge & Kegan Paul, 1975).

Atkins, P. W., *The Creation* (Oxford: W. H. Freeman, 1981).

Augustine (St), *Confessions*, tr. and intro. by R. S. Pine-Coffin (Harmondsworth: Penguin Books, 1961).

Austin, J. L., *Sense and Sensibilia*, reconstructed from the manuscript notes by G. J. Warnock (Oxford: Clarendon Press, 1962).

Ayer, A. J., *Language, Truth and Logic* (London: Victor Gollancz, 1936).

Bache, Christopher M., "On the Emergence of Perinatal Symptoms in Buddhist Meditation", *J. Sc. Stud. Rel.* 20 (1981), 339–50.

Baillie, John, *Our Knowledge of God* (London: OUP, 1939).

Baker, Mark and Richard Gorsuch, "Trait Anxiety and Intrinsic-Extrinsic Religiousness", *J. Sc. Stud. Rel.* 21 (1982), 119–22.

Barbour, Ian G., *Myths, Models and Paradigms: The Nature of Scientific and Religious Language* (London: SCM, 1974).

Batson, C. Daniel and W. Larry Ventis, *The Religious Experience: A Social-Psychological Perspective* (New York: OUP, 1982).

Batson, C. Daniel, Stephen J. Naifeh, and Suzanne Pate, "Social Desirability, Religious Orientation, and Racial Prejudice", *J. Sc. Stud. Rel.* 17 (1978), 31–41.

Beardsworth, Timothy, *A Sense of Presence: The Phenomenology of Certain Kinds of Visionary and Ecstatic Experience, Based on a Thousand Contemporary First-hand Accounts* (Oxford: The Religious Experience Research Unit, 1977).

Beit-Hallahmi, Benjamin, "Psychology of Religion—What Do We Know?" *Archiv für Religionspsychologie* 14 (1980), 228–36.

Benfey, O. Theodor, "August Kekule and the Birth of the Structural

Theory of Organic Chemistry in 1858", *Journal of Chemical Education* 35 (1958), 21–3.

Bernard of Clairvaux, *Five Books on Consideration: Advice to a Pope* (De consideratione ad Eugenium papam tertiam libri quinque), tr. John D. Anderson and Elizabeth T. Kennan (Cistercian Fathers Series No. 37; Kalamazoo: Cistercian Publications, 1976).

Berry, J. W. and P. R. Dasen (eds.), *Culture and Cognition: Readings in Cross-Cultural Psychology* (London: Methuen, 1974).

Bhagavad Gita, translations. [1] Franklin Edgerton (New York: Harper & Row, 1944). [2] W. D. P. Hill (London: OUP, 1928). [3] Juan Mascaró (Harmondsworth: Penguin Books, 1962). [4] R. C. Zaehner (London: OUP, 1969).

Boehme, Jacob, *Dialogues on the Supersensual Life*, tr. and ed. Bernard Holland (London: Methuen, 1901).

Bolton, Neil, *Concept Formation* (Oxford: Pergamon Press, 1977).

Bourne, Lyle E., Jr., *Human Conceptual Behaviour* (Boston: Allyn & Bacon, 1966).

Bowers, Malcolm B., Jr. and Daniel X. Freedman, "'Psychedelic' Experiences in Acute Psychoses" (1966), ch. 31 of Tart (ed.), *Altered States of Consciousness*, pp. 463–76.

Bowker, John, *The Sense of God* (Oxford: Clarendon Press, 1973).

Braithwaite, R. B., "An Empiricist's View of the Nature of Religious Belief", in Hick (ed.), *The Existence of God*, pp. 229–52 (full reprint of CUP, 1955, publication).

Broad, C. D., *Religion, Philosophy and Psychical Research: Selected Essays* (London: Routledge & Kegan Paul, 1953).

Brown, David, *The Divine Trinity* (London: Duckworth, 1985).

Brown, L. B. (ed.), *Psychology and Religion: Selected Readings* (Harmondsworth: Penguin Education, 1973).

Brümmer, Vincent, *What are we doing when we pray? A Philosophical Inquiry* (London: SCM Press, 1984).

Bruner, Jerome S., *Beyond the Information Given: Studies in the Psychology of Knowing*, selected and ed. Jeremy M. Anglin (New York: Norton, 1973).

Buber, Martin, *I and Thou*, tr. R. G. Smith (Edinburgh: T. & T. Clark, 1937).

Carrithers, Michael, *The Forest Monks of Sri Lanka: An Anthropological and Historical Study* (Delhi: OUP, 1983).

Carroll, Michael P., "Visions of the Virgin Mary: The Effect of Family Structures on Marian Apparitions", *J. Sc. Stud. Rel.* 22 (1983), 205–21.

Catherine of Genoa (St), *Catherine of Genoa: Purgation and Purgatory; The Spiritual Dialogue*, tr. and notes by Serge Hughes, intro. by Benedict J. Groeschel (The Classics of Western Spirituality; London: SPCK, 1979).

Chisholm, Roderick M., *Perceiving: A Philosophical Study* (Ithaca, NY: Cornell Univ. Press, 1957).

Clark, Ralph W., "The Evidential Value of Religious Experiences", *Int. J. Phil. Rel.* 16 (1984), 189–202.

The Cloud of Unknowing. [1] Ed., with an intro., by James Walsh, S J, preface by Simon Tugwell, OP (Classics of Western Spirituality; London: SPCK, 1981). [2] Tr. into modern English, with an intro., by Clifton Wolters (Harmondsworth: Penguin Books, 1961).

Cook, Mark, *Perceiving Others: The Psychology of Interpersonal Perception* (London: Methuen, 1979).

Cygnar, Thomas E., Donald L. Noel, and Cardell K. Jacobson, "Religiosity and Prejudice: An Interdimensional Analysis", *J. Sc. Stud. Rel.* 16 (1977), 183–91.

Daniélou, J., *From Glory to Glory*, tr. H. Musurillo (London: John Murray, 1962).

Day, R. H., *Human Perception* (Sydney: John Wiley & Sons, 1969).

Deikman, Arthur J., "Bimodal Consciousness and the Mystic Experience", in Woods (ed.), *Understanding Mysticism*, pp. 261–9. Reprinted from P. Lee *et al.*, *Symposium on Consciousness*, 1976.

—— "Deautomatization and the Mystic Experience", in Woods (ed.), *Understanding Mysticism*, pp. 240–60. Reprinted from *Psychiatry* 29 (1966), pp. 324–38.

Dionysius the Pseudo-Areopagite, *Dionysius the Areopagite on the Divine Names and the Mystical Theology*, tr. C. E. Rolt (London: SPCK, 1920).

Donnellan, Keith S., "Reference and Definite Descriptions", *The Philosophical Review* 75 (1966), 281–304.

—— "Speaker Reference, Descriptions, and Anaphora", in Peter Cole (ed.), *Syntax and Semantics*, vol. 9 (New York: Academic Press, 1978).

Donovan, Peter, *Interpreting Religious Experience* (Issues in Religious Studies; London: Sheldon Press, 1979).

Douglas-Smith, Basil, *The Mystics Come to Harley Street* (London: Regency Press, 1983).

Eckhart (Meister). [1] *Meister Eckhart: The Essential Sermons, Commentaries, Treatises, and Defense*, tr., with an intro., by Edmund Colledge, O.S.A. and Bernard McGinn (The Classics of Western Spirituality; London: SPCK, 1981). [2] Some use was made of Franz Pfeiffer, *Meister Eckhart*, vols. i and ii (Leipzig, 1857), by C. de B. Evans (London: Watkins, 1956).

Farrer, Austin, *The Glass of Vision* (Bampton Lectures; Westminster: Dacre Press, 1948).

—— *Love Almighty and Ills Unlimited: An Essay On Providence and Evil* (Garden City, NY: Doubleday, 1961).

—— *A Science of God?* (London: Geoffrey Bles, 1966).

Ferré, Frederick, *Basic Modern Philosophy of Religion*, ch. 12, "The Linguistic Key" (London: Allen & Unwin, 1968).

Festinger, L. and J. M. Carlsmith, "Cognitive Consequences of Forced Compliance", *Journal of Abnormal and Social Psychology*, 58 (1959), 203–11.

Fishman, J. A., "A Systematization of the Whorfian Hypothesis" (1960), in Berry and Dasen (eds.), *Culture and Cognition*, pp. 61–85.

Flew, Antony, *God and Philosophy* (London: Hutchinson, 1966).

—— and Alasdair MacIntyre (eds.), *New Essays in Philosophical Theology* (London: SCM Press, 1955).

Foley, Richard, *The Facts About Medjugorje* (London: The Medjugorje Centre).

Forgus, Ronald H. and Lawrence E. Melamed, *Perception: A Cognitive Stage Approach* (New York: McGraw-Hill, 1976).

Francis, L. J., "Psychological Studies of Religion Head for Derailment", *Religion* 13 (1983), 127–36.

Frankl, Viktor E., *Man's Search for Meaning: An Introduction to Logotherapy*, tr. Ilse Lasch (New York: Washington Square Press, 1963).

Franks Davis, Caroline, "The Devotional Experiment", *Rel. Stud.* 22 (1986), 15–28.

Frazier, L. Scott, "The Psychodynamics of Religion: An Inquiry Based on a Kleino-Freudian Interpretation, with Special Reference to the Life of T. S. Eliot", D.Phil. thesis (Oxford, 1978).

Freud, Sigmund, *The Future of an Illusion*, tr. W. D. Robson-Scott; rev. and newly ed. by James Strachey (London: Hogarth Press, 1962).

—— *Totem and Taboo: Some Points of Agreement between the Mental Lives of Savages and Neurotics*, tr. James Strachey (London: Routledge & Kegan Paul, 1950).

Garside, Bruce, "Language and the Interpretation of Mystical Experience", *Int. J. Phil. Rel.* 3 (1972), 93–102.

Geach, Peter, *Providence and Evil* (The 1971–2 Stanton Lectures; Cambridge: CUP, 1977).

al-Ghazālī, *The Faith and Practice of Al-Ghazālī*, tr. of *Deliverance from Error* and *The Beginning of Guidance* by W. Montgomery Watt (London: Allen & Unwin, 1953).

Gibbons, Don. E. and James De Jarnette, "Hypnotic Susceptibility and Religious Experience", *J. Sc. Stud. Rel.* 11 (1972), 152–6.

Gimello, Robert M., "Mysticism and Meditation", in Katz (ed.), *Mysticism and Philosophical Analysis*, pp. 170–99.

Godin, A. (ed.), *From Religious Experience to a Religious Attitude* (Lumen Vitae Studies in Religious Psychology III; Brussels: Lumen Vitae Press, 1964).

Good, Robert C., "Ninian Smart and the Justification of Religious Doctrinal Schemes", *Int. J. Phil. Rel.* 13 (1982), 69–75.

Gorsuch, Richard L. and Craig S. Smith, "Attributions of Responsibility to God: An Interaction of Religious Beliefs and Outcomes", *J. Sc. Stud. Rel.* 22 (1983), 340–52.

Gorsuch, Richard L. and Daniel Aleshire, "Christian Faith and Ethnic Prejudice: A Review and Interpretation of Research", *J. Sc. Stud. Rel.* 13 (1974), 281–307.

Grice, H. Paul, "The Causal Theory of Perception", in G. J. Warnock (ed.), *The Philosophy of Perception* (London: OUP, 1967).

—— "Logic and Conversation", in Peter Cole and Jerry L. Morgan (eds.), *Syntax and Semantics*, vol. 3 (New York: Academic Press, 1975), pp. 41–58.

Gutting, Gary, *Religious Belief and Religious Scepticism* (Notre Dame: Univ. of Notre Dame Press, 1982).

Hamlyn, D. W., *The Psychology of Perception: A Philosophical Examination of Gestalt Theory and Derivative Theories of Perception* (London: Routledge & Kegan Paul, 1957).

Hanson, Norwood Russell, *Patterns of Discovery: An Inquiry into the Conceptual Foundations of Science* (Cambridge: CUP, 1958).

—— *Perception and Discovery* (San Francisco: Freeman, Cooper & Co., 1969).

Happold, F. C., *Mysticism: A Study and an Anthology*, rev. edn. (Harmondsworth: Penguin Books, 1970).

Hardy, Alister, *The Spiritual Nature of Man: A Study of Contemporary Religious Experience* (Oxford: Clarendon Press, 1979).

Harré, R. and P. F. Secord, *The Explanation of Social Behaviour* (Oxford: Basil Blackwell, 1972).

Hay, David and Ann Morisy, "Reports of Ecstatic, Paranormal, or Religious Experience in Great Britain and the United States: A Comparison of Trends", *J. Sc. Stud. Rel.* 17 (1978), 255–68.

Hepburn, Ronald W., *Christianity and Paradox: Critical Studies in Twentieth-Century Theology* (London: Watts, 1958, 1966).

Hesse, Mary, *Revolutions and Reconstructions in the Philosophy of Science* (Brighton: Harvester Press, 1980).

Hick, John, *Evil and the God of Love*, 2nd edn. (London: Macmillan, 1977).

—— *Philosophy of Religion* (Englewood Cliffs, NJ: Prentice-Hall, 1963).

—— "Religious Faith as Experiencing-As", in Schedler (ed.), *Philosophy of Religion*, pp. 278–90. (Reprinted from *Royal Institute of Philosophy Lectures* 2, pp. 20–35.)

—— (ed.), *The Existence of God: Readings* (New York: Macmillan, 1964).

—— (ed.), *Faith and the Philosophers* (London: Macmillan, 1966).

Hinton, J. M., *Experiences: An Inquiry into Some Ambiguities* (Oxford: Clarendon Press, 1973).

Holm, Nils. G., "Mysticism and Intense Experiences", *J. Sc. Stud. Rel.* 21 (1982), 268–76.

Hood, Ralph W., Jr., "The Construction and Preliminary Validation of a Measure of Reported Mystical Experience", *J. Sc. Stud. Rel.* 14 (1975), 29–41.

—— "Hypnotic Susceptibility and Reported Religious Experience", *Psychological Reports* 33 (1973), 549–50.

—— "Psychological Strength and the Report of Intense Religious Experience", *J. Sc. Stud. Rel.* 13 (1974), 65–71.

Humphreys, G. W. and M. J. Riddoch, *To See But Not To See* (London: Erlbaum, 1987).

Hutch, Richard A., "Are Psychological Studies of Religion on the Right Track?" *Religion* 12 (1982), 277–99.

Inge, William Ralph, *Christian Mysticism* (The 1899 Bampton Lectures; London: Methuen, 1912).

Irvine, S. H., "Contributions of Ability and Attainment Testing in Africa to a General Theory of Intellect", in Berry and Dasen (eds.), *Culture and Cognition*, pp. 247–59.

Jahoda, G., "Supernatural Beliefs and Changing Cognitive Structures Among Ghanaian University Students" (1970), in Berry and Dasen (eds.), *Culture and Cognition*, pp. 142–57.

James, William, *The Varieties of Religious Experience: A Study in Human Nature* (The 1901–2 Gifford Lectures; Glasgow: Collins Fount Paperbacks, 1977).

—— "The Will to Believe", in his *The Will to Believe and Other Essays in Popular Philosophy*, pp. 1–31 (New York: Longmans Green, 1902).

Jantzen, Grace, "Conspicuous Sanctity and Religious Belief", in Abraham and Holtzer (eds.), *The Rationality of Religious Belief*, pp. 121–40.

Johnson-Laird, P. N. *Mental Models: Towards a Cognitive Science of Language, Inference, and Consciousness* (Cambridge: CUP, 1983).

Julian of Norwich, *Revelations of Divine Love*, tr. into modern English and with an intro. by Clifton Wolters (Harmondsworth: Penguin Books, 1966).

Kalansuriya, A. D. P., "Two Modern Sinhalese Views of Nibbāna", *Religion* 9 (1979), 1–11.

Katz, Steven T., "Language, Epistemology, and Mysticism", in Katz (ed.), *Mysticism and Philosophical Analysis*, pp. 22–74.

—— (ed.), *Mysticism and Philosophical Analysis* (London: Sheldon Press, 1978).

Kenny, Anthony, *The God of the Philosophers* (Oxford: Clarendon Press, 1979).

King, Morton B. and Richard A. Hunt, "Measuring the Religious Variable: Replication", *J. Sc. Stud. Rel.* 11 (1972), 240–51.

King, Winston L., *Buddhism and Christianity: Some Bridges of Understanding* (London: Allen & Unwin, 1962).

Koestler, Arthur, *The Act of Creation* (London: Hutchinson, 1964).

Kripke, Saul, "Speaker's Reference and Semantic Reference", in P. A. French *et al.* (eds.), *Contemporary Perspectives in the Philosophy of Language* (Minneapolis: Univ. of Minnesota Press, 1979), pp. 6–27.

Laski, Marghanita, *Ecstasy: A Study of Some Secular and Religious Experiences* (London: Cresset Press, 1961).

Lewis, C. S., *Surprised by Joy* (London: Goeffrey Bles, 1955).

Lewis, H. D., *Our Experience of God* (London: Allen & Unwin, 1959).

Lloyd, Barbara B., *Perception and Cognition: A Cross-cultural Perspective* (Harmondsworth: Penguin Books, 1972).

Lott, Eric, *Vedantic Approaches to God* (London: Macmillan, 1980).

Louth, Andrew, *The Origins of the Christian Mystical Tradition: From Plato to Denys* (Oxford: Clarendon Press, 1981).

Mackie, J. L., *The Miracle of Theism: Arguments For and Against the Existence of God* (Oxford: Clarendon Press, 1982).

—— "Evil and Omnipotence", ch. 5 of B. Mitchell (ed.), *The Philosophy of Religion*.

Maclay, H., "An Experimental Study of Language and Nonlinguistic Behaviour", in Berry and Dasen (eds.), *Culture and Cognition*, pp. 87–97.

MacPhillamy, Douglas J., "Some Personality Effects of Long-Term Zen Monasticism and Religious Understanding", *J. Sc. Stud. Rel.* 25 (1986), 304–19.

Mallik, Gurdial, *Divine Dwellers in the Desert* (Bombay: Nalanda Publications, 1949).

Martin, Michael, "The Principle of Credulity and Religious Experience", *Religious Studies* 22 (1986), 79–93.

Maupin, Edward W., "On Meditation", in Tart (ed.), *Altered States of Consciousness*, pp. 177–86.

Metuh, Emefie Ikenga, *God and Man in African Religion: A Case Study of the Igbo of Nigeria* (London: Geoffrey Chapman, 1981).

Michotte, A., *The Perception of Causality*, tr. T. R. and E. Miles (London: Methuen, 1963).

Miles, T. R., *Religious Experience* (London: Macmillan, 1972).

Mitchell, Basil, *The Justification of Religious Belief* (New York: OUP, 1981).

—— (ed.), *Faith and Logic: Oxford Essays in Philosophical Theology* (London: Allen & Unwin, 1957).

—— (ed.), *The Philosophy of Religion* (London: OUP, 1971).

Moore, Peter, "Mystical Experience, Mystical Doctrine, Mystical Technique", in Katz (ed.), *Mysticism and Philosophical Analysis*, pp. 101–31.

Moray, Neville, *Attention: Selective Processes in Vision and Hearing* (London: Hutchinson Educational, 1969).

Nielsen, Kai, *Contemporary Critiques of Religion* (London: Macmillan, 1971).

Nielsen, Kai, "In Defense of Atheism", in Schedler (ed.), *Philosophy of Religion*, pp. 251–78 (reprinted from *Perspectives in Education, Religion, and the Arts*, SUNY Press).

Nock, A. D., *Conversion: The Old and the New in Religion from Alexander the Great to Augustine of Hippo* (Oxford: Clarendon Press, 1933).

Otto, Rudolf, *The Idea of the Holy: An Inquiry into the Non-rational Factor in the Idea of the Divine and its Relation to the Rational*, tr. J. W. Harvey (London: OUP, 1936).

—— *Mysticism East and West: A Comparative Analysis of the Nature of Mysticism*, tr. Bertha L. Bracey and Richenda C. Payne (London: Macmillan, 1932).

Owen, H. P., *The Christian Knowledge of God* (London: Athlone Press, 1969).

Pahnke, Walter N. and Wm. A. Richards, "Implications of LSD and Experimental Mysticism" (1966), ch. 27 of Tart (ed.), *Altered States of Consciousness*, pp. 399–428.

Parrinder, Geoffrey, *Mysticism in the World's Religions* (London: Sheldon Press, 1976).

Patrick, John W., "Personal Faith and the Fear of Death Among Divergent Religious Populations", *J. Sc. Stud. Rel.* 18 (1979), 298–305.

Penelhum, Terence, *Survival and Disembodied Existence* (London: Routledge & Kegan Paul, 1970).

Piaget, Jean, *The Child's Construction of Reality*, tr. Margaret Cook (London: Routledge & Kegan Paul, 1955).

Pike, Nelson (ed.), *God and Evil: Readings on the Theological Problem of Evil* (Englewood Cliffs, NJ: Prentice-Hall, 1964).

Plantinga, Alvin, *God and Other Minds: A Study of the Rational Justification of Belief in God* (Ithaca: Cornell Univ. Press, 1967).

—— *The Nature of Necessity* (Oxford: Clarendon Press, 1974).

—— "The Free Will Defence", ch. 6 of Mitchell (ed.), *The Philosophy of Religion*.

—— "Justification and Theism", *Faith and Philosophy* 4 (1987), 403–26.

—— "Reason and Belief in God", in Plantinga and Wolterstorff (eds.), *Faith and Rationality*, pp. 16–93.

—— and Nicholas Wolterstorff (eds.), *Faith and Rationality: Reason and Belief in God* (Notre Dame and London: Univ. of Notre Dame Press, 1983).

Polanyi, Michael, *Personal Knowledge* (London: Routledge & Kegan Paul, 1962, 1958).

Prado, Carlos G., *Illusions of Faith: A Critique of Non-credal Religion* (Dubuque, Iowa: Kendall/Hunt, 1980).

Prince, Raymond H. and C. Savage, "Mystical States and the Concept of Regression" (1965), in John White (ed.), *The Highest State of Consciousness* (Garden City, NY: Doubleday Anchor Books, 1972, pp. 114–34.

Proudfoot, Wayne, *Religious Experience* (Berkeley: Univ. of California Press, 1985).
—— and Phillip Shaver, "Attribution Theory and the Psychology of Religion", *J. Sc. Stud. Rel.* 14 (1975), 317–30.
Pye, Michael and Robert Morgan (eds.), *The Cardinal Meaning: Essays in Comparative Hermeneutics: Buddhism and Christianity* (The Hague: Mouton, 1973).
Ramakrishna. [1] *Life of Sri Ramakrishna*, "Compiled from various authentic sources" (6th edn.; Mayavati: Advaita Ashrama, 1948). [2] *Memoirs of Ramakrishna*, compiled by Swami Abhedananda (2nd. edn.; Calcutta: Ramakrishna Vendanta Math, 1957).
Ramsey, Ian T., *Models for Divine Activity* (London: SCM Press, 1973).
Raven, C. E., *Natural Religion and Christian Theology*, vol. ii (Cambridge: CUP, 1953).
Robin, Robert W., "Revival Movement Hysteria in the Southern Highlands of Papua New Guinea", *J. Sc. Stud. Rel.* 20 (1981), 150–63.
Robinson, Edward, *The Original Vision: A Study of the Religious Experience of Childhood* (Oxford: Religious Experience Research Unit, 1977).
Rokeach, Milton, *The Three Christs of Ypsilanti: A Psychological Study* (London: Arthur Barker, 1964).
Rolle, Richard, *The Fire of Love*, tr. into modern English with an intro. by Clifton Wolters (Harmondsworth: Penguin Classics, 1971).
Rowe, William L., "Religious Experience and the Principle of Credulity", *Int. J. Phil. Rel.* 13 (1982), 85–92.
Russell, Bertrand and F. C. Copleston, "The Existence of God, A Debate Between Bertrand Russell and Father F. C. Copleston", in Hick (ed.), *The Existence of God*, pp. 167–91 (originally publ. by Allen & Unwin, 1957).
Sabom, Michael B., *Recollections of Death: A Medical Investigation* (Corgi Books, 1982).
St George, Arthur and Patrick M. McNamara, "Religion, Race and Psychological Well-Being", *J. Sc. Stud. Rel.* 23 (1984), 351–63.
Sanders, E. P., *Jesus and Judaism* (London: SCM Press, 1985).
Sanford, Anthony J., *Cognition and Cognitive Psychology* (London: Weidenfeld and Nicolson, 1985).
Sargant, William, *Battle for the Mind: A Physiology of Conversion and Brainwashing* (London: Heinemann, 1957).
Schachter, Stanley and Jerome E. Singer, "Cognitive, Social and Physiological Determinants of Emotional State", *Psych. Review* 69 (1962), 379–99.
Scharfstein, Ben-Ami, *Mystical Experience* (Baltimore, Md.: Penguin Books, 1973).
Schedler, Norbert O., "Talk About God-Talk: A Historical Introduction", in Schedler (ed.), *Philosophy of Religion*, pp. 221–50.

Schedler, Norbert O. (ed.), *Philosophy of Religion: Contemporary Perspectives* (New York: Macmillan, 1974).

Scholem, Gershom G., "General Characteristics of Jewish Mysticism", ch. 11 of Judah Goldin (ed.), *The Jewish Expression* (excerpt from Scholem's *Major Trends in Jewish Mysticism*; New York: Bantam Books, 1970).

Scobie, Geoffrey E. W., *Psychology of Religion* (London: Batsford, 1975).

Shor, Ronald E., "Hypnosis and the Concept of the Generalized Reality-Orientation" (1959), ch. 15 of Tart (ed.), *Altered States of Consciousness*, pp. 233–50.

Sivananda, Swami, *Concentration and Meditation* (Yoga Sadhana Series No. 8; Rikhikesh: The Sivananda Publication League, 1945).

Smart, Ninian, *Beyond Ideology* (London: Collins, 1981).

—— *A Dialogue of Religions* (London: SCM Press, 1960).

—— *Doctrine and Argument in Indian Philosophy* (London: Allen & Unwin, 1964).

—— *Reasons and Faiths: An Investigation of Religious Discourse, Christian and Non-Christian* (London: Routledge & Kegan Paul, 1958).

—— *The Religious Experience of Mankind* (London: Collins/Fontana, 1969).

—— "Interpretation and Mystical Experience", *Rel. Stud.* 1 (1965), 75–87.

—— "Understanding Religious Experience", in Katz (ed.), *Mysticism and Philosophical Analysis*, pp. 10–21.

Smith, Margaret, *The Way of the Mystics: The Early Christian Mystics and the Rise of the Sūfīs* (London: Sheldon Press, 1976; first publ. 1931).

Society of Friends, *Christian Faith and Practice in the Experience of the Society of Friends* (London Yearly Meeting of the Religious Society of Friends, 1960).

Soskice, Janet Martin, *Metaphor and Religious Language* (Oxford: Clarendon Press, 1985).

Spilka, Bernard and Greg Schmidt, "General Attribution Theory for the Psychology of Religion: The Influence of Event-Character on Attributions to God", *J. Sc. Stud. Rel.* 22 (1983), 326–39.

Stace, W. T., *Mysticism and Philosophy* (London: Macmillan, 1960).

Stanley, Gordon, W. K. Bartlett, and Terri Moyle, "Some Characteristics of Charismatic Experience: Glossolalia in Australia", *J. Sc. Stud. Rel.* 17 (1978), 269–78.

Streeter, B. H. and A. J. Appasamy, *The Sadhu: A Study in Mysticism and Practical Religion* (London: Macmillan, 1921).

Streng, Frederick J., *Emptiness: A Study in Religious Meaning* (Nashville: Abingdon Press, 1967).

Strickland, Bonnie R. and Sallie Cone Weddell, "Religious Orientation, Racial Prejudice, and Dogmatism: A Study of Baptists and Unitarians", *J. Sc. Stud. Rel.* 11 (1972), 395–9.

Suzuki, Daisetz Teitaro, *Essays in Zen Buddhism*, 2nd. series (London: Luzac & Co., 1933).

—— *An Introduction to Zen Buddhism*, ed. Christmas Humphreys, foreword by C. G. Jung (London: Arrow Books, 1959).

—— *Mysticism Christian and Buddhist* (London: Unwin, 1957, 1979).

Swain, Marshall (ed.), *Induction, Acceptance, and Rational Belief* (Dordrecht, Holland: Reidel, 1970).

Swinburne, Richard, *The Coherence of Theism* (Oxford: Clarendon Press, 1977).

—— *The Existence of God* (Oxford: Clarendon Press, 1979).

—— *Faith and Reason* (Oxford: Clarendon Press, 1981).

—— "Does Theism need a Theodicy?", *Canadian Journal of Philosophy* 18 (1988) 287–311.

Tao Tê Ching, a new translation by Ch'u Ta-Kao (London: Unwin Books, 1970; 1st edn. 1937).

Tart, Charles T. (ed.), *Altered States of Consciousness: A Book of Readings* (New York: John Wiley & Sons, 1969).

Taylor, A. E., *Does God Exist?* (London: Collins/Fontana, 1945, 1961).

—— Excerpts from "The Vindication of Religion" in Hick (ed.), *The Existence of God*, pp. 153–64.

Teresa of Avila (St), *The Complete Works of Saint Teresa of Jesus*, vol. 1, *Life*, tr. and ed. E. Allison Peers, from the critical edn. of P. Silverio de Santa Teresa, C. D. (London: Sheed & Ward, 1946).

—— *Interior Castle*, tr. and ed. E. Allison Peers, from the critical edn. of P. Silverio de Santa Teresa, C. D. (Garden City, NY: Image Books (Doubleday), 1961).

Thouless, Robert H., *An Introduction to the Psychology of Religion*, 3rd. edn. (Cambridge: CUP, 1971).

—— *The Lady Julian: A Psychological Study* (London: SPCK, 1924).

Tooker, Elisabeth (ed.), *Native North American Spirituality of the Eastern Woodlands: Sacred Myths, Dreams, Visions, Speeches, Healing Formulas, Rituals and Ceremonials* (Classics of Western Spirituality; London: SPCK, 1979).

Toulmin, Stephen, "Concept-Formation in Philosophy and Psychology", ch. 22 of Sidney Hook (ed.), *Dimensions of Mind: A Symposium* (London: Collier-Macmillan, 1960), pp. 191–203.

Trankell, Arne, *Reliability of Evidence: Methods for Analysing and Assessing Witness Statements* (Stockholm: Beckmans, 1972).

Tyrrell, G. N. M., *Apparitions* (London: Duckworth, 1943, rev. edn. 1953).

Underhill, Evelyn, *Mysticism: A Study in the Nature and Development of Man's Spiritual Consciousness* (London: Methuen, 1911, 12th. edn. rev. 1930).

Upanishads [1] *The Thirteen Principal Upanishads*, tr. from the Sanskrit, with an outline of the philosophy of the Upanishads, by Robert E. Hume. (2nd. edn., rev. London: OUP, 1931). [2] *The Upanishads*, tr. from the

Sanskrit with an intro. by Juan Mascaró (Harmondsworth: Penguin Books, 1965).

Verma, S. B., "Comment: Scientific Study of Religion in India", *J. Sc. Stud. Rel.* 17 (1978), 173–9.

Wainwright, William J., *Mysticism: A Study of Its Nature, Cognitive Value and Moral Implications* (Brighton: Harvester Press, 1981).

—— "Mysticism and Sense Perception", *Rel. Stud.* 9 (1973), 257–78.

Wapnick, Kenneth, "Mysticism and Schizophrenia", in Woods (ed.), *Understanding Mysticism*, pp. 321–37.

Ward, Colleen A. and Michael H. Beaubrun, "The Psychodynamics of Demon Possession", *J. Sc. Stud. Rel.* 19 (1980), 201–7.

Weiskrantz, L., "Varieties of Residual Experience", *Quarterly Journal of Experimental Psychology* 32 (1980), 365–86.

Wesley, John, *The Journal of the Rev. John Wesley A. M.*, vol. 1, ed. Ernest Rhys (London: J. M. Dent & Co., Everyman's Library).

Wiles, Maurice, *The Remaking of Christian Doctrine* (The 1973 Hulsean Lectures; London: SCM, 1974).

Williams, Michael, *Groundless Belief: An Essay on the Possibility of Epistemology* (Oxford: Blackwell, 1977).

Wilson, J. Cook, *Statement and Inference*, II (Oxford: OUP, 1926).

Wilson, J. R. S., *Emotion and Object* (Cambridge: 1972).

Wisdom, John, "Gods" (1953), ch. 10 of Wisdom's *Philosophy and Psychoanalysis* (Berkeley: Univ. of California Press, 1969).

Witkin, H. A., "Cognitive Styles across Cultures" (1967), in Berry and Dasen (eds.), *Culture and Cognition*, pp. 99–117.

Wolters, A. W. P., *The Evidence of our Senses* (London: Methuen, 1933).

Wolterstorff, Nicholas, "Can Belief in God be Rational if it has no Foundations?", in Plantinga and Wolterstorff (eds.), *Faith and Rationality*, pp. 135–86.

Woods, Richard (ed.), *Understanding Mysticism* (Garden City, NY: Doubleday/Image Books, 1980).

Wright, Derek S., Ann Taylor, *et al.*, *Introducing Psychology: An Experimental Approach* (Harmondsworth: Penguin Books, 1970).

Yee, Margaret M., "The Validity of Theology as an Academic Discipline: A Study in the Light of the History and Philosophy of Science and with Special Reference to Relevant Aspects of the Thought of Austin Farrer", D.Phil. thesis (Oxford, 1987).

Zaehner, R. C., *Mysticism Sacred and Profane: An Inquiry into Some Varieties of Praeternatural Experience* (Oxford: Clarendon Press, 1957).

INDEX